Praise for  the Second Edition:

"It's hard enough to wrestle with Zionism as a secular Jew, but far more anguishing to do so as a rabbi. *Wrestling in the a Daylight* is a must read. It offers a unique opportunity for Jews and non-Jews alike to follow the evolution in thinking of a deeply spiritual Jewish rabbi as he breaks with long-cherished beliefs about Zionism and embraces the liberation of the Palestinians. As a secular Jew, I find solace in Rosen's writing. It shows me that Jews who hold truly sacred, compassionate values must, sooner or later, reject the Zionist dream. Brant's construction of a new dream, one in which no ethnic group holds privilege over another, is indeed a dream worth wrestling for."

—MEDEA BENJAMIN
author, co-founder of CODEPINK for Peace

"Deeply grounded in the Jewish tradition of questioning one's own and one's community's conscience, *Wrestling in the Daylight* is a work of extraordinary moral reckoning from America's bravest rabbi. With great compassion, rigorous intellectual engagement, and an unfailing sense of justice, Brant Rosen documents his own struggles with the most urgent issue facing American Jews today. Rosen writes as he acts: with clarity, courage, and conviction."

—BEN EHRENREICH
author, *The Way to the Spring: Life and Death in Palestine*

"A heroic rabbi who risked a great deal to stand in solidarity with the people of Palestine and in support of justice and peace in the region; one of the righteous voices that demonstrate the true meaning of Judaism, transcending tribal identities and committed to social justice and human love."

—NAOMI WOLF
author, social critic, and political activist

Praise for the First Edition:

"Rosen wrestles openly, 'in the daylight' with his deepest moral dilemma: reconciling the classic Zionist narrative that has informed him his entire life with Israel's inexcusable treatment of the Palestinians (and the liberal Zionism often used to rationalize it). We accompany him on his journey. The result is an eye-opening, much-needed contribution to the discourse surrounding Zionism in the American Jewish community. A critical work."

—LAILA EL-HADDAD
co-author, *The Gaza Kitchen: A Palestinian Culinary Journey*

"In *Wrestling in the Daylight*, Rosen patiently challenges the ways so many in the Jewish community seek to bend Judaism's liberationist themes to the goal of justifying Israeli repression. His intervention is a revolutionary and prophetic act."

—**ADAM HOROWITZ**
co-editor, Mondoweiss.net

"Brant Rosen is at once a courageous rabbi and the voice of a new generation of American Jews who are refusing to concede that loyalty to the Jewish people requires blind loyalty to the policies of the State of Israel... If you want to understand the inner struggle of American Jews about Israel, this is a must read."

—**Rabbi MICHAEL LERNER**
editor, *Tikkun Magazine*

"It was fascinating to read Brant's book and see in how many ways the process of breaking ranks and overcoming your tribal identity is so similar, whether you are an officer in 'the most moral army in the world' or a rabbi in Chicago. I would give this book as a gift to many Jewish Americans, rabbis, and others who, despite their doubts, have chosen to carry on being 'good soldiers' in the service of the Israeli occupation."

—**YONATAN SHAPIRA**
Israeli human-rights activist

WRESTLING
IN THE DAYLIGHT

A RABBI'S PATH TO
PALESTINIAN SOLIDARITY

Second Edition

BRANT ROSEN

Just World Books
Charlottesville, Virginia

Development editing: Grey Editing
Project management and proofreading: Marissa Wold Uhrina
Typesetting: PerfecType, Nashville, TN
Cover concept and front cover design: Micah Bazant
Back cover design: Wordreams

Publisher's Cataloging-in-Publication
(Provided by The Donohue Group, Inc.)

Names: Rosen, Brant. | Rosen, Brant. Shalom Rav.
Title: Wrestling in the daylight : a rabbi's path to Palestinian solidarity / Brant Rosen.
Description: Second edition. | Charlottesville, Virginia : Just World Books, an imprint of Just World Publishing, LLC, [2017] | Summary: A selection of posts from the author's blog, Shalom Rav.
Identifiers: ISBN 978-1-68257-065-4 | ISBN 978-1-68257-071-5 (ePub) | ISBN 978-1-68257-072-2 (mobi) | ISBN 978-1-68257-073-9 (PDF)
Subjects: LCSH: Arab-Israeli conflict--1993---Blogs. | Jews--United States--Attitudes toward Israel--Blogs. | Palestinian Arabs--Crimes against--Israel--Blogs. | Zionism--Blogs. | Rosen, Brant--Blogs.
Classification: LCC DS119.76 .R667 2017 (print) | LCC DS119.76 (ebook) | DDC 956.9405/4--dc23

Contents

A Note on the Text

The blog posts in this book were written between December 2008 and July 2015. With minor exceptions, they are presented in chronological order. The comments that are included are by no means exhaustive, but I selected them to offer readers a sense of the tenor and breadth of the discussion provoked by each post. The comments presented here have been edited only to correct spelling and grammar, and for length. All posts and comments can be read in their original, full form at www.rabbibrant.com.

The opinions in my posts are mine alone and do not represent the views of any institution with which I am affiliated.

—B.R.

Preface to the 2017 Edition

When I wrote the blog posts presented in the first edition of *Wrestling in the Daylight*, I hoped they might help to widen the discourse on Israel/Palestine in the American Jewish community. In the five years since that edition was published, I'm encouraged to be able to say this discourse has indeed widened in significant ways.

To cite just a few examples: Jewish Voice for Peace, an organization that openly supports Palestinian human rights and endorses the Palestinian civil society call for boycott, divestment, and sanctions (BDS), has experienced explosive growth in the past several years and has become a force to be reckoned with by the Jewish community. Open Hillel, an initiative initiated by Jewish college students to "promote pluralism and open discourse on Israel/Palestine and beyond," is increasingly active in campuses across the country. Another rapidly growing organization created by young Jews, IfNotNow, is challenging American Jewish communal support of Israel's occupation through public acts of civil disobedience.

I do believe we are witnessing the growth of a very real Jewish movement of resistance to the status quo in the American Jewish community and Israel. Led largely by a younger generation, it is openly challenging Israel's brutal occupation and in some cases, even the very premise of Zionism itself. Notably, it is growing and thriving outside the mainstream Jewish institutional world, finding common cause with other movements (such as Black Lives Matter) that struggle against systems of oppression.

As I write these words, Israel is currently ruled by the most right-wing government in its history and is doubling down on its brutal occupation. In Europe, extreme nationalist parties are on the rise, and in the United States, the so-called "alt-right" has become politically normalized following the election of Donald Trump. White liberal Americans have suddenly been forced to confront the reality of institutional oppression that has been long familiar to black and brown people, gay, lesbian, queer, and trans people, undocumented people, and First Nations peoples—as well as those who live at the intersections of those identities.

If my participation in the Palestine solidarity movement has taught me anything over the past several years, it is that the fight for justice in Palestine is inseparable from the fights for justice in Chicago, Ferguson, Baltimore, Standing Rock, and too many other places around the world. If I have any hope at all in this fearful political moment, it comes from all that I've learned from those who live every day with the reality of institutional oppression and the allies and accomplices who stand in solidarity with them. I take heart in the knowledge that there is an active Jewish presence within this new movement of resistance—and I'm immensely proud to be part of it.

This second edition of *Wrestling in the Daylight* contains a few editorial changes and updates the book with two new chapters: "Toward a New Model of Interfaith Relations" and "Tzedek Chicago." The former chapter also contains some posts and comments that were written during "Operation Protective Edge," Israel's military assault on Gaza during the summer of 2014. Later that year, I decided to resign from my congregation to devote myself to activism full time. In 2015, I founded a new non-Zionist congregation, Tzedek Chicago.

As it has turned out, *Wrestling in the Daylight* is now bookended by two ruinous "operations" waged by Israel against Gaza. Nearly ten years since the first words of this book were written, two million Palestinians (the majority of them children) remain imprisoned in a tiny strip of land, subjected to increasingly subhuman conditions and regular onslaughts at the hands of the Israeli military. If the past is any indication, it is only a matter of time before Israel launches its next assault.

It is our collective shame that the world allows this outrage to continue—and it is to the people of Gaza that I dedicate this new edition of this book.

Brant Rosen
November 2016

Preface to the 2012 Edition

Jacob was left alone. And a man wrestled with him until the break of dawn.
—Genesis 32:25

This well-known Biblical episode leaves behind tantalizing questions. Who is the mysterious "man" with whom Jacob wrestles? What is his identity, and where did he come from? One popular interpretation suggests that the night stranger with whom Jacob struggles at this critical moment is none other than Jacob himself—perhaps his alter ego or his shadow self.

But why must the wrestling match necessarily take place at night? Why does the night stranger say so desperately to Jacob in the next verse, "Let me go, for dawn is breaking"? Perhaps this detail is teaching us that our deepest struggles invariably occur in the most private of places. After all, whenever we publicly wrestle with our deepest dilemmas, doubts, or fears, we take a very real risk. That's why we tend to engage in our most challenging struggles internally—"in the dead of night."

This book is, among other things, a record of the moment I personally began to wrestle in the daylight. It documents a two-year period during which I publicly struggled, as a congregational rabbi, with one of the most difficult and painfully divisive issues facing the American Jewish community.

I've identified deeply with Israel for most of my life. I first visited at a very young age and have been back to visit more times than I can even count. In my early twenties, I spent two years there studying, working, and living on *kibbutzim*. I have family members and many dear friends who live in Israel. My Jewish identity has been profoundly informed by the classic Zionist narrative: the story of a small underdog nation forging a national and cultural rebirth out of the ashes of its near-destruction. The redemptive nature of this narrative has at times assumed a quasi-sacred status for me, as it has for many American Jews of my generation and older.

Politically speaking, I've identified with what tends to be referred to today as "liberal Zionism." I've long been inspired by Israel's Labor Zionist origins, and I've generally aligned myself with positions advocated by the Israeli left and the Israeli peace movement. When it came to the ongoing conflict with the Palestinians, I'd invariably intone a familiar refrain of liberal Zionists: "It's *complicated*."

If I found myself occasionally troubled by ill-advised or even unjust Israeli policies, I tended to view them as "blemishes" on an otherwise stable democracy and a noble national project. At the end of the day, I understood the essence of this conflict to be a clash between two national movements, each with compelling and valid claims to the same small piece of land. In the end, the only viable, equitable solution would be its division into two states for two peoples.

Over the years, however, I confess, I struggled with nagging, gnawing doubts over the tenets of this liberal Zionist narrative. Although I was able to keep these doubts at bay—for the most part—I was never able to successfully silence them. I experienced the earliest of these doubting voices when Israel invaded Lebanon in 1982, unleashing a shocking degree of military firepower that shook my naive "David vs. Goliath" assumptions to their core. Several years later, the voices grew even louder as I witnessed the brutality with which Israel put down the nonviolent Palestinian demonstrations of the First Intifada. And they grew more insistent still when I began to witness firsthand the darker truths of Israel's oppressive occupation of the West Bank and Gaza.

Truth be told, however, if I was troubled by these things, it was less out of concern for the well-being or safety of Palestinians per se than it was the tribal notion that the occupation was "corrupting Israel's soul" and endangering Israel's future existence as a "Jewish and democratic state." Like many liberal Zionists, I dealt with such concerns by retreating to the safety of political pedagogy: these troubling realities simply proved to us all the more that we needed to redouble our efforts toward the peace process and an eventual two-state solution.

When I was ordained as a rabbi in 1992, the stakes were raised on my political views—particularly when it came to Israel/Palestine. Given the ideological centrality of Zionism in the American Jewish community, my inner conflicts over Israel's oppressive treatment of Palestinians now carried very real professional consequences. Rabbis and Jewish leaders are under tremendous pressure by the American Jewish organizational establishment to maintain unflagging support for the state of Israel. Congregational rabbis in particular take a very real professional risk when they criticize Israel publicly. To actually stand in solidarity with Palestinians would be tantamount to communal heresy.

Shortly after I was ordained, I began reading the newly published English translations of Israel's "New Historians"—important scholars, such as Benny Morris, Tom Segev, Avi Shlaim, and Ilan Pappe—who exposed the darker truths about the establishment of the Jewish state and the birth of the Palestinian refugee problem. These books had a powerful, even radicalizing, impact upon me. I became increasingly struck by the sheer injustice that accompanied Israel's birth, an injustice that was not only historical but, as I was coming to believe, still very much present and ongoing.

From here, I began to entertain difficult questions about the ethnic nationalism at the heart of Zionism—and became more and more troubled that Israel's identity as a Jewish state was entirely dependent upon the maintenance of a Jewish majority within its borders. In the United States, the very suggestion of a "demographic time bomb" (an oft-used term used by liberal Zionists to advocate the critical importance of a two-state solution) would be considered incorrigibly racist. In my more unguarded moments, I'd ask myself: Why, then, do we bandy this concept about so freely when it pertains to the Jewish state?

Despite the questions, I nevertheless found a safe and comfortable home in liberal Zionism for the first decade of my rabbinate, affiliating with such organizations as Americans for Peace Now, Brit Tzedek v'Shalom, and J Street. All the while, the gnawing voices continued. Although I shared the elation of many at the signing of the Oslo Accords in 1993, my optimism was short-lived. In due time, Israel expanded its settlement regime over the Palestinian territories, Israeli Prime Minister Yitzhak Rabin was assassinated, and the Clinton-brokered peace talks at Camp David crashed and burned.

When the horrors of the Second Intifada began in the fall of 2000, I dealt with my anguish through a carefully cultivated avoidance of the Israel/Palestine issue. Whenever I addressed the subject in writings or sermons, it was usually with a vague but essentially substance-free plea for "peace and coexistence" on both sides. I would mourn the loss of life for both peoples and advocate redoubling our efforts at a peace process I increasingly feared was empty at the core.

Israel's second military campaign in Lebanon during the summer of 2006 jolted me temporarily out of my avoidance. As I read and watched another military bombardment of Beirut—and my e-mail inbox filled up with Jewish Federation blasts exhorting me to support the Israel Emergency Campaign—I was deeply saddened that my community showed precious little concern about the sheer magnitude of the violence Israel was unleashing yet again against the people of Lebanon. Although I certainly felt compassion for—along with a certain tribal solidarity with—the citizens of Northern Israel suffering under Hezbollah rocket fire, I was unable to accept the utter destruction the IDF was inflicting upon Lebanon in the name of national security. Still, I kept my silence. The pressure to present a united Jewish communal front during a time of war still trumped my own inner struggle.

In October 2006, I started keeping a blog I called *Shalom Rav*. (The title is a pun: *Shalom Rav*, or "abundant peace," is the name of a well-known Jewish prayer—but the Hebrew can also be taken to mean "hello, Rabbi.") At the time, my intention was simply to hold forth on anything or everything I thought to be worthy of sharing over the blogosphere. As a congregational rabbi serving in Evanston, Illinois, I also thought it would be an effective way for my congregants to hear more regularly from their rabbi.

Because social action had always played an important role in my rabbinate, I intended to devote a significant percentage of my blog posts to current issues of social justice and human rights. As a result, a reader perusing *Shalom Rav* in those early years could read my thoughts on subjects as wide-ranging and diverse as the wars in Iraq and Afghanistan, fair-trade coffee, torture at Guantánamo, poverty and hunger in sub-Saharan Africa, and human rights in Darfur.

Soon, however, the focus of my blog changed dramatically.

On December 28, 2008, I read the first news report of Israel's military assault on Gaza—a campaign that would soon be well-known as Operation Cast Lead. On the first day of operations, the Israeli Air Force destroyed Hamas security facilities in Gaza, killing more than 225 people, most of whom were new police cadets participating in a graduation ceremony. Numerous civilians, including children, were also among the dead. By the end of the day, it was clear we were only witnessing the beginning of a much longer and even more violent military campaign that would drive much farther into Gaza.

I remember reading this news with utter anguish. At the same time, oddly enough, I realized that I was finally observing this issue with something approaching true clarity: this is not about security at all—*this is about bringing the Palestinian people to their knees.*

Once I admitted this to myself, I realized how utterly tired I had become. Tired of trying to excuse the inexcusable. Tired of using torturous, exhausting rationalizations to explain away what I really knew in my heart was sheer and simple *oppression.*

After staring at my screen for what seemed like an eternity, I logged on to my blog and typed out a post entitled "Outrage in Gaza: No More Apologies." I ended with a declaration—and a question:

What Israel has been doing to the people of Gaza is an outrage. It has brought neither safety nor security to the people of Israel and it has wrought nothing but misery and tragedy upon the people of Gaza.

There, I've said it. Now what do I do?

Although it was a simple and not particularly eloquent post, I knew full well what it would mean when I clicked "publish." It represented a very conscious and public break from the liberal Zionist fold that had been my spiritual and political home for almost my entire life. But although I was finally very clear about what I was leaving behind, I was not at all sure about where I now belonged. Hence the final line of my post: *Now what do I do?*

Although I expected my words to make waves, I was still astonished by what happened next: The post immediately went viral, eliciting 125 comments in less than a month—far more than I have ever received before or since. Although some of the initial commenters were congregants, I ultimately received responses from all over the world. Predictably, some lashed out against my post, but as the comments continued to roll in, I was surprised to read the words of many more—congregants, Jews, and non-Jews alike—expressing their immense thanks for what I had written. The comment thread was peppered with a palpable sense of gratitude and relief that a Jewish leader—a rabbi, no less—had finally crossed a significant line so publicly.

My post was not, as many assumed at the time, a temporary burst of emotion on my part. As Israel intensified its military assault on Gaza throughout January 2009, my anguish only deepened. I read news reports of Apache helicopters dropping hundreds of tons of bombs on 1.5 million people crowded into a besieged 140-square-mile patch of land. I learned about the bombing of schools and homes in which entire families were destroyed, about men, women, and children literally burned to the bone with white phosphorus. Throughout it all, I continued to blog openly about the outrages I believed Israel was committing in Gaza—and about my increasing sense of solidarity with Gazan civilians.

Over the months following Cast Lead, I broadened my scope, writing numerous posts addressing my changing relationship to Israel. As the months went by, I brought all my nagging, gnawing doubts out into the bright light of day. It soon became clear to me that Cast Lead was simply the final tipping point of a domino line I'd been setting up steadily over the years. I became increasingly involved in Palestinian solidarity work, founding, with my colleague Rabbi Brian Walt, an initiative called Jewish Fast for Gaza and taking on a leadership role in the rapidly growing national organization Jewish Voice for Peace. Along the way, I recorded and commented upon my newfound activism in *Shalom Rav*.

Although I knew I was taking a risk on many levels by publishing my initial post, the conversation that has resulted fills me with hope. I am immensely proud of the relatively high and eloquent level of the debate on my blog, and I am regularly awed by the willingness of so many of my commenters to be fundamentally challenged over such a difficult issue. Over the years, I've been humbled and excited to convene this lively, almost Talmudic discussion between members of my congregation along with countless others: Jews, Israelis, Palestinians, Muslims, Christians, and citizens of various ethnicities and nations, many of whom I have never actually met—and most likely never will.

Today, I continue to serve my congregation in Evanston. I continue to "wrestle in the daylight," and I continue to advocate for a just peace in Israel/Palestine. I'm often asked where I stand now—that is, now that I've officially broken ranks with liberal Zionism. Although it's not a simple answer, I *do* know this: My primary religious motivation comes from my inherited Jewish tradition, in which God commands me to stand with the oppressed and to call out the oppressor. I know that the American Jewish community is my spiritual home *and* that I stand with the Palestinian people in their struggle against oppression. And I know that I fervently desire a just and peaceful future for Israelis *and* Palestinians.

I also know that my constituency is not as narrow as some might think. Through my work, I have come to discover increasing numbers of Jews—particularly young Jews—who genuinely seek a home in the Jewish community but cannot countenance the Jewish establishment's orthodoxy on Israel. I have also met many non-Jews—including Palestinians, interfaith colleagues, and fellow political activists—who constitute a new, exciting, ever-growing community of conscience.

Along the way, I've come to believe that too many of us have been wrestling in the dark on this issue for far too long. I believe we simply *must* find a way to widen the limits of public discourse on Israel/Palestine, no matter how painful the prospect. It is my fervent hope that the conversations presented here might represent, in their small way, a step toward the light of day.

Chapter 1

In the Wake of Cast Lead

December 2008–March 2009

I wrote the first post in this chapter immediately upon hearing the initial reports of Israel's military attacks on Gaza, which began on December 27, 2008. The post resulted in a flurry of comments ranging from appreciative to angry to utterly unprintable. As Israel's war intensified over the next three weeks, my posts focused almost exclusively on the increasingly tragic events unfolding in Gaza.

Outrage in Gaza: No More Apologies[1]

December 28, 2008

The news today out of Israel and Gaza makes me just sick to my stomach. I know, I can already hear the responses: Every nation has a responsibility to ensure the safety of its citizens. If the Qassams stopped, Israel wouldn't be forced to take military action. Hamas also bears responsibility for this tragic situation . . .

I could answer each and every one of these claims in turn, but I'm ready to stop this perverse game of rhetorical ping-pong. I don't buy the rationalizations any more. I'm so tired of the apologetics. How on earth will squeezing the life out of Gaza, not to mention bombing the living hell out of it, ensure the safety of Israeli citizens?

We good liberal Jews are ready to protest oppression and human-rights abuses anywhere in the world but are all too willing to give Israel a pass. It's a fascinating double standard, and one I understand all too well. I understand it, because I've been just as responsible as anyone else for perpetrating it.

So, no more rationalizations. What Israel has been doing to the people of Gaza is an outrage. It has brought neither safety nor security to the people of Israel and it has wrought nothing but misery and tragedy upon the people of Gaza.

There, I've said it. Now what do I do?

Discussion

lostandconfused
Hey, can someone give me a hand with the search function on the blog? I'm trying to find your outraged piece about rockets shot from Gaza killing civilians, and I am not having a whole ton of luck. I can't help but get the feeling you learned a little too much in Iran.[2]

jb
Not by might and not by power, but by my spirit, said the Lord of Hosts. (Zechariah 4:6)

The Haftarah for the Shabbat of Hanukkah. This is something to think about in the wake of these useless and dangerous attacks.

Lisa
I also must have missed the occasions of your hand-wringing over rocket attacks on Israeli citizens, which are war crimes.

Frankly, I'm having a hard time working up sympathy for Gaza. Someday, maybe the people who live there will throw out the thugs (the ones who refused to let their injured be evacuated across the border to Egyptian hospitals) instead of electing them. In the meantime, Israel has every right, according to international law, to respond to acts of war.

To jb: [Rabbi Gunther] Plaut comments that the angel's words in Zechariah were inserted into the Hanukkah Haftarah as a way to placate the ruling Romans by shifting the emphasis toward the spiritual and away from commemorating a time when Israel had military and political power.[3] I, for one, am not sorry to live in a time when Israel is again a sovereign nation with the power to defend its citizens.

martin
I agree with you that this is a mistake. Rather than commenting on whether this is justified, or justifiable (I happen to think the response is disproportionate, but I don't want to be drawn into fruitless

legalistic or moralistic arguments that will never lead to resolution), instead, what is the point of this? Does anybody seriously think that Hamas is going to stop the rockets because of this offensive? Is Israel going to reoccupy Gaza? (That worked out well, didn't it?) What is the exit strategy?

I don't pretend to have the answers, but if there is simply repeating and continuing the flawed strategies that led to this, the results will be more of the same.

Kat

You are going to catch hell for telling it like it is, but thank you for taking a stand. As to what to do now? You answered it and are doing it: Stop engaging in the perverse rhetorical ping-pong; stop engaging in the hypocrisy and double standards. You are to be commended and not condemned. Please remember in the coming days that you have a lot of support in your refusal to be baited by comments here and in the real world.

Jesse

I was proud to read your statement as a former JRC member (I moved to Philadelphia). I am wrestling with and haunted by your final question of what you should do. I know what I do, and I know I have been wishing that one of the many rabbis in my life would make a post/sermon like that. I want to believe that such an act of moral courage will have long ripple effects and be evidence of a larger upwelling of principled stands. However, I am questioning the inevitability of some of my own assumptions and hear your hunger for effective action to take. I would be happy to discuss the question of what you will do next with you though!

CShapiro

I don't get it. When my older and stronger kid is beating on my younger kid, I make him stop. I make him stop even if the younger kid did something purely and deliberately provocative, like take a precious possession without permission, or even something violent, like kick him. I don't tell my older child that it's okay to beat on his brother if the brother provoked him and in order to deter or (worse!) disable his brother. I make them find another way to work it out.

I realize that Israel is not a child, nor is Hamas. But the analogy it seems to me is stronger than it might appear. Were I to take the option of allowing my older child to physically deter his brother from future provocation, what do you think would happen? They would both become horrific human beings. This, writ large, is what we see happening before our very eyes. It breaks my heart.

Abigail

I'm so happy that the synagogue I grew up in now has a rabbi willing to openly support the Jewish values I thought I'd learned.

What can you do? A whole lot, or, rather, if you can't do anything, then no one can do anything. You can start by calling your senators and representatives, the State Department, the Israeli embassies and consulates. You can submit your beautifully written pieces to mainstream media. You can organize a meeting so that many people can come together and make these sorts of phone calls and draft letters and sign petitioners (feed them and have the addresses and phone numbers listed and talking points ready). It feels hopeless, but we must try.

Eric G

Shalom. It is the appropriate word. I am an ex-JRC member, live in Chicago, and went to the demonstration Friday night downtown in support of the people of Gaza. The pre-rally had four speakers; the first and third (or fourth?), all Muslim leaders, specifically reached out to us as Jews to stand on our principles of peace and justice. I was moved and made an impromptu sign that read "Jews Against Occupation," which I held high during the rally and march. The march was almost entirely Arab, no doubt mainly Palestinian. As I walked around with the sign, many people told me "thank you." A Palestinian teacher asked me if she could take my picture so that her students (many of whom are Palestinian) would know there was a difference between Judaism and Zionism. I said yes and told her I wanted people to know that, too.

Thank you, Rabbi, for having the courage to make this statement. We need to stand clearly on the side of justice. Yes, I wish that Hamas's political strategy was one of high moral ground, no rockets, a push for international pressure, boycott, sanctions, whatever, on Israel, like the movement to support South African liberation against apartheid. But I am not in the position the people of Gaza are in, and I can only have an impact on my government, and, as a Jew, on Jewish opinion and Israel. Your stand is an inspiration and powerful.

Arlene

I write this from Israel, and I know how mistaken you are in what you say. But I will not argue with you, because you refer to discussion as a "perverse game of rhetorical ping-pong."

Instead, I want to ask a question. And if you are as moral as you aspire to be, you will answer me forthrightly:

You say, "We good liberal Jews are ready to protest oppression and human-rights abuses anywhere in the world."

I would like to know when is the last time you took on the issue of human-rights abuses committed by Arabs?

Have you ever spoken out about Arab female-genital mutilation, or Arab family-honor killings, or the fact that Egypt sometimes shoots in the back refugees from Sudan who are trying to make their way to Israel, where they will be safe?

Have you ever decried the killing by the Palestinian Authority of so-called collaborators? Have you ever expressed concern about the fact that the PA does not allow freedom of the press?

Have you ever grappled with the severe deprivation of human rights suffered by Arab children who are forced into participation in war or terrorist activities—this coercion being forbidden by Geneva conventions?

Tom

Beautiful piece. As a Jew, the son of a Holocaust survivor, and, most of all, as a human being, I thank you for speaking out. As to what you should do now, I think the most important thing is just to continue to do so.

Abdul

Thank you so much for finally giving voice to my sadness and frustration with what is going on in Gaza.

I am (despite my name) a Jew (of Russian and Sierra Leonean descent), and I have struggled with my mixed emotions regarding how the state of Israel treats the Palestinian nation.

I have often been reluctant to criticize Israel, understanding how important the defense of Israel is to Jews around the world. And, not having been raised in a traditional White/Ashkenazi Jewish environment, I cannot pretend to understand how/why Israel is so important that her actions must be defended at all costs. Regardless, I have bitten my tongue out of respect for all those who have such a strong emotional connection to Israel.

But I've been getting less and less comfortable with my silence and the silence of other liberal Jews on the question of Israel's treatment of the Palestinians.

It's good to know I'm not alone. And neither are you.

> You've said it. What's next, I don't know. But know that you've got 100% of my support.
>
> Keep fighting the good fight!
>
> **Infidelicious**
> I'm sorry, but this just doesn't move me in the slightest. The people of Gaza sowed the seeds of terror when they elected Hamas, and now they are reaping the whirlwind. I feel no sympathy for them.

Israel and Gaza: In Search of a New Moral Calculus[4]

December 30, 2008

I knew my last post would generate passionate comments—and I confess that I did hesitate before posting something so patently emotional. I went ahead, though, because as I read the increasingly tragic news about the Israel-Gaza conflict, I'm consciously resisting the knee-jerk impulse to paper over my emotions with dispassionate analysis. It's becoming clear to me that our attempts to be "rational" keep us from facing the inherent irrationality of this conflict.

Of course the Qassam attacks against Southern Israel have been intolerable. Of course Hamas bears its share of responsibility for this conflict. But beyond the rhetorical "well, he started it" arguments (which could stretch well back to 1948 and beyond), there remains the central question: What will bring safety, security, and ultimately peace to this tortured region? I realize there are no easy answers, but I believe to my marrow that it will not come by sending in the war planes and reducing what's left of Gaza to rubble.

Does anyone in his right mind truly think this abject destruction will ultimately bring safety and security to Southern Israel? In the end, every Gazan killed equals that many more family members and friends who will now be forever enraged and inflamed against the Jewish state. If peace depends largely on cultivating moderates on the other side, what does blowing them to smithereens accomplish? Believe me, if Israel ultimately thinks their attacks will turn Gazans against Hamas, they will be sorely disappointed. If forced to choose between Israel and Hamas, who do we really think they will choose now?

But even more than the strategic considerations, I am infinitely more troubled by the deeper moral implications of Israel's military actions. Yes, it is unclear who was responsible for breaking the cease-fire, and yes, Israel has few good options. But it was ultimately Israel who made the decision to bombard Gaza with a massive air attack, loosing many several hundreds of bombs into a densely populated city center, virtually guaranteeing widespread civilian carnage and death.

As I write these words, I can already predict the standard moral calculus: "Yes, but Hamas purposely launches Qassams into civilian areas, while Israel tries to minimize civilian casualties whenever possible." I'm coming to realize that pat rhetorical equations like these might serve to help us sleep better at night, but they don't change some basic unavoidable truths: That in the Israeli-Palestinian conflict, the military power dynamic is heavily weighted in Israel's favor; that Hamas's Qassams are but peashooters against Israel's armed might; and ultimately, as traumatic as it undoubtedly is to live in Sderot, that Palestinian civilian casualties vastly outnumber Israeli. And in the end, it matters little to the loved one of a dead civilian whether his or her death was caused intentionally or by "collateral damage."

From what I can tell, Israel's response to this latest bloody go-round amounts to: "We regret if civilians are killed, but they started it, and anyhow that's what happens in war." I certainly understand how Israel, a nation that has been in a constant state of war and conflict since its inception, might develop such a moral trope. But whatever comfort it might afford us in the short term, it will not ultimately provide us with a path to peace—only a rationalization for prolonging the bloody status quo.

That's all for now. Thank you for your comments, and please keep them coming. And let's pray for better news tomorrow.

Discussion

CShapiro

The issue to me is not who started it—which (as you said) is a hopeless discussion, with recriminations going back more than 60 years ("a land without a people for a people without a land"). And the issue to me is not whether Israel's response is proportionate or not.

The only issue that matters, it seems to me, is what course is most likely to lead to an end to bloodshed in the region. And this ain't it, as you say. Israel's claim that they are going to topple Hamas is, in my view, completely delusional. Please. This will only make Hamas stronger in the long run. Israel is making new terrorists by the dozen.

security, two states living side by side—are very separate matters from this short-term campaign, which the great majority of Israelis feel is entirely justified. Does the answer to Israel's and Palestine's quest for peace lie in a military solution? Most decidedly not—it must be a political solution, but nobody is pretending that the Gaza campaign is a solution to anything other than the immediate protection of the citizens of Southern Israel and an open door to a solid cease-fire.

Lynn

I am so grateful to you, Brant, for sharing your anguish and grief with us and the world.

Perhaps, as Elaine suggests, we should sit shiva—at a public event at JRC, mourning:

The deaths of innocent Palestinians

The deaths of innocent Israelis

The death (for some) of a dream of an Israel that is a "light unto the nations"

The thousands injured, the hundreds of thousands who can't sleep at night, the many who have stopped speaking, the children and their parents who are in the throes of traumatic stress syndrome

I am ashamed at the lies coming out of the mouths of people who claim to speak for American Jewry. We need to help people see beyond the talking points of this propaganda (and I've seen the talking points), including the drastic misrepresentation of Gaza, as if the 1.5 million people there chose their fate of occupation and the slow strangulation—drastic shortages of food, medicine, and fuel—that Israel has imposed on Gaza since their withdrawal of troops and settlers in 2005.

I urge everyone to venture out of your own comfort zone. (I have done this myself, recently visiting Sderot.)

Read *Ha'aretz* daily. Read the *Electronic Intifada*. Go to the website of B'Tselem (the Israeli human-rights organization) and click on "statistics." Dwell for a while on the numbers of Palestinians in Gaza who have been killed. Read their bios. Note their ages.

Before the truce began in August of this year, between January and July 2008, the Israeli Army had already killed more than 400 Palestinians in Gaza, 75 of whom were children. I guess because no one seemed to be protesting these deaths too much, Israel felt emboldened that if they killed nearly as many in just a few days, no one would care. Please, please, let's prove them wrong!

Write a letter to your congressperson. To Bush. To Obama. To the newspaper. Identify yourself as a Jew who is appalled at this tragedy and in so doing give someone else the courage to speak out. Let's build a movement of intolerance for this disregard for human life. *Dayenu! Halas!*

Go to a demonstration and begin to understand the pain and anger the Palestinian diaspora is feeling. It's a close community—the ties between Palestinians in Chicago and in the Occupied Territories are deep. (Friday, January 2—at the Tribune Plaza, 3:00 p.m.)

I hope to see you there.

Danielle

I so appreciated these last two posts and have e-mailed them to several friends in the West Bank (I don't know anyone in Gaza), because I think they will give them hope.

I consider your willingness to take the risk to post with such intellectual and emotional honesty a deeply religious act, a leap of faith in the idea that that which connects us as humans (and as Jews) will outweigh divergences in political opinion.

Particularly, one line really made me think. You write: "It's becoming clear to me that our attempts to be 'rational' keep us from facing the inherent irrationality of this conflict."

I think it is incredibly important to point out that this conflict is rooted in our common, human irrationality. Both Israeli and Palestinian identities were to some extent constructed in juxtaposition to the "irrational" other, and both Israelis and Palestinians use the many irrational actions that have composed the decades-long "cycle of violence" between them to justify "reactions" that serve to increase the violence. . . . We've all heard this before. But maybe your statement alludes to what is the really relevant cycle in this conflict: You can't count the casualties inflicted by what I'd call the "cycle of dehumanization," but I would argue that it is just as relevant, just as real, and just as violent. And it is the only way that I can understand what is happening right now in Gaza.

It goes like this: Those who commit irrational acts are less human ("terrorists"/"Zionists" used in the pejorative sense), those who are less human lead lives that are less valuable (420 Gazan deaths are acceptable collateral damage/it is all right to target civilians with rockets), the pain of those who are less valuable is less worth analyzing, their voices less worth hearing, their actions are irrational.

Where and why did we learn to think that as humans we should be rational, that to be irrational is to be, somehow, less human? In a conflict with such deep ties to religion, why are we able to forget that what makes us human is exactly the part of us that is not rational?

Shlomo

I am an American and an Israeli. I believe Jews should live morally. I criticize a lot of things that Israel has done and is continuing to do. But as the call for "proportionality" is heard, I feel compelled to respond differently. Take this:

White Jewish Americans: Living on a beautiful land (actually, it was much more beautiful before it was cruelly and horribly taken away from the Native Americans), singing "This land is your land, this land is my land," etc., in a true peacenik spirit (are you including the Native Americans in the "you and me" of your song?), living in a make-believe leftist world, where they can experience all these feelings of love and compassion for humanity (especially for innocent people) and criticize Israel for all the bad things it does.

American Jews, living the good life, which was achievable only with the price of millions of people's deaths and sufferings throughout the world (whether by killing natives to steal their lands or by destroying nations for their oil and other material goods, whether by acts of war or by acts of economic rape), feel good about their beautiful conscience when they criticize Israel for its evilness. After all, beating your own is the highest act of morality.

You can only afford that spirit because the raped Native Americans have been subdued way before your lifetime, and there is no outside force (like Iran, Russia, or whoever) that keeps fueling them with weapons and propaganda.

But what if Native Americans were living in densely populated reservations, shelling rockets daily on your towns, homes, kindergartens, schools, hospitals, synagogues? What if they cowardly used their own mothers and babies as human shields against retaliation? What if their deadly weapons were to traumatize your 2-year-olds, your 5-year-olds, your 10-year-olds? What if you could not sleep at night or lead normal lives?

I am sure that in that same peacenik spirit of yours, you would have risen up and pleaded with the American government and army: Please do not harm these innocent people anymore! They have suffered enough!! Better we suffer now! Better we let them play Russian roulette with our lives and our babies' lives! Or better yet, let's all wash ourselves into the Atlantic and the Pacific, so they don't have to do the dirty work! Please let them have their beloved country back!!! After all, we have no right to be here!!

Oh, how lucky you are that this is not the case. . . . I am sure you will discount everything I say, as good Jews know how to do. I am sure you will not be able to actually imagine a terrible scenario such as I suggest above. And why should you? You will never have to live under such a threat.

Go ahead. Bash Israel. Power to you.

Jonathan

This is a very thoughtful forum, and I commend the rabbi and participants. However, I do not agree with most of my fellow Jews' condemnation of the Gaza offensive.

I am against war unless it is, truly, in self-defense. I was against Vietnam, Korea, intervention in Central America, and was out protesting the war in Iraq well before the USA launched its invasion.

Yet I see Israel's action as truly in self-defense.

I cannot ask my fellow Jews in Israel to practice peace when it is their lives, and the lives of their loved ones, that are continually threatened and killed by Hamas and their fundamentalist brethren.

Gaza is not Iraq, and Israel is not the USA. Hamas has stated its continual war with Israel from the beginning; their objective is to kill every Jew in Palestine, a geographic region that includes everything that is now Israel and Palestine. Why is it that liberal American Jews refuse to judge Hamas and Islamic fundamentalists by their murderous actions and their unambiguous words?

I am against the Israeli settlements and was against cluster bombs and civilian bombings in Lebanon last time. This is different.

In the security of our American homes, we speak of peace, as though Hamas has *ever* expressed an interest in peace for any stated objective beyond. I lived in Lower Manhattan through September 11; I have read what the Islamic fundamentalists want. It has nothing to do with peace.

Many ask how this will end: My hope is that Hamas will be defeated militarily, will lose the power to suppress and to intimidate the many Palestinians who do, through the Palestinian Authority, truly support a lasting peace with Israel.

Israel and Gaza: One Geographer's Prediction[6]

January 6, 2009

I am enormously grateful to those who've commented on my last two posts, which inspired the longest and liveliest conversation I've ever seen on this blog. I know that my words struck a nerve, but I'm grateful to have facilitated at least a small measure of open discussion.

Speaking personally, my own anguish over this tragedy has only deepened during the past week—particularly as Israel's ground invasion begins, the civilian death/casualty toll increases, and headlines scream things at us like "Cease-fire Rejected" and "No End in Sight." Still and all, I seem to have retained a uniquely masochistic impulse to devour every news report and analysis that comes my way.

Amid the myriad of articles, news reports, and blog posts I have read this past week, the one that has stuck with me the longest is a five-year-old *Jerusalem Post* interview with Israeli geographer Arnon Soffer. Soffer is widely regarded as the architect of [former Israeli Prime Minister Ariel] Sharon's disengagement plan and his insights (as morally repugnant as they are) are critical for our understanding of the actual intentions behind Israel's pullout from Gaza. In their tragically ironic way, I believe Soffer's words are profoundly important in helping us understand why it shouldn't be such a surprise that things have now come to this.

A brief excerpt:

How will the region look the day after unilateral separation?
The Palestinians will bombard us with artillery fire—and we will have to retaliate. But at least the war will be at the fence—not in kindergartens in Tel Aviv and Haifa.

Will Israel be prepared to fight this war?
First of all, the fence is not built like the Berlin Wall. It's a fence that we will be guarding on either side. Instead of entering Gaza, the way we did last week, we will tell the Palestinians that if a single missile is fired over the fence, we will fire 10 in response. And women and children will be killed, and houses will be destroyed . . .
Second of all, when 2.5 million people live in a closed-off Gaza, it's going to be a human catastrophe. Those people will become even bigger animals than they are today, with the aid of an insane fundamentalist Islam. The pressure at the border will be awful. It's going to be a terrible war. So, if we want to remain alive, we will have to kill and kill and kill. All day, every day.[7]

Discussion

Ann

I was curious to see what the demonstration looked like that Lynn promoted on a previous post. There are numerous videos on YouTube of the demonstration at Tribune Plaza on January 2.[8] [You can] see a blue and white flag with a blue swastika.

For any of you who would like to attend a rally in support of Israel in this trying time, there will be one Friday, January 9, at noon. Federal Plaza.

Rabbi Brant Rosen

Without question, many of the images from that rally are incendiary and repugnant. It is important, however, to point out that neither side of this conflict is innocent from using this kind of odious rhetoric. A few years ago I attended the annual Walk for Israel in Chicago—it took place shortly before Israel's Gaza disengagement. I vividly remember walking with my children past scores of Jewish protesters handing out flyers and loudly proclaiming, "Sharon is a Nazi!"

Sad to say, with an issue this profoundly emotional, this kind of hateful speech is fairly inevitable. The important thing, I believe, is not to judge any movement by the words of its angriest constituents, but rather by the justice of its cause.

Lynn

It's difficult to control messaging at a large demonstration and relatively speaking, there were just a few really offensive signs. In almost every case, those holding hateful signs were asked to put them down. For example, there was one being held by some young Palestinian girls, and my Palestinian colleague went up to them and asked if they understood how offensive their sign would be. The girls immediately threw their sign away and took one of the official ones, calling for an immediate cease-fire.

One of the main reasons I urged readers of Brant's blog to go to that demonstration, as you may recall, was to face the pain and anger that the Arab-American community feels as their relatives and friends in Gaza are under attack and dying by the hundreds with absolutely no place to flee. We Jews expect people to understand our fears and need for security but are too often indifferent or dismissive of the fear and suffering that the conflict with Israel inflicts upon Palestinians.

There will continue to be demonstrations throughout the week, including large ones with lots of angry people and people who just don't know what to do with that anger. Inevitably there will be a few outrageous signs, but I'm confident that the organizers of the events will make efforts to remove those signs.

Ann
Point taken.

Last night, commentators on Fox News completely overemphasized a chant by a Palestinian demonstrator calling for Jews to go back to the ovens. You are correct. You can't judge a movement by singled-out comments.

There were several parts of the video, though, that were disturbing. Do you think "Free, free Palestine" just refers to Gaza? When I have heard it in the past, it refers to all of Israel. Hamas is clear in its intentions.

"Justice of its cause," you say? What is it in the recent behavior of Hamas that you find just? Is their vision of society one that you feel comfortable supporting? The organizers of this demonstration clearly weren't supporting Jewish self-determination alongside a Palestinian state.

Rabbi Brant Rosen
I think the words "Free Palestine" mean different things to different Palestinians. For some I believe it means an independent Palestinian state alongside an independent Jewish state. For others I'm sure it means one secular democratic state with equal rights for all its citizens, both Jewish and Palestinian. For still others it might mean one free Palestinian state with no room for Jews at all.

Yes, there are some who hold this latter position, but most polls show that this is clearly a minority view. Most analysts point out that the majority of Palestinians who voted for Hamas in the last elections did not favor them because of their extreme position toward Israel, but as a rejection of the inefficient, corrupt nature of Fatah. However, if there is no progress made in the status quo very soon, I genuinely fear that the extreme view will gain in popularity for a growing number of Palestinians.

Israelis Protest Attack on Gaza[9]

January 9, 2009

I've decided I'm not going to attend the [Jewish] Federation's "Solidarity with Israel" rally tomorrow in downtown Chicago. Instead I'm going show my solidarity with Israel's soul by watching this video[10] over and over and over and over again. . . .

Discussion

Lisa

I am disappointed but not surprised. I will be down there, and shame on you for staying home.

Larry

Far easier to sit home on a high horse.

Those children in Sderot deserve our support. Israel's actions are rational. Rabbi Rosen, you have called for more emotion and less rationality. Where is your emotion for the terrified children of Sderot who have lived every moment for years wondering which bomb shelter or which doorway they will rush to if the warning siren sounds while they take their next breath?

Sitting at home helps neither the children of Israel (about 20 percent of whom are Palestinian) nor the children of Gaza (not one of whom is Jewish, unless you count Gilad Shalit). How many years should we keep assuring them that nonviolence and vulnerability will eventually persuade Hamas to stop trying to kill them?

Yes, theoretically, force solves nothing, there's always a talking cure and everyone wants the same thing we want. But, however much we wish it were not so, force works. Israelis have tried everything else that they have been told would work. History shows that in such a case, force and only force works. And talking is nice. But listening is even more important. Listen to what Hamas says. See how they have reacted to all the concessions and attempts at peace that Israel has made. Hamas does not want the same things Israelis want.

Year after year, Rabbi Rosen and his ideological compatriots tell us that Palestinians are only reacting to Israelis, as if they have no aspirations of their own, no values of their own, and no ability to assert their own will aside from reacting to Israelis. Aside from being a fairly narcissistic and borderline racist view, it is also factually wrong.

Hamas (and [PLO chairman Yasser] Arafat and [Palestinian National Authority president Mahmoud] Abbas before them) tell us with their plain words and deeds what they want and what they believe in their souls: Muslim states are good. Arab states are good. Any Jewish state is immoral. And they do not want peace in the Levant until a Palestinian state occupies all the land from the Jordan to the sea; depending upon the state's ruler, a few Jews might be allowed to live in it in a state of dhimmitude. Not because of anything any Jews have done or not done. But just because that's how Hamas's rulers read the Koran.

Stay home if you will, Rabbi Rosen, and keep the tarnish from your gleaming sense of morality. Thousands of other Jews and non-Jews will rally Friday to support Israeli and Palestinian children and the real peace that they deserve.

Eric

I strongly disagree with both of you, Lisa and Larry.

This rally will not support Palestinian children or the children of Sderot. It will support this war in Gaza. That is its purpose, whatever the motives of those who attend. And it does sound like both of you approve of this war, so there's no great difficulty there.

I, for one, would have been ashamed of Brant for going or for "standing with Israel" when his moral judgment says that Israel is doing something very, very wrong. (So does the moral judgment of a large number of Israelis, as the video shows.)

Had more American rabbis been this brave for the last 60 years, things would look very different over there now—and, I believe, much better for everyone concerned.

For those who prefer their rabbis with a comfortably tarnished sense of morality, there are plenty to choose from. I thank God, on a regular basis, that I have one of the other ones.

There are more of us than you know, Brant—and we're with you.

Rabbi Brant Rosen

I know that my words on this post were glib, and I apologize for that. I know that this situation calls for more thoughtful discussion. However, I can't apologize for deciding not to attend the rally, which was a decision I made in good faith.

I simply don't agree with the "official" Jewish community position that Israel's actions are justified acts of self-defense, and I reject the notion that attending Federation rallies should be a litmus test for one's loyalty to Israel or the Jewish people. There are many ways to support Israel and Israelis at this terrible time. (There are also many reasons to be proud of Israel and Israelis, and for me, the words and images on this video are a prime example.) Personally, I think the most meaningful way we can support children in Sderot is not by standing with a sign in Daley Plaza but by contributing to the ongoing relief efforts currently being organized (which I have urged my congregation to do).

Is my response an emotional one? I don't know, I think this is an emotional issue for us all. And I do believe that Israel's overwhelming military response to Hamas's threat smacks of emotionality in a very real way. If we're going to be "rational" as Larry suggests, I submit that we must redouble our efforts, as difficult as it is, to find another way out of this tragic, tragic crisis.

Who Am I to Criticize?[11]

January 11, 2009

You have no idea what it is like to live here. You don't understand what we live with every day. We are the ones who have to live with the consequences of this war. Who are you to criticize us?

In a very real way, of course, they're absolutely right. Although I visit Israel frequently and have spent a significant amount of time there, I have no idea what it is like to live and to work and to raise a family and to make one's home in a country that is in a constant state of war against enemies within and without.

And I certainly cannot even begin to imagine what it must be like to live in Southern Israel during this most current crisis: to try to live a life with some sense of normalcy knowing that at any moment an air-raid siren could go off and afford you and your family mere moments to await the possibility of an incoming missile.

It is true, and I must acknowledge it. American Jews do not live with the traumatic reality of this conflict. It is very different to relate to the war in Gaza from the comfort of our homes a world away rather than mere kilometers from the border. At the end of the day, I do admit to my Israeli friends that I cannot and will never understand what it must be like to live there.

But as someone who has identified deeply with Israel for his entire life, someone who has dear friends and family there, I write this with utmost honesty and respect: I reject the suggestion that I have no place speaking out against Israel's actions simply because I don't actually live there.

Who am I to criticize? I am a Jew—one of the many millions of diaspora Jews for whom the Jewish state was created. According to the official Zionist narrative, Israel is my Jewish inheritance, my Jewish national home. As a Jew living outside Israel, I have been given the right to receive instant citizenship if I ever decide to actually move there (something, by the way, that scores of Palestinians whose families have lived in that land for generations cannot do). If Israel purports to relate to me thus, do I not have a voice in the discussion over the actions the Jewish state takes in the name of my people?

Who am I to criticize? I am an American. I am a citizen whose country, the world's largest superpower, supports Israel with significant economic and military aid. My tax dollars thus implicate me in a very real way with Israel's national decisions—not least of which are its military actions. I am also the citizen of a nation whose government has essentially given Israel a blank check to take numerous measures that I believe are counter to the cause of peace, including the expropriation of Palestinian lands, destruction of homes, injustice in military courts, and widespread building of settlements in occupied Palestinian territory, to name but a few.

As I have written in earlier posts, I believe Israel's response to Hamas's missile attacks have been disproportionate and outrageous. I believe their actions only further endanger the security of Israelis while inflicting collective punishment and a severe humanitarian crisis upon Gazans. Indeed, just as I cannot understand what it must be like to be a citizen of Sderot, I cannot even begin to imagine what it must be like to be a Gazan citizen at the moment, living under constant air attack, with no running water or electricity and dwindling food, as hospitals fill up with wounded and corpses lie rotting in the streets because relief workers are unable to reach them.

Do I believe that Palestinians bear their share of the blame in this crisis? Absolutely. As the cliché goes, there is certainly enough blame to go around. But as a Jew and an American, I am uniquely implicated in the actions Israel takes. We Jews and Americans must bear our share of responsibility for this crisis. How far are we willing to go to contribute to a solution?

Discussion

Anya

I want to thank you for your reflections, which I've been following and encouraging others to read.

I want to share my thoughts after continually hearing Israeli spokespeople talking of the civilian dead and wounded in Gaza. They repeatedly claim they don't intend to harm civilians, that Hamas puts them in harm's way intentionally, that civilians should rid themselves of Hamas, and that, unfortunately, "this is war."

- If a gunman grabbed one of our own children or loved ones as a "human shield," we would not, seeing our own beloved innocent in danger, shoot through our loved one to destroy the gunman. The fact of the innocent civilians has to change the game rules—or it should!
- If a heart surgeon routinely damaged all the surrounding organs while working on damaged hearts, he would not keep his job and patients, and he would be held to account for knowing that each time he did surgery, he caused so much "collateral damage" to living tissue.
- Without options, resources, freedom of movement, what do we expect Gazan children to be able to do—eradicate Hamas? That's absurd and cruel.
- For the last eight years, we've had leadership that vast numbers of us didn't vote for or endorse—who have wrought all sorts of violence upon innocent people. Because we were not able to eradicate them from office, should bombs have dropped on us?
- Would any of us raise children as siblings to believe that the way a bigger brother ought to handle being poked by a smaller brother is to grab a bat and smash all the younger brother's fingers, so he can never poke anyone again? (This reiterates an earlier commentator.)

Additionally, I urge all to write to the Obama team, as I did, asking him to speak out. Certainly, if he is speaking out on the economy as president-elect, because it is such a pressing matter, he can/should also be speaking out on what is a major world security issue with far-reaching implications.

Larry

Anya—Interesting analogy. I don't think anyone would intentionally shoot the child. I don't think we would tell the kidnapper to go ahead and have a good life with our child.

And if the kidnapper told us that in 10 seconds he was going to shoot the child, then I think most of us would be happy for a sharpshooter to try to kill the kidnapper.

Gazans have had options and resources for the last century—repeated offers of peace, repeated offers to share the land and resources, repeated offers of more resources, such as the houses Israelis built for Gazans trapped (by their Egyptian then-rulers) in camps (now they are trapped by their own Palestinian rulers), and on and on and on. No, the children have no options. But their parents do. They could choose compromise and peace. They could choose to live in peace with their neighbors.

As for proportionality, not sure what [that] would be. Would that mean lobbing 6,000 crude missiles into Gaza regardless of what they hit? Would it mean randomly killing and terrorizing the population of Gaza until as many were hurt as Hamas had made suffer in Israel?

Finally, what is the better way? It is all well and good to vow to "redouble" our efforts. But if you have criticism of what Israel is doing, then you have an obligation to suggest a better way, one that hasn't been tried and failed, one that has a reasonable chance of working.

Louis

I am an Israeli, I live in Jerusalem, and I am against the war. Who are you to criticize Israel, for its Occupation, the war, etc.? You are the right person to do so. For far too long the only Jewish voice that was afforded any sort of authenticity was the voice that supported the settlements, the Occupation, and Israel without question. For who were they to criticize, safely from their living rooms, their sanctuaries, and their Federations?

Well, look where that has gotten us now. . . .

Pablo

I'll follow up on your analogy of the kidnapper telling us that she/he will shoot our child.

Of course I'd like a sharpshooter to take him down. But would we be happy sending *our* other children to destroy the kidnapper's house and kill his friends and neighbors?

For the analogy to reflect the situation, I think we would need to describe the guy a little better . . . because he is not just some random guy passing by. A lot of questions come to mind. . . . Did our security guard kill his son or daughter? Did our good friend bulldoze his home? Did he used to be our neighbor? Does he have running water? Is his life hell? Are there another 2 million people on the brink of becoming as crazy as he is?

Barbara

I am shocked and saddened by the gaping blind spot we Jews have about Israel. When I attend Torah study, the high holidays, and

Passover, I am taught, discuss, and think about these stories as meta-phor, fable, myth, object lessons. All very powerful versions of *behave*.

To me, "Israel" is a state of righteousness and lovingkindness inde-pendent of any physical place. It is like thinking about the Messiah: a human being, no? A messianic era brought about by collective *tikkun olam*, yes. The worship of a piece of land, any piece of land, to this degree is idolatry.

Is the cost of keeping a piece of land worth even one innocent human life? And every time a piece of land is fused with man-made religion (and this I do mean literally, as in male-dominated), this will continue to happen.

There was another time in history when "innocents" stood by and did nothing in the face of brutal oppression. Why are we now doing the same, with different rationalizations?

Again, I know the arguments—no land is worth the killing.

Israel and Gaza: Speaking about the Unspeakable[12]

January 14, 2009

Stayed up until the wee hours last night surfing the Web, reading report after report about Gaza. Despite my better judgment, I couldn't take my eyes off the horrific reports that Israel was using white phosphorus in densely populated civilian areas. After seeing a picture in the *New York Times*[13] of a 10-year-old boy who had lost his eyesight and most of the skin from his face from phosphorus burns, I turned to reports on B'Tselem and Human Rights Watch. I'm ashamed to report I was reading this stuff well past the time it would have made sense to go to bed. . . .

Needless to say, as I read, my mind and emotions reacted a mile a minute, ranging back and forth from defensiveness to righteous anger and everything in between. Is it really true? Perhaps the reports are mistaken? Burning children alive in the streets? Couldn't there possibly be another explanation?

It's been all the more upsetting because there has been a near-total absence of any honest communal discussion about these kinds of reports. On one end of the spectrum, some can discount upsetting news like this by placing exclusive responsibility upon Hamas for cynically using civil-ians as human shields. On the other end, others will excoriate Israel for the barbaric genocide it is perpetrating against the Palestinian people. The rest, I imagine, simply bury the news deep down and move on.

This morning upon arriving at work, I read one of the weekly e-briefings that I regularly receive from a well-known American Jewish organization. It purported to give an up-to-date status report/analysis on the situation in Gaza, but it was essentially yet another excuse to dispassionately analyze Israel's successful military "operation" in Gaza.

In the meantime, there was nary a hint of the untold civilian suffering and loss that this horrid war has wrought. I don't know what I expected, really. I shouldn't underestimate how hard it is for a community to find the wherewithal to speak about the unspeakable. Is it too much to hope that we find a way to start?

The Arrow Cannot Be Taken Back[14]

January 20, 2009

When an arrow leaves the hand of a warrior he cannot take it back.
(Mechilta of Rabbi Ishmael, Beshallach, Shirah)

From this classic Jewish teaching, we learn that violence unleashes a myriad of consequences that we can neither control nor reverse. Apropos of recent events, I take this to mean many things:

- When you loose tons and tons of bombs on a small patch of land inhabited by 1.5 million people, you will invariably kill a myriad of civilians.
- We cannot begin to fathom the depths of grief and loss that Israel's actions have brought upon scores of Gazans, their families, and loved ones. Indeed, even in the wake of a fragile cease-fire, the death toll continues to rise. (Read this article from today's *New York Times*, which documents heartbreaking scenes of victims continuing to be pulled from the rubble weeks after they were killed.[15])
- We cannot comprehend the anger and fury Israel's actions have inspired in Gazans, Palestinians, and the Arab world at large. Yesterday I spoke with a Palestinian-American friend who told me he had never seen the Arab streets so inflamed against Israel—and in many cases, against their own governments. (The anger of Egyptian citizens toward their government is frightening to behold.)
- It is impossible to underestimate the damage this war has done to the already tenuous prospects for peace between Israel and Palestine. Most analysts seem to agree that no matter whoever might be considered the military

"victor" in this war, the moderate Fatah (at present, Israel's only Palestinian peace partner) is the heaviest political casualty. Moderate Arab countries are all the queasier about supporting the peace process, and the Saudis are now under fire to pull their plan from the table.

This quote from the *Times* article above sums up the tragic new reality on the ground:

In the upper middle-class neighborhood of Tal al-Hawa, Ziad Dardasawi, 40, a wood importer, was trying to process what had happened. As a supporter of Fatah, a political rival of Hamas, Mr. Dardasawi said that he despised Hamas, but that its rocket fire was no justification for Israel's military response.

"Let's say someone from Hamas fired a rocket—is it necessary to punish the whole neighborhood for that?" he said, standing in a stairway of his uncle's house, where furniture had been smashed, and all the windows broken.

He drew on an analogy he thought would strike a chord: "In the U.S., when someone shoots someone, is his entire family punished?"

The Israeli actions made the situation more intractable, he said. "How can I convince my neighbors now for the option of peace? I can't."

He added: "Israel is breeding extremists. The feeling you get is that they just want you to leave Gaza."

Discussion

BF

Arab anger, Palestinian anger, inflammation on the streets are not compelling reasons to change behavior. Anger is by definition an irrational response. Anger often begets violence, which necessitates a response to protect one's self against that violence, which often begets more anger. Just because someone is angry doesn't mean I should not defend myself from his violence.

Elaine

I have to disagree. Anger is *not* an irrational response, especially when basic conditions of living are not being met. There is no question that the residents of Gaza do not enjoy even the most basic of human rights at this point—e.g., food, water, let alone freedom of movement. We can all argue endlessly about why that is, who started what, etc., but the fact remains that unless the underlying causes of tension on both sides are addressed, violence will continue. There is little evidence that continued aggressive military action on the part of Israel results in better long-term security for Israelis, just as the Palestinians are not served in the long run by the violent actions of Hamas. (And by the way, I think we all have to be very careful not to lapse into characterizing all Palestinians or Arabs as equivalent with Hamas.) I truly believe the only way forward—away from the endless cycle of violence—requires a vision as radical as that of MLK's or Gandhi's or Mandela's. Those leaders showed that real anger against oppression can beget radical change, without violence. Unfortunately, I have no idea where that is going to come from in *either* Palestine or Israel.

Rabbis on the Third Rail[16]

January 29, 2009

Having nothing better to do, I spent a fair amount of time last week trying to spearhead a Rabbinical Statement on Gaza. Sorry to report that after several days of back and forth, we had to fold the entire project when it became clear that we wouldn't find a wording that would satisfy a critical mass of rabbis. (To make matters even worse, an early version of the statement was precipitously posted on the Net before we had consensus. I'm fairly sure it's still floating around out there in cyberland in all its unauthorized glory. . . .)

There were several motivations for the statement. First and foremost, it came from a desire to express a rabbinical voice of opposition to Israel's military action in Gaza, which we felt was strategically disastrous and morally outrageous. It was also important to us that Jewish community leaders publicly expressed sorrow not just for the loss of Israeli life but also for the massive devastation experienced by Gazans during the past three weeks:

> We condemn the firing of missiles from Gaza that forced so many Israelis to live in fear and we mourn the loss of life that resulted from these attacks. However, we are devastated by Israel's disproportionate use of force, killing a myriad of people, including over 450 children. In the wake of such overwhelming civilian bloodshed, we can only ask, in the words of the Talmud, "How do we know that our blood is redder than the blood of our fellow?"

Additionally, because we felt we could not address the tragedy of the war while ignoring the larger political context of the conflict, our statement contained a strong message for the new American administration:

> We urge our new President to turn back the policies of previous administrations—policies which have given Israel permission to take numerous measures that we believe are counter to the cause of peace, including the expropriation of Palestinian lands, destruction of Palestinians' homes and businesses, and the widespread building of settlements in occupied Palestinian territory.

The most controversial aspect of our statement was our call for the new administration to take an assertive diplomatic approach with Israel and not to rule out the withholding of military aid "as necessary." As anyone familiar with American Jewish community politics must surely know, withholding aid is the "third rail" for organized Jewry—that is, the line that can never be crossed.

And it was this sentence more than any other that confounded our core group of signers. We tried various different wordings: "if the administration deems it necessary," "withholding of aid as a last resort," "withholding aid for noncompliance"—but in the end, no wording seemed to suffice. Some felt that this was going too far, and others refused to sign unless a strong statement about withholding aid was included.

I can certainly understand why this issue pushes such profound buttons for American Jews. It plays on our deepest fears as well as our abiding sense of Jewish vulnerability. For many American Jews, the withdrawal of aid would be tantamount to abandonment by Israel's most significant ally. But there are other Jews—and I believe their ranks are growing—who simply do not want to be party to Israel's growing militarism and are not afraid to admit it.

For my part, I was less concerned about this particular issue, and perhaps that just reflects my own naiveté. Although I understand our community's fears, I also believe that withholding aid is probably the strongest diplomatic "stick" America can wield with Israel—and in the end it may be the only one that will ever really get Israel's attention. But whatever we might think about this issue, I just don't agree that it must be ipso facto off the table for mere discussion in our community—and I deeply resent those in our community who reserve the right to excommunicate others who hold this opinion in good faith.

It's all moot anyhow. No matter how we worded the statement, we couldn't retain our core of signers. Some asked to have their names removed for various reasons. Many told me they would have loved to have signed but couldn't for organizational or professional reasons. After several days, we called it quits.

I know there are some decent lessons in all of this, but mostly I'm just frustrated and very, very sad. I know for a fact that there are many Jews out there who were waiting for rabbis to make a statement of this kind, regardless of the final wording. I still believe that whatever the political realities, those of us who care about the shared fate of Israelis and Palestinians will have to find the courage of our convictions.

For me it really comes down to this: Two of our most sacred Jewish values are *ahavat yisrael* (love for the Jewish people) and *ahavat habriot* (love for all people). Should it really be that hard for us to promote both with equal passion?

Discussion

Thomas

Dear Rabbi,

What do you mean with "Having nothing better to do"? This was, this is important, what could you do better than to work to protect innocent people?

Israel was—many years ago—a reference for me: a democratic society surrounded by Arab countries that mostly are not democratic (to phrase it politely). But in the course of the past 25 years or so, I have seen Israel slipping toward a militaristic country, a country where Jewish lives are more highly valued than non-Jewish lives.

Please, understand me right: The rockets fired on Sderot and other places are pure terrorism and justify a response. But Palestinian children and Palestinian people are also created by God and are protected by the word in the Decalogue (not to speak of the Fourth Geneva Convention).

Please, Rabbi, I do not think that your efforts, your thoughts about these wasted lives are worthless! Peace can only come to Israel if Jews and Muslims accept that they must live together, that they must respect each other and give each other the chance of living in dignity. Your voice must not be silenced, and I hope that other rabbis will see that what you are doing is important.

I hope with all my force that peace will come, that Arabs and Israelis, that Muslims and Jews will live together and respect each other's right to live, even if they don't "love" each other. This implies respect for innocent lives—please do all that you can to defend this view of a better world! I know, it requires a lot of courage to do so, and I am sure that many people will support you even when they don't speak out.

Marge

Perhaps we need to wait and see what the new administration's diplomatic approach to Israel will be before inserting the word "assertive" or threatening to withhold aid. After all, they've only been in office for one week, and it seems to me that the president's reaching out to the Arab world and appointing George Mitchell to the region are first positive steps. Why now, at this new hopeful beginning, should the rabbinical statement be so aggressive?

Soldiers Speak Out[17]

March 20, 2009

Once permission has been given to the destroyer to do harm, it does not discriminate between the guilty and the innocent. (Mechilta, Bo)

Today the *New York Times* reported on an issue that has gripped the Israeli press and public for some time now:

> In the two months since Israel ended its military assault on Gaza . . . testimony is emerging from within the ranks of soldiers and officers alleging a permissive attitude toward the killing of civilians and reckless destruction of property . . . . On Thursday, the military's chief advocate general ordered an investigation into a soldier's account of a sniper killing a woman and her two children who walked too close to a designated no-go area by mistake, and another account of a sharpshooter who killed an elderly woman who came within 100 yards of a commandeered house.[18]

In reading these accounts, I'm especially struck by the powerfully defensive reaction of many within Israel—insisting that these were either isolated incidents or that they were simply untrue. Witness Defense Minister [Ehud] Barak's recent statement on Israel radio:

> The Israeli Army is the most moral in the world, and I know what I'm talking about because I know what took place in the former Yugoslavia, in Iraq.[19]

I don't know if Israel's army is the "most moral" in the world. I'm not sure if I even know what that means. I don't know what we really expect when we train young men and women to kill, give them the most sophisticated killing instruments on Earth, and then demonize their enemies before sending them off to battle.

Israel has long claimed its army follows the military war ethic of *tohar haneshek* ("purity of arms"). Whether or not this was ever true, there seems to be growing evidence that in the heat of battle (or, if you prefer, the "fog of war"), the difference between "legal killing" and "war crimes" becomes increasingly fuzzy to those who wield the weapons. And I'm fairly sure that this is the case whether or not the soldiers in question happen to be Jewish.

Even more disturbing are the reports from Israeli soldiers that the Israeli rabbinate is urging them to view this conflict as nothing less than a holy war. Richard Silverstein, blogging over at *Tikun Olam*, has translated some of the Hebrew press accounts, uncovering this jaw-dropping testimony from a commander named Ran:

> The military rabbis sent us lots of material and in these articles the message was clear: we are the nation of Israel. We arrived by a miracle in Israel. God returned us to the Land (of Israel). Now we must battle to remove the non-Jews who disturb us in our conquest of the Holy Land. That was the main message. And the sense of many of the soldiers in this operation was that it was a religious war. From my perspective as a commander, I tried to talk about politics and various strains within Palestinian society. That not everyone in Gaza was Hamas and not every resident wants to conquer us. I wanted to explain to them that this war was not about Kiddush Hashem (sanctifying the name of God), but about stopping Qassam fire.[20]

Expect more horrifying news in the coming weeks. . . .

Discussion

Ron

The IDF has just abandoned its official investigation, or probe, into the conduct of IDF soldiers during the assault on Gaza.[21]

Apparently it's sufficient to conclude that the soldiers' testimony is hearsay without investigating to see whether it is or isn't.

Lisa

So now that the two stories and videos have proved to be hearsay and/or manufactured propaganda, will any of you retract or refine your comments? Or will you be like the *New York Times* and not bother?

Rabbi Brant Rosen

Lisa,

Thus far the only investigation into these allegations was a hastily concluded one that the IDF itself conducted. I agree with the Israeli human-rights org B'Tselem, which stated, "The speedy closing of the investigation raises suspicions that the very opening of this investigation was merely the army's attempt to wipe its hands of all blame for illegal activity during Operation Cast Lead."[22]

With all due respect, a military investigating itself is no investigation at all. A significant coalition of Israeli human-rights organizations has called upon the attorney general to appoint an independent investigation into these alleged abuses. Until that happens, I think it will be premature to conclude that these allegations are "hearsay" or "manufactured propaganda."

Chapter 2

The Dominos Fall

February–June 2009

After expressing my honest response to Israel's actions during Operation Cast Lead, I broadened my scope to address a variety of subjects pertaining to Israel and Palestine, including the Palestinian call for boycott, divestment, and sanctions (BDS); my feelings toward Israeli Independence Day; Palestinian nonviolent resistance in the West Bank; and the increasing failure of the American-brokered peace process.

The Contradictions of Ethnic Nationalism[1]

February 10, 2009

It's the last day before the Israeli elections, and there seems to be widespread agreement that Yisrael Beiteinu party chairman Avigdor Lieberman is going to win big—perhaps as many as 19 or 20 seats. They've already pulled ahead of the Labor party, and by now it's virtually a foregone conclusion that Lieberman will emerge from these elections with considerable political influence.

It's also fair to say that those of us who cherish the values of liberal democracy are recoiling at the prospect of a politically ascendant Avigdor Lieberman, whose most notorious campaign promise is a requirement for all Arab citizens of Israel to sign a loyalty oath to the Jewish state:

> [Lieberman's] loyalty oath would require all Israelis to vow allegiance to Israel as a Jewish, democratic state, to accept its symbols, flag and anthem, and to commit to military service or some alternative service. Those who declined

to sign such a pledge would be permitted to live here as residents but not as voting citizens.

Currently Israeli Arabs, who constitute 15 percent to 20 percent of the population, are excused from national service. Many would like to shift Israel's identify from that of a Jewish state to one that is defined by all its citizens, arguing that only then would they feel fully equal.

Mr. Lieberman says that there is no room for such a move and that those who fail to grasp the centrality of Jewish identity to Israel have no real place in it.[2]

These are disturbing ideas, to be sure, and it's even more troubling that they seem to be finding traction with increasing numbers of the Israeli electorate.

And yet . . .

. . . and yet in the wee hours of the night, I just can't shake the nagging feeling that the real reason Lieberman makes us squirm is that he shines a bright light on the logical contradictions of political Zionism: an ethnic nationalist movement that has always sought to create a Jewish state in a land that also happens to be populated by millions of non-Jewish inhabitants.

Take, for example, Israel's Declaration of Independence, which refers specifically to Israel as a "Jewish state" committed to the "ingathering of the exiles" but also promises complete equality of political and social rights for all its citizens, irrespective of race, religion, or sex.[3] Therein lies the tension: The first principle emphasizes the creation of a state that privileges the Jewish people, and the latter promises equal rights for all its citizens.

I don't say this easily: I'm not sure this is a nut that Israel will ever be fully able to crack. It is indeed notable that Israel has repeatedly tried and failed to create a constitution that legally guarantees equality for all citizens of this exclusively Jewish state. In the meantime, Israel's Arab citizens suffer from what we Americans would consider significant institutional discrimination with only limited recourse to the rule of law.

So as a nice liberal American Jew fully prepared to voice my outrage at Lieberman's likely Tuesday morning success, here are some questions I feel compelled to ponder:

As proud citizens and beneficiaries of a secular, multicultural nation, are we ready to face the deeper implications of Israel's ethnic nationalism?

Will it ever truly be possible, in a country defined as exclusively Jewish, for its Arab citizens to be considered as anything but second-class citizens (or, at worst, traitors)?

If it does indeed come down to a choice between a Jewish or a democratic state, which will we ultimately support?

Discussion

Stan

Wow—you really opened up the big questions with this one. . . .
A few thoughts:

1) I personally remain appalled at any attempt in any democratic state to have people register a vow of allegiance. If there is not the faith in each other, then no vow will work and will only promote an increasing "us" vs. "them" mentality. Institutional discrimination can be worked on. Traitor mentalities are bitter, hateful, divisive, and directly contrary to plurality and inclusiveness.

2) I think, in the end, you set up a false dichotomy. The question is not whether you can be a religious democracy, but rather how do you work on it so that you can indeed be true to both. Any democracy can and should guarantee a voice and rights of protection to minority viewpoints. And yes, I believe it *is* possible to allow all its Arab citizens to be afforded full citizenship.

3) I think the issue relates more strongly to the perpetual war mentality that both Jews and Arabs find themselves in. I remember before the pullout of settlements in Gaza a story I saw about a settler who had moved into Gaza some 30 to 40 years ago and was welcomed by the surrounding Arab community and until about 20 years ago had very good relations with her Arab neighbors. It is the fear mentality, the omnipresent sense that there are your people and there [is] the other, that leads to the sense of making sure "they" are put in their place.

4) The underlying question, which I take to be whether or not any society can be a religious democracy, depends largely on exactly your definition of democracy. Any organized society will have members who have fewer or more privileges—what's more important is to ensure that everyone can have a voice and that everyone has equal rights to justice. These seem, at their best, to be inherently Jewish ideals and so don't seem to contradict a Jewish state. Much of the early Israeli state philosophy was more along the lines of socialist ideals—you could also ask if a true socialist democracy is possible.

5) Ultimately, as I said above, I believe the Jewish/democracy choice is a false choice. We have a secular democracy here—what we need is a Jewish state. We need to fight for a Jewish state that lives up to the ethical, practical, and compassionate behaviors so lacking

in many of its recent leaders. We need to fight for a Jewish democratic state that is Jewish in the best sense of our ideals and not
the worst sense of our self-righteousness, isolationist and nationalistic fear-mongering, and dogmatism. We don't have to accept the
politics of fear in Israel any more than we do in the US, nor do we
have to accept its practice as forcing us to choose between Israel's
being Jewish and being democratic.

Thanks, as always, for forcing us to open up our minds as well as
our souls.

Lesley

Stan, two questions: Are we talking about "Jewish" as a religion or as
an ethnic identity? Many of the most ardent Zionists and indeed a large
portion of Israel's Jewish population consider themselves more secular
than religious.

Second, whether it's a religious or an ethnically Jewish state, is it
really possible to have a functioning democracy that privileges one
group, that insists the country exists primarily for that group? Would
you feel that you were a full citizen of a Christian democratic state,
one that gave you legal rights but also stated its intent that you would
always remain a minority? Isn't that why a lot of us came to the US?

"Any organized society will have members who have fewer or more
privileges. . . ." Yes, but all citizens should have the same privileges,
or at least the same hope of achieving them through work, education,
etc. In a democracy, privileges should not be based on ethnicity.

Would your ideal democratic Jewish state have a law of return? If so,
how is it democratic to offer citizenship based on ethnicity or religion?

If Israel is truly democratic, what is going to happen if the Arab
population becomes a majority, which, given demographic trends, is a
distinct possibility?

Ron

The key issue to me is not what a given nation-state (people or laws)
considers itself to be so much as who its laws are for. "For" both in the
sense of whom they benefit and the sense of who is subject to their
enforcement.

For instance, Sweden's official national religion is Lutheranism.
Lutheran values may be found in details of its legal system and many
details of historical policy. It is a "Lutheran state," or hey, take away
the quotation marks, as they don't need to be there.

However, nothing about people's religion, or the way they practice it, has anything to do with civic life in Sweden. The laws apply to everyone, and every citizen is equal in participation. Over the past five years, Sweden has accepted many Iraqi refugees—many may well become citizens. Although some Swedes react with ethnic suspicion (call it what it is, prejudice), they also know that the laws of the land are not going to be two-tiered for those Muslim or eastern-church Christian citizens when the day comes.

I suggest that the phrase "Jewish state," as written in Israel's Declaration of Independence, is straightforwardly interpreted in a completely different way from Sweden's Lutheran state. It is two-tiered: for Jews, but against everyone else. Also, as I see it, that is unacceptable from the outset to my sensibilities—here speaking as a member of the citizenry [that] currently pays [for] the lion's share of Israel's military and settlement policies without any political voice in that process.

There isn't any way 'round that. It could be called a Jewish state or not, and the issue remains: Either Israel's policies are bigoted and discriminatory, or they aren't. And the only way they wouldn't be is if the laws applied to all, fairly and equally. In this, I strongly agree with Susan Nathan's excellent book *The Other Side of Israel* that the current laws and their practice are egregiously Jim Crow. If Israel were a Jewish state in the same sense that Sweden is a Lutheran one, that would be different and quite reasonable. My chief conclusion is that the phrase "Jewish state" currently serves as a red herring, such that criticizing Israel's discriminatory policies is shunted into challenging the Jewish character of its founding. This trap should be called out for what it is, a rhetorical trick, and defied.

All right, perhaps there is a good place to stop, but I might as well nab the goat as well as the kid. . . .

I know of no substantial modern state (i.e., not a tiny island somewhere) that is characterized by a single ethnicity or way of life. In various literature regarding Israel, references are often made to "the French have France, the English have England," and similar. It's nonsense. All those nations are characterized by gradients and pockets of diverse ethnicities (or religious practices, or other distinct cultural tags), some very keenly felt. To go back to Sweden, there exists a smooth gradient of Swede-to-Finn across the islands and coastlines of both nations, including a substantial number of ethnically Swedish Finnish citizens, despite strong stereotypes, prejudices, and a mild myth of separatism within each. Or, the very notion of "Switzerland for the Swiss!" should clarify the point: Thinking of Swiss-ness in exclusive language, ethnic, or religious terms is silly to the point of outright laughter. Or, if you don't mind being punched in the nose, ask a Welshman if he's English.

That one-people-one-state concept has been idealized as an entitlement by various splinter groups since the early 19th century, and it's sadly entered (and tainted) the recognition of former colonial states since the inception of the UN, for instance in Africa. It is a chimera and, in addition, a recipe for oppression and bloodshed. It results in the current affairs in the Congo, or, in the case of a state propped up by a foreign superpower, the astonishingly cruel, spoiled, and ignorant culture of Saudi Arabia. Saudi Arabia perfectly illustrates what happens when a nation does privilege one group/religion as the nation's reason for being. It is widely as well as domestically perceived as a single Arab community bound by a single application of Wahhabi religious law, but that is incorrect, because it overlooks the marginalized non-Wahhabi Sunni and Shi'a populations as well as the imported army of [South Asian] labor. Saudi Arabia is not unified as a one-people-state; rather, its laws are brutally discriminatory and oppressive to preserve the illusion of "pure" national identity.

Given that, the very notion of "the Jewish state's" being associated with a Jewish-only population, and in lieu of that, being only for the benefit of the Jews there to the exclusion of anyone else there . . . it's not emulating other nations, such as Sweden. An Israel such as envisioned by [Jewish Defense League founder] Meir Kahane or Avigdor Lieberman, or as permitted by centrists who ally with them, would either implode under civil strife or come to resemble Saudi Arabia.

Steve

I may be ignorant, but Israel's Arab population has had about 10 seats in the Israeli parliament. However, the Arab parties that hold those seats do not seem to be using them to promote a progressive social and economic agenda for Israel's Arab electorate.

Is there a list of public works, health care, or educational improvement projects put forth by the elected representatives of the Arab minority that repeatedly languishes in the Israeli budgeting process? If so, I haven't heard of them.

Can it be that despite living side by side with their Jewish brothers and sisters these past 65 years, the Arab electorate in Israel still has not developed the civic tools that allow them to be well represented in the Israeli political process?

I can't help but think that if there were, indeed, widespread institutionalized discrimination preventing the implementation of a progressive Arab-sector social and economic agenda, we'd be hearing much more about it from the all-too-vocal anti-Zionist left, if not from the leaders of the Israeli Arab electorate itself.

Please don't respond with platitudes about its being the responsibility of Israel's Jews to care for the needs of its Arab citizens. Israel is a very open democracy, with each interest group—whether ethnic or age or religious or interest based—obliged to organize and to represent its own interests. Ten parliamentary seats are nothing to sneeze at in the context of Israeli political life—but only if that political platform is used to benefit its constituents.

The social and economic culture of Israel's Arab communities— vague and largely out of the spotlight as they have chosen to remain— still seem to mirror the undemocratic social and political structures of the neighboring Arab nations.

Israel's Jewish majority is not to blame for these cultural differences that result in significant differences in the allocation of public resources.

We must expect Israel's Arab electorate to speak for itself. They must play the Israeli political game. They must vote in greater numbers, increasing the number of seats in parliament that represent their community's (as yet uncrystallized?) social and economic goals.

If Arab Israelis want to show Jewish Israelis that they see themselves as a productive part of Israeli society for the long haul, it would be easy for them to convincingly reject Palestinian and Arab-Muslim irredentism, vocally ally themselves with progressive forces in the Arab-Muslim world and with the Peace Camp in Israel, and take other equally convincing steps to ally themselves with their Jewish-Israeli neighbors, while working equally hard to advance their own domestic agenda for communal progress.

Ron

Steve, I think you've answered your own question with the phrases you chose:

1. They've "chosen" to remain out of the spotlight.
2. The "Jewish majority is not to blame. . . ."
3. ". . . it would be easy for them. . . ."

Given those, I am not optimistic that my point will mean much to you, but at least I can provide a reference if you're interested.

The book *The Other Side of Israel,* by Susan Nathan, addresses this issue in extreme detail. It does not concern the West Bank or Gaza. Nathan is not an ideologue but an empiricist; as a Jewish immigrant from England and a life-long Zionist, as well as an impeccable rights activist in South Africa, she knew what she was looking at when she finally arrived. She provides such clear details on both trends and instances that her conclusion is inescapable: Israeli society is discriminatory to an onerous degree, refuting claims such as yours that the non-Jewish Arab citizens can't seem to handle democracy. She also carefully documents how the activist Jewish groups in Israel focus on the Occupied Territories and ignore the Israeli Arabs just outside town, which is itself discrimination as strong as any other.

Israeli Arabs face quasi-legal, institutional discrimination similar to those faced by black Americans during the Jim Crow era. Few law books of that time actually explicitly forbade certain actions, property ownership, participation in elections, or other aspects of being American citizens. However, specific combinations of local statutes and practices, some authoritative (police, law) and some informal (habitual disinformation or lack of access), resulted in barriers that were simply too high to climb for most people's circumstances. Also, many rights or opportunities that exist on paper are not practically available.

One of her most important points is the distinction between citizens and nationals. The non-Jewish native citizens are not considered nationals, and a wide variety of services and access to resources are reserved for nationals alone.

At the policy and representation level, I have heard many times, "The Arabs vote, so what excuse do they have?" and it does not stand up to critique based on what really happens. Arab parties (a bit of a misnomer: Jewish members are not barred and can be found there) are routinely excluded from coalitions. You may interpret this as "they're not ready," or "they don't know how to participate," or whatever you like, but US history provides very clear lessons regarding statements of that kind. First among those lessons is that separate is not equal. A marginalized group cannot improve its circumstances via its (isolated) mainstream representation alone.

Gil

Ron, Israeli Arabs participate in Israeli politics outside the Arab parties. As members of the Labor party and Likud, they have participated and have even been ministers in Israeli governing coalitions.

The formal and informal barriers to full equality largely stem from two factors. Preexisting socioeconomic differences (most of the Arabs that remained in Israel after 1948 were peasants and villagers, most of the urban middle class left), which Israel has made great strides in reducing, e.g., educational attainment, infant mortality, life expectancy; and secondly, real security concerns. You completely ignore [the fact that] Israel has been in conflict with its Arab minority's co-nationals for the entirety of existence. Can you think of a single analogous situation where the minority has been treated better than the Arabs in Israel, or do you hold Israel to a standard that no one else is actually expected to meet?

The comparison with Sweden is laughable. The average Israeli 10-year-old has experienced more racial, ethnic, religious, and linguistic diversity than the average Swede will in her lifetime. Israel has accepted thousands of non-Jewish and even Muslim refugees just like Sweden. The Israeli Declaration of Independence isn't "against everybody else," and it is malicious of you to say so. And anyway, the series of basic laws as interpreted by the Supreme Court, not the Declaration of Independence, governs civic life. The court is renowned for ensuring that discriminatory laws or government actions don't stand.

Finally, although the Jim Crow analogy is novel, it is about as accurate as the more common apartheid and Nazi libels Israel faces and disgraces those who utter and publish it.

Rabbi Brant Rosen

As Ron pointed out, Jim Crow refers to institutional discrimination that undercuts formal rights "guaranteed" by a state. You are free to agree or to disagree with his analysis, but you are crossing the line when you label his words (or my publishing them) as "libel." Moreover, your association of them with Nazism is profoundly offensive. This kind of incendiary rhetoric only contributes to the muzzling of honest debate that is so critical to this conflict.

In the meantime, you've conveniently dodged my central questions about the contradictions inherent in Israel's ethnic nationalism. As I understand your argument, because Israel has raised the standard of living of its Arab citizens, they shouldn't complain about their status as second-class citizens. And the reason for the socioeconomic disparity between Arab and Jew in Israel is because Israel's founding forced the more middle-class Palestinians from their homes? I'd say that begs even more troubling questions.

Finally, I strongly disagree with your assertion that the laws issued by Israel's Supreme Court "govern its civil life." As long as Israel has no constitution upon which the Court can base its rulings, these laws exist in a legal vacuum—and there will never be a true foundation that guarantees equal rights for all its citizens.

Is BDS Anti-Semitism?[5]

April 1, 2009

For many Jews, no three letters seem to conjure up rage and fury as effectively as BDS. Still, I have a strong suspicion that we'll be hearing them bandied about increasingly in the coming months.

Since the Gaza war, the movement for global boycott/divestment/sanctions against Israel seems to have gained new momentum. Among its prominent new supporters is economic journalist/activist Naomi Klein, who made a passionate call for BDS at the peak of the crisis:

> Every day that Israel pounds Gaza brings more converts to the BDS cause, and talk of cease-fires is doing little to slow the momentum. Support is even emerging among Israeli Jews. In the midst of the assault roughly 500 Israelis, dozens of them well-known artists and scholars, sent a letter to foreign ambassadors stationed in Israel. It calls for "the adoption of immediate restrictive measures and sanctions" and draws a clear parallel with the anti-apartheid struggle. "The boycott on South Africa was effective, but Israel is handled with kid gloves. . . . This international backing must stop."
>
> Yet even in the face of these clear calls, many of us still can't go there. The reasons are complex, emotional and understandable. And they simply aren't good enough. Economic sanctions are the most effective tools in the nonviolent arsenal. Surrendering them verges on active complicity.[6]

Count longtime peace activist Rabbi Arthur Waskow as one of those who "still can't go there." The current issue of *In These Times* contains a fascinating debate between Klein and Waskow on the merits of BDS. For his part, Waskow opposes it primarily for tactical reasons:

> [The] BDS approach is not the way to bring about the change that is absolutely necessary. The most important, and probably the only effective, change that can be brought about is a serious change in the behavior of the U.S. government. That means we need to engage in serious organizing within the United States. . . . Boycotts and divestment are not going to do it. I understand that they express a kind of personal purity—"not with my money you don't"—but they won't change U.S. policy, which is exactly what needs to be changed.[7]

Klein and Waskow's conversation is edifying as far as it goes, but to my mind it doesn't address the main concern over BDS articulated by so many American Jews: Namely, that given all the odious regimes throughout the world, the unique singling out of Israel for sanction is an expression of flat-out anti-Semitism. This point of view was well summed up by Thomas Friedman in the *New York Times* back in 2002, at a time when student movements were increasingly pressuring universities to divest from Israel:

> How is it that Egypt imprisons the leading democracy advocate in the Arab world, after a phony trial, and not a single student group in America calls for divestiture from Egypt? (I'm not calling for it, but the silence is telling.) How is it that Syria occupies Lebanon for 25 years, chokes the life out of its democracy, and not a single student group calls for divestiture from Syria? How is it that Saudi Arabia denies its women the most basic human rights, and bans any other religion from being practiced publicly on its soil, and not a single student group calls for divestiture from Saudi Arabia?
>
> Criticizing Israel is not anti-Semitic, and saying so is vile. But singling out Israel for opprobrium and international sanction—out of all proportion to any other party in the Middle East—is anti-Semitic, and not saying so is dishonest.[8]

For his part, Alan Dershowitz expressed a similar critique in response to recent reports (later retracted) that Hampshire College was divesting from six companies that profit from Israel's occupation:

> The divestment campaign applies to Israel and Israel alone. Hampshire will continue to deal with companies that supply Iran, Saudi Arabia, China, Cuba, North Korea, Zimbabwe, Libya, Syria, Sudan, Belarus and other brutal dictatorships around the world that routinely murder civilians, torture and imprison dissenters, deny educational opportunities to women, imprison gays and repress speech. Indeed many of those who support divestiture against Israel actively support these repressive regimes. This divestment campaign has absolutely nothing to do with human rights. It is motivated purely by hatred for the Jewish state.[9]

Klein is absolutely right when she writes of BDS that "many of us can't go there." The reasons for this are complex and painful—and Friedman and Dershowitz do a compelling job of spelling out just how deeply painful and divisive they are. I must admit I have serious hesitation in taking on an issue that pushes so many of my own Jewish fear-buttons. (I'm not unmindful of the tragic historic specters that boycotts against Jews and Jewish institutions conjure up for us.) Still and all, I can't help but wonder whether by dismissing BDS as simple, abject hatred of Jews and Israel, we are misunderstanding the essential point of this movement. Even more fundamentally, I wonder if our rejection of BDS simply papers over our inability to face the more troubling aspects of the Jewish state.

I'll start here: In a way, Dershowitz is correct when he writes that BDS has "nothing to do with human rights." This particular movement did not in fact arise out of the international community's concern over human rights in Israel/Palestine: It was founded in 2005 by a coalition of Palestinian groups who sought to fight for self-determination through nonviolent direct action. It arose out of their frustration over Israel's continued refusal to comply with international law on any number of critical issues—and the oppressive manner in which Israel has occupied and ruled over Palestinians. In other words, it is absolutely true that BDS is not an international human-rights campaign. It is, rather, a liberation campaign waged by the Palestinian people—one for which they are seeking international support.

Yes, there are many oppressive nations around the world—and if a call came from indigenous, grassroots movements in these nations calling for international support of BDS to support their struggle, I'd say most of us would seriously consider lending them our support. To use a partial list of nations mentioned by Friedman and Dershowitz, if any constituencies of the oppressed in Egypt, Syria, Saudi Arabia, Libya, Zimbabwe, or Belarus called for nonviolent global boycott/divestment/sanction campaigns to force change in their countries' policies, yes, I think we might well agree that they would be worthy of our backing.* However, the absence of such movements does not necessarily negate the justice of the Palestinians' current campaign. And it doesn't seem to me that support of their call automatically constitutes hatred of Israel or Jews.

What I think Friedman and Dershowitz—and so many of us—fail to grasp is this: Even as we recoil from nations that "choke the life out of their democracies" and "routinely murder civilians, torture and imprison dissenters, deny educational opportunities to women, imprison gays and repress speech," the only way we can help truly address this kind of oppression is to support the people who struggle for rights within these countries themselves—it is not for us Westerners to determine what is best for them. (And I particularly fear that when we frame this as a fight for "democracy," as Friedman does, this is really just a code for "imposing Western influence"—but perhaps that is a discussion for another day.)

The bottom line? Although I believe there are undoubtedly those out there who will support BDS out of hatred pure and simple, I think it is just too easy to dismiss this movement as ipso facto anti-Semitism. Beyond the fears articulated by Friedman, Dershowitz, and so many others like them, I think there's an even deeper fear for many of us in the Jewish

---

* Indeed, this did prove to be the case during the Arab Spring uprisings in 2011, as a global protest movement emerged in solidarity with activists in Egypt, Tunisia, Libya, and other countries.

community: the prospect of facing the honest truth of Israel's oppression of Palestinians.

For so many painful reasons, it is just so hard for us to see Israel as an oppressor—to admit that despite all the vulnerability we feel as Jews, the power dynamic is dramatically, overwhelmingly weighted in Israel's favor. Although a movement like BDS might feel on a visceral level like just one more example of the world piling on the Jews and Israel, we need to be open to the possibility that it might more accurately be described as the product of a weaker, dispossessed, disempowered people doing what it must to resist oppression.

I have to say it feels like I'm going out on a serious limb by writing these words. I'm only raising these issues, as always, in the hope of starting a wider discussion in the Jewish community. Somehow, I feel that it is only by facing the stuff we prefer not to have to face that we might begin to find a way out of this painful reality.

Discussion

Sydney

I've been anti-occupation for many years. I left Israel primarily because of it.

Intellectually I also understand the right of Palestinians to attack and to kill Israeli soldiers in the West Bank. (That's *not* the same as blowing up civilians inside Israel.) Ehud Barak, among other Israeli leaders, said that if he had been born a Palestinian, he would have joined a terrorist group.

But there is a difference between understanding, even sympathizing with, a legitimate tactic and supporting it. I myself served in the Israeli Army. I have friends and relatives in Israel with kids in the army. I don't agree with their politics, but I can't support an activity that gets their kids killed.

I feel the same about BDS. How can I support destroying the livelihood of friends and relatives? Some of whom have bad politics and some of whom have good politics. How could I ever explain to them what I was doing?

Sometimes I feel like Israel is like a brother who has become a drug addict. I wouldn't buy him drugs, but I can't see having him arrested either. Or [letting him] become homeless. You want to give him a kick in the ass, a major intervention, send him to detox; but you also want him to have a bed to sleep in.

Perhaps it's an illogical reaction. But it's to an impossible dilemma.

Rebekah

Thank you for speaking out so thoughtfully on this issue. Like the letter from the 500 Israelis in support of BDS, we need to find the most expedient and powerful way to mobilize large numbers of American Jews to speak out in equally thoughtful ways about the value in supporting BDS. Having spent years in the slow process of educating people (Jews and non-Jews) about the realities in Israel/Palestine, we need to figure out ways to help these individuals and groups turn their understanding into action. The BDS movement may be a good mechanism.

Martha

It is misguided to object to BDS actions undertaken toward Israel on the grounds that other nations are not targeted. Syria is now targeted with the "Syria Accountability Act" passed by Congress. Iraq was heavily sanctioned under Saddam Hussein. Google this and read: "Since 1987, U.S. agencies have implemented numerous sanctions against Iran." Cuba, North Korea, Sudan, others.

Perhaps most relevantly, the Palestinians have been sanctioned/embargoed systematically, most stringently since the elections that brought Hamas to power. Opponents of BDS gestures toward Israel have their argument upside down: The Palestinians have been ostracized for their acts of violence against civilians and their failures to meet diplomatic commitments, while Israel has not.

Eric

Ordinarily I'm to the left of you, Brant, but on this issue, I'm skeptical.

Not one of the sanctions campaigns I can think of other than the one against South Africa has done any good, and many have done considerable harm (Iraq, Cuba, even Gaza itself). This suggests to me that the crucial variable in South Africa wasn't the divestiture movement: It was the leadership of Mandela and (eventually) De Klerk. At the moment, I see no evidence of comparable leaders on either side. In their absence, I'm very skeptical about the good this campaign will do and worried about the injury.

Why I Didn't Celebrate Yom Ha'atzmaut[10]

April 29, 2009

I've decided not to celebrate Yom Ha'atzmaut today. I don't think I can celebrate this holiday anymore.

That doesn't mean I'm not acknowledging the anniversary of Israel's independence—only that I can no longer view this milestone as a day for unabashed celebration. I've come to believe that for me, Yom Ha'atzmaut is more appropriately observed as an occasion for reckoning and honest soul-searching.

As a Jew, as someone who has identified with Israel for his entire life, it is profoundly painful to me to admit the honest truth of this day: That Israel's founding is inextricably bound up with its dispossession of the indigenous inhabitants of the land. In the end, Yom Ha'atzmaut and what the Palestinian people refer to as the Nakba are two inseparable sides of the same coin. And I simply cannot separate these two realities any more.

I wonder: If we Jews are ready to honestly face down this "dual reality," how can we possibly view this day as a day of unmitigated celebration? But we do—and not only in Israel. Indeed, there is no greater civil Jewish holiday in the American Jewish community than Yom Ha'atzmaut. It has become the day we pull out all the stops—the go-to day upon which Jewish Federations throughout the country hold their major communal Jewish parades, celebrations, and gatherings.

I wonder: How must it feel to be a Palestinian watching the Jewish community celebrate this day year after year on the anniversary that is the living embodiment of your collective tragedy?

I can't yet say what specific form my new observance of Yom Ha'atzmaut will take. I only know that it can't be divorced from the Palestinian reality—or from the Palestinian people themselves. Many of us in the coexistence community speak of "dual narratives"—and how critical it is for each side to be open to hearing the other's "story." I think this pedagogy is important as far as it goes, but I now believe that it's not nearly enough. It's not enough for us to be open to the narrative of the Nakba and all it represents for Palestinians. In the end, we must also be willing to own our role in this narrative. Until we do this, it seems to me, the very concept of coexistence will be nothing but a hollow cliché.

Toward a new understanding of Yom Ha'atzmaut, I recommend to you this article by Amaya Galili, which was published today in the Israeli newspaper *Yediot Achronot*. Galili is affiliated with Zochrot, the courageous Israeli organization whose members work tirelessly to raise their fellow citizens' awareness about the Nakba.

An excerpt:

Accepting responsibility for the Nakba and its ongoing consequences obligates me to ask hard questions about the establishment of Israeli society, particularly about how we live today. I want to accept responsibility, to correct this reality, to change it. Not to say, "There's no choice. This is how we've survived for 61 years, and that's how we'll keep surviving." It's not enough for me just to "survive." I want to live in a society that is aware of its past, and uses it to build a future that can include all the inhabitants of the country and all its refugees.[11]

Discussion

Mark

Thank you for this, Brant, and it's hard to convey how deeply I mean that. What you have expressed here gives me hope—and it's hard to convey how much it means to say that in the midst of the pain and the despair and horror that I have felt in the situation in which we find ourselves. Taking in and taking on the condition of the Palestinian people is the only way through to whatever lies beyond the current condition of war, separation, and spiral of violence. And you are so right: It is not about "two narratives," or "interfaith" or "intercultural" understanding. No—in order to understand ourselves, what we have done, and what we are doing, we have to understand the experience of the other and fully see and accept our responsibility. And if the other side bears any responsibility, that is for them to understand and to deal with. It has no bearing on our responsibility for ourselves. Yom Ha'atzmaut, in order to have any meaning at all, must be devoted to *heshbon hanefesh*—a self-accounting. And the day before Yom Ha'atzmaut, and the day after, and every day, until we find ourselves clearly and squarely on the path of taking responsibility for what this state has cost.

Joel

Thank you so much for this blog. I'm an (older) rabbinic student at Boston's Hebrew College and found myself avoiding the school's celebrations this week. I knew why, but I also felt uncomfortable doing so: After all, it's not like I hate Israel, just the way many in government and among the citizenry conduct themselves. Your saying that "Yom Ha'atzmaut is more appropriately observed as an occasion for reckoning and honest soul-searching" gave me the balance I was looking for, and

I will work during the next year to try to redirect the school's celebrations to just this kind of discussion.

Evin
Thanks so much for having the courage to post this, Brant. While I was living in Washington, DC, for the last few years, my close friends and I never affiliated with a synagogue and instead formed our own independent *minyan*—in part because we felt so alienated by the complete lack of dissent or meaningful discussion about Israel within the organized Jewish community. But I've followed and forwarded your blog postings for years, because I find them so heartening and truly brave. The discussion of your prompt makes me feel like there may actually still be a place for me and my views within the institutional Jewish community. I'm really proud that you are my hometown rabbi.

BF
Wouldn't your reasoning for not "celebrating" Israel Independence Day also preclude "celebrating" American Independence Day?

Isn't it also the "honest truth" that the founding and growth of the United States of America "is inextricably bound up with its dispossession of the indigenous inhabitants of the land"? What will be the new form of your observance of American Independence Day?

Is there no ethical rationale for the existence of the state of Israel? It seems that's where you are heading.

I'll never get there.

Rabbi Brant Rosen
I'm not sure that the American Independence Day and Yom Ha'atzmaut are so historically comparable. If we're going to look for parallels, it's probably more apt to compare Yom Ha'atzmaut to Thanksgiving (inasmuch as it also involves the acquisition of a land at the expense of its indigenous peoples).

And here I would say yes, we Americans would probably do well to consider Thanksgiving to be a day of reckoning (and not simply a day to stuff our faces and watch football). I wonder how many Americans actually know that most Native Americans consider this to be an official day of mourning—check out this link, for instance: www.pilgrim-hall.org/daymourn.htm.

You ask, "Is there no ethical rationale for the existence of the State of Israel?" To be honest, I don't believe that any nation can ultimately claim an "ethical rationale" for its existence. Nationalism is by its very nature an ethically messy business. At best, one might claim it's a "necessary evil," but I personally struggle with even that.

It's worth pointing out that Jews have historically been the victims of nationalistic movements. Now that we've gotten into the nationalism business ourselves, it would behoove us at least to seriously consider what we've wrought before we break out the party hats.

Richard

A few weeks ago, I went on a trip to Bethlehem. We visited various Palestinian institutions and met with different groups. I learned that the Nakba is central to their identity and that they do see themselves as victims.

That said, I celebrated Yom Ha'atzmaut. I'm in Israel right now. I danced in the streets at night and in the morning, I attended two barbecues. I prayed festively with better *kavanna* than I have ever had.

I recognize that the founding of Israel is tied to suffering. I can even take responsibility for that suffering. But I refuse to muffle my emotions.

I am ecstatic that there is a state of Israel, a country that I can call home. I am ecstatic that the hundreds of thousands of Jews who were in this country in 1948 were not slaughtered by the incoming Arab armies. (Do you have any doubt that that would have been the result had Israel lost?) I sit at my computer looking over the beautiful Jezreel Valley and know that what happened in 1948 is responsible for my safety and ability to take advantage of my spiritual homeland.

I will not argue that Israel has [not] committed sins in the past. I'm not suggesting that we can't represent with the Palestinians in their suffering. I'm not suggesting that we shouldn't help them. But I am saying that we have every right to rejoice in our freedom. Even if the creation of the state is inextricably bound with suffering, it was created in a war! Wars are the definition of suffering. I suggest you stop celebrating Hanukkah, Purim, Pesach, and Veterans' Day. Your claim that your values only restrict holidays based on land being taken is rather absurd. People suffer for other reasons.

The Jewish people have a state, something we haven't had for 2,000 years. I'm happy, and I wish you were, too.

Rabbis Remembering the Nakba[12]

May 17, 2009

These I remember and I pour out my soul. . . . (Psalm 42:4)

Last Thursday night I welcomed 14 people—9 Jews and 5 Palestinians—into my home for what turned out to be a powerful and sacred experience. The timing of our gathering was significant. May 14, 1948, the date the State of Israel was declared, is a joyful milestone for Israel and Jews around the world. For the collective memory of the Palestinian people, however, this date represents their displacement and dispossession—an event they refer to collectively as the Nakba ("catastrophe").

The gathering in my home was one of four events that took place throughout the country on Thursday evening sponsored by Rabbis Remembering the Nakba, a new ad hoc group of rabbis and rabbinical students who seek to create a Jewish context for remembering this tragic event. Even more crucially, we believe it is critical that the Jewish community find a way to honestly face the painful truth of this event—and in particular, Israel's role in it.

In the words of a statement that was read at each gathering:

> Our gathering tonight, "Rabbis Remembering the Nakba," is part of a series of programs occurring simultaneously around the country. It was originated by an ad hoc group of American rabbis who desire to seriously reflect upon the meaning of Israel's Independence Day. We are united in our common conviction that we cannot view Yom Ha'atzmaut—or what is for Palestinians the Nakba—as an occasion for celebration. Guided by the values of Jewish tradition, we believe that this day is more appropriately an occasion for *zikaron* ("memory"), *cheshbon nefesh* ("soul-searching"), and *teshuvah* ("repentance").
>
> These spiritual values compel us to acknowledge the following: that Israel's founding is inextricably bound up with the dispossession of hundreds of thousands of indigenous inhabitants of the land, that a moment so many Jews consider to be the occasion of national liberation is the occasion of tragedy and exile for another people, and that the violence begun in 1948 continues to this day. This is the truth of our common history—it cannot be denied, ignored, or wished away.
>
> Jewish tradition teaches that peace and reconciliation can only be achieved after a process of repentance. And we can only repent after an honest accounting of our responsibility in the wronging of others. While it is true that none of the Jews present tonight were actively involved in the dispossession of Palestinians from their homes in 1948, it is also true that if we deny or remain silent about the truth of these events, past and present, we remain complicit in

this crime. In the words of Rabbi Abraham Joshua Heschel, "In a free society some are guilty, but all are responsible."

Our gatherings this evening bring together Jews and Palestinians in this act of remembrance. This coming together is an essential, courageous choice. To choose to face this painful past together is to begin to give shape to a vision of the future where refugees go home, when the occupation is ended, when walls are torn down, and where reconciliation is underway.

In addition to the event I hosted in Chicago, "Rabbis Remember the Nakba" gatherings were held simultaneously in Berkeley, New York, and Philadelphia.[13] Though each event was organized separately and involved the additional participation of various local peace and justice groups, each gathering was linked by a few important common factors: Each was led by a rabbi or rabbinical student, each involved the participation of both Jews and Palestinians, and each incorporated aspects of Jewish ritual into their ceremonies.

At the Chicago gathering, the guiding value of our ritual was *zikaron*—remembrance. As part of our ceremony, we bore witness by reading the history of the eight Palestinian villages that were destroyed on May 14, 1948. (In all, more than 400 villages were depopulated of their inhabitants over the course of that year.) In addition to learning about the events that transpired on the Nakba, we also learned about the history, culture, and communal life of each village. (Palestinian historian Walid Khalidi's exhaustive and highly recommended work *All That Remains*[14] was an essential resource for our ceremony.) After hearing the history and fate of each village, a memorial candle was lit, and we recited the following line from the Yom Kippur liturgy together: "These I remember and I pour out my soul."

On the whole I would describe our evening as a modest first effort that nonetheless contained some profound and indelible moments. By incredible coincidence, Shafic, one of the Palestinian participants, mentioned that his wife's family was from al-Bassa—one of the eight villages we commemorated in our ceremony. (Al-Bassa was a large village in Acre District, near the northwest coast of Palestine.)

As we read about al-Bassa's fate during the Nakba, we learned this tragic account relayed by Palestinian eyewitnesses: After occupying the village, Haganah forces lined up some of the townspeople outside a church, shot them, and ordered others to bury the bodies. Shafic said he has heard numerous stories about al-Bassa from his mother-in-law over the years, including her traumatic recounting of the massacre on May 14. He added that his mother-in-law now has Alzheimer's and has lost most of her adult memory—her only remaining memories are of her childhood village.

After our ritual, other Palestinian participants spoke at length about the stories of their own families. One man told us about the experiences of his mother, who was a survivor of an infamous massacre in the village of Deir Yassin, outside Jerusalem. Our gathering also included a Christian Palestinian from the north of the country who experienced the Nakba personally. Another Palestinian participant told us about his father, who was saved by a Jewish friend during the Irgun's attack on Jaffa.

In the end, the Palestinian participants were quite obviously moved that they were given this opportunity to have this conversation with Jews, as part of a ceremony convened by a rabbi. To put it mildly, it was obviously something quite unprecedented in their experience. For the Jewish participants, there were a myriad of complex and powerful emotions. I'm personally still trying to sort through them all.

Whatever cognitive dissonance I might feel over this issue, I truly believe that this kind of reckoning is utterly essential for us as Jews. When it comes to the Nakba, most of us tend to respond through denial, avoidance, or dismissive rationalization ("That's just how nations are made—what can you do?"). The reason seems fairly clear: to face the painful truths of this history means to admit that our people—a people that has been the victim of dispossession and dehumanization for centuries—have now become the perpetrator. And if we do indeed manage to face these truths, where does that leave the Zionist narrative that has been so deeply cherished by so many of us for so long?

I don't know where we will go from here, but everyone present agreed that this was the tentative beginning of something enormously important. Our humble gathering resonated with a myriad of implications that ranged from the personal to the political. But by the end of the evening, it was clear that whatever happens next, Jews and Palestinians must do it together.

P.S.: Just learned that Yisrael Beiteinu, the party of Avigdor Lieberman, seeks to make it illegal for Arabs in Israel to commemorate the Nakba.[15] This is what it has now come to: Memory is not only denied, it is now deemed against the law. . . .

Discussion

Lesley

I am awestruck. Most of what I have read about Deir Yassin in Jewish sources has been denials, equivocations, and minimizations. Your gathering sounds like the start of a much-needed truth and reconciliation process for everyone involved in this ongoing tragedy.

I know you will hear angry voices demanding that Arabs and Palestinians need to accept their share of responsibility for the violence. That is true, but if we keep waiting for "someone else" to take the first step, we will never get anywhere. Thank you Brant, and your fellow rabbis, for taking that first step.

Stan

First—I agree totally that if we are to have peace we must come together—Jews and Palestinians—to make the next steps. We must do it together. And I completely agree that as part of that, we must have honest and open dialogue about the actions of everyone—both past and present.

However, it seems that the balance on the evening is precisely what was missing. It is proper and important that the day be one of remembrance for what was lost and resolve for trying to make things right. But just as it is important for Jews to know what [effect] their actions have had on the Palestinians, isn't it also important for the Palestinians to know what Israel has meant for those who had nowhere else to go?

I applaud your efforts for leading toward a true sense of co-awareness and ultimately (hopefully) reconciliation. But if it is to occur it must—equally as honestly—allow the Palestinians to understand why Israel is so important to so many Jews. Just as it is naive and disingenuous for Jews to dismiss the pain and suffering we have caused, so it is equally disingenuous to disavow the political, historical, and social needs for Jews that have led them to cling so desperately to a homeland.

Although I certainly respect and admire your honesty and strength in arranging such an event, I also completely disagree with the inability to celebrate the day.

You need not accept the process by which the State of Israel was founded to accept the joy of its presence. I oppose the way that the United States has treated the Native Americans—the dispossession of their peoples, the diminution of their cultures, and the breaking of their treaties. Yet this does not keep me from celebrating the presence of a country where I can openly study these facts, openly disagree with the government, and actively work for a society that is better.

Similarly I find the State of Israel, even with its flaws of action and omission, to be a blessing, just as I would find the foundation of a Palestinian state to equally be a blessing. In Passover we celebrate our freedom yet remember the pain we have caused. At Yom Kippur we end with a joyous celebration, even though we have spent days self-reflecting on the pain and suffering we have caused others and wish to avoid in the future. Judaism is nothing if not a religion of contrasts, and I find no conflict in celebrating our blessings while simultaneously cursing our own evils and remembering the pain we have inflicted.

I believe that the path to peace lies not in just remembering together our tragedies and pain but also imagining together the blessings we can share. That is why I will continue to celebrate with joy Israel's Independence Day—while simultaneously renewing myself toward ridding the pain and suffering of others.

May the day come speedily where Israelis and Palestinians can together celebrate their Independence Days and work together for peace and prosperity for all their people.

Rabbi Brant Rosen

Thank you, Stan, for an eloquent and thoughtful response, as always. I agree with much of what you say, of course. I would only add that I don't think we agree on what constitutes "balance" in this particular conflict.

If there was parity in the power dynamic between Israel and Palestine, then perhaps I would agree with you that a balanced "co-awareness" would be necessary for reconciliation. But that is not the case here. In the case of Israel/Palestine, there is a radically imbalanced power dynamic between the two parties. And a big part of the problem comes from the fact that while this imbalance is patently obvious to most Palestinians, most Jews/Israelis simply just don't see it. Most of us good liberal Jews tend view the conflict simply as a conflict between two equal sides with two equal claims to the same piece of land.

Part of my own evolution on this issue is my own coming to grips with the reality that the playing field is not actually level at all—that Israel is the infinitely more powerful party here. And even more to the point (and much more painful to admit) that Israel has, in a very real way, committed an injustice against the Palestinians and continues to oppress them to this day.

And if we do accept these painful realities, then what does coexistence ultimately mean in this context? What does it mean for the oppressor to "coexist" with the oppressed? And what do we mean by reconciliation? Cannot reconciliation only truly occur when the offending party admits and takes responsibility for its past and present offenses and makes an effort to make repair? This is precisely the step that is so horribly difficult (if not unthinkable) for so many Jews and Israelis.

The reason I organized this gathering was precisely because I don't think most Jews understand the true source of the Palestinian people's pain—and the depth of the injustice that was committed against them. And until we Jews honestly come to grips with our role in perpetrating and perpetuating this injustice, I don't see how we will ever achieve balance or reconciliation going forward.

Yotam

First of all, let me thank you again, Rabbi, for hosting this powerful event in your home. I found it very meaningful, and I personally greatly appreciated having a Jewish context for such a commemoration.

I think it was a testament to how earnestly your intentions came across that the Palestinians present felt comfortable sharing such clearly painful first- and secondhand experiences. I think it's incredibly important that we Jews take the initiative when we can in things like this, because it is the only way to overcome the skepticism seen in many Palestinians. Miryam and I were talking about this on the way to your house. We agreed that while we can understand why there is this skepticism—years of overtures of reconciliation have only yielded more dispossession and bereavement—still it is important whenever possible to expose Palestinians to Jews who are in the process of acknowledging and accepting their share of responsibility for the long-suppressed narrative of the Nakba.

On the other hand, it was clear that the Jews present were sympathetic enough to what the Palestinians there had to share that we could have a successful memorial without it becoming too much of a debate. On that note, most of the debating happened between the Palestinians there! I am especially grateful that we had the kind of dynamic where the Palestinian participants were the ones who brought up the Holocaust and other persecution of the Jewish people in an attempt to bridge a gap between our two narratives (and *not* in an attempt to equate). The fact that we had to remind ourselves that it was getting late and we all needed sleep is a good sign that we all wanted to continue the conversation about what happened and what we can realistically do now to actively acknowledge and redress the Nakba.

I felt especially connected to this experience, because we accessed it through Jewish values. As in a Shiva, we participated in the sorrow and pain the Palestinians were expressing. Furthermore, it is my belief that our value of remembering (never forgetting) is only strengthened by serving that function to others, especially those whom we have injured. The pain and loss we have suffered in our Jewish narrative will only be made more legitimate by our acknowledgment of and participation in the pain and loss of others, especially the Palestinians.

Lisa K

I feel so blessed to have been invited to share your Nakba commemoration last Thursday. I also felt so humbled and fortunate to have earned the trust of my Palestinian friends, that they could share their very painful personal stories. It is a testament to you, Brant, that you created such a safe environment for them to do so—as so often, they are silenced in either subtle or blatantly cruel ways in our society. My journey from growing up in the Reform Zionist movement to becoming an activist for Palestinian human rights and a just peace in Israel/Palestine was for so many years an extremely lonely one. Although many in the Jewish community speak of "peace," there is a conspicuous absence of honest soul-searching and coming to grips with the true history of how Israel came to be, what it is today, and how we got here. I have often felt that I focus my anger, outrage, shame, and grief into activism. What was missing was a moment to reflect, to mourn, to commemorate. Thursday night provided that much-needed opportunity. You and the other rabbis who remember the Nakba are true spiritual leaders, and I hope many more follow your example.

Miryam

The gathering and Nakba commemoration at your home Thursday night was incredibly meaningful to me in so many different ways. Your initiative felt so genuine and grounded that as a Palestinian, I was "at home" discussing and reflecting on this painful situation with you.

I read a previous comment about the gathering's being unbalanced. But demanding or expecting balance in a situation that's so acutely unequal and unbalanced prevents a necessary coming to terms with the major injury and injustice that was done and continues to be done to the Palestinian people on a daily basis. There are few Palestinians who haven't experienced the effects of dispossession or occupation. I don't think my experience of having lived under military occupation is different than most Palestinians in that it is that much more difficult to get to a place of healing when the wound is ongoing.

I think you're exactly right when you say it's important that we work and move forward together as Arabs and Jews. When all is said and done, there will be a major reservoir of painful memories and experiences for people to draw on when carving out a future. It's critical that we build another kind of historic memory now, as we work in solidarity to end the occupation and support human rights and equal rights for all.

> I hope you know how important your leadership felt in furthering a
> new kind of relationship.

In Search of Perspective in Bil'in[16]

May 27, 2009

Recently read a piece on *Ynet* describing the experience of IDF soldiers
stationed in Bil'in—a Palestinian village that has been the site of a weekly
demonstration for the past four years. I was particularly intrigued by a
quote from one soldier, who described the detail as "more terrifying for us
than dealing with terrorists in Gaza inside a tank":

> In Gaza you spot a terrorist, fire a shell, and it's over. Here you face citizens
> who hurl a stone or a Molotov cocktail, but your ability to respond is limited.
> It may appear that we are the ones using force here, but in reality that's not the
> case, as we are subject to very difficult restrictions.[17]

I completely understand the perspective of an individual soldier who
is ordered to perform an incomprehensibly difficult duty such as this.
But I understand that there is also more to understand—so much more.
I certainly don't begrudge the experience of individuals caught up in
this bitter struggle. But I believe we do ourselves a huge disservice when
we neglect—as this article did—the larger context in which this struggle
occurs.

Some context: The Bil'in demonstration was born in response to Israel
placing its separation barrier so that it now separates 60 percent of the
village from its farming land—land that Israel is using to expand its settlement of Modi'in Illit, which lies immediately to the west.

In 2007, the Israeli Supreme Court ordered the government to reroute
the barrier, which it called "highly prejudicial" to the villagers of Bil'in.
Although Israel's Defense Ministry has said it will abide by the ruling,
the fence has yet to be moved. Just last month, the state submitted a new
proposal to the Court to redraw the route of the barrier. According to this
plan, however, only 700 of the original 1,700 dunams of farmland will be
returned to the villagers of Bil'in.

The Bil'in demonstration is a nonviolent direct action that began in
January 2005 and has taken place every Friday since then. Although Bil'in

is a local initiative, it is an integral part of the larger Palestinian nonviolence movement—a significant sociopolitical phenomenon that is chronically underreported by the Western media. Indeed, it is important to note that Palestinian nonviolent action vastly predates Bil'in—this is a movement that coalesced in large part during the years of the First Intifada. (I highly recommend Mary Elizabeth King's excellent book *A Quiet Revolution*[18] for more on this important history.)

It has been well reported that the Bil'in demonstrations have witnessed tragedy in recent months. Four Palestinians, including two children, have been killed in the area since last summer, and dozens have been injured. Last month, Bassem Abu Rahmeh, a Palestinian demonstrator, was killed by a tear-gas canister that sliced through his chest. A month earlier, an American demonstrator named Tristan Anderson was critically injured in a similar demonstration in the nearby village of Ni'ilin.

As the *Ynet* article attests, some Palestinian demonstrators have indeed become increasingly violent. In a sense, we are witnessing the classic spiral. As any student of nonviolent activism knows, it is difficult to contain the frustration that invariably sets in when an action settles in for the long haul—particularly when there is so little progress along the way. This recent article from the *Guardian* illuminates the challenges the Bil'in protesters face in this regard—including the generational split in the villagers' attitudes toward nonviolence:

> The Bil'in demonstration was always intended to be nonviolent, although on Friday, as is often the case, there were half a dozen younger, angrier men lobbing stones at the soldiers with slingshots. The Israeli military, for its part, fires tear gas, stun grenades, rubber-coated bullets, and sometimes live ammunition at the crowd.
>
> There have long been Palestinian advocates of nonviolence, but they were drowned out by the militancy of the second intifada, the uprising that began in late 2000 and erupted into waves of appalling suicide bombings.
>
> Eyad Burnat, 36, has spent long hours in discussions with the young men of Bil'in, a small village of fewer than 2,000, convincing them of the merits of "civil grassroots resistance."
>
> "Of course it gets more difficult when someone is killed," said Burnat, who heads the demonstration. "But we've faced these problems in the past. We've had more than 60 people arrested and still they go back to nonviolence. We've made a strategic decision."[19]

As always, perspective is everything. The *Ynet* article did a fine job of documenting the perspective of scared, frustrated young soldiers who find themselves in an impossible position. But there are other equally valid and compelling perspectives we cannot ignore: the perspective of the farmers whose access to their own lands and livelihood has been taken from them, the perspective of villagers seeking justice in an inherently unjust situation, the perspective of nonviolent activists trying to rise above the frustration and rage that inevitably surface during the course of their struggle.

As for us Jews, I only hope we can go beyond our narrow perspective of Palestinians as nothing more than violent terrorists who want nothing more than to wipe Jews off the face of the map. Is that a step we might be willing to take?

Confessions of a Peace Process Cynic[20]

June 2, 2009

Don't get me wrong. I'm on board. I'm in there with the American Jews who are reassuring Obama that we've got his back. But I have to say it's all I can do to resist my cynicism when I read about Peace Process, version 5.0. (And for safety's sake, let me just reiterate my blog's disclaimer: I'm writing this merely as a snarky private citizen—not on behalf of any organization with which I'm affiliated.)

As I've written before, I'm encouraged by Obama and Clinton's tough talk on the settlements. Nevertheless, I've increasingly been wondering if/ how the administration would back up its tough words with meaningful action.

Thus I confess to a distinctly familiar sinking sensation when I read this in the *New York Times* this morning:

> As President Obama prepares to head to the Middle East this week, administration officials are debating how to toughen their stance against any expansion of Israeli settlements in the West Bank.
>
> The measures under discussion—all largely symbolic—include stepping back from America's near-uniform support for Israel in the United Nations if Prime Minister Benjamin Netanyahu of Israel does not agree to a settlement freeze, administration officials said.
>
> Other measures include refraining from the instant Security Council veto of United Nations resolutions that Israel opposes and making use of Mr. Obama's bully pulpit to criticize the settlements, officials said. Placing conditions on

loan guarantees to Israel, as the first President Bush did nearly 20 years ago, is not under discussion, officials said.[21]

Call me cynical, but "symbolic measures" simply aren't going to cut it. Not when you're up against the juggernaut that is Israel's settlement movement. (Read Akiva Eldar's book *Lords of the Land*[22] if you think "juggernaut" is too strong a word.) And certainly not when you are dealing with the most pro-settlement Israeli administration in recent memory. Already several Israeli officials are complaining loudly that the demand for a settlement freeze is "unfair." ("There are reasonable demands and demands that are not reasonable," Bibi said today.[23])

I found it interesting that the *New York Times* article cited George H. W. Bush and the loan guarantees—now that brought back some memories. Remember the last time an American president tried to tie US aid to Israel's settlement activity?

> For many in the Jewish community, Bush's presidency could be encapsulated in his offhand quip to reporters in September 1991 during an AIPAC lobbying effort on Capitol Hill in support of the proposed $10 billion loan guarantee to Israel: "I'm one lonely little guy" up against "some powerful political forces" made up of "a thousand lobbyists on the Hill."
>
> Bush had opposed the loan guarantees as long as Israel continued settlement in the West Bank and Gaza. The president finally agreed to a loan guarantee package in August 1992, requiring as a set-off any funds Israel spent to build housing or infrastructure in the territories. Despite this action, the political damage was done. The loan guarantee controversy later motivated Jewish opposition to President Bush, who received no more than 12% of the Jewish vote in the 1992 election (down from close to 35% in 1988).[24]

More than 15 years later, you'd still be hard-pressed to find anyone in the American Jewish establishment supporting the withholding of aid to Israel under any circumstances. As I've written before, this is the "third rail" in the American Jewish community. But trust me on this: It may well be the only diplomatic stick that will get Israel's attention at the end of the day.

Now, is Obama up to that level of political courage? And even more to the point: Will the American Jewish community still have his back if and when that time comes?

The Dominos Fall | 61

Discussion

Mick

There is no peace process underway, just domestic politics. If you really want a peace process, you have to be prepared to boycott, disinvest, isolate, and sanction. Are you up for that?

Bibi's History Tutorial[25]

June 15, 2009

I'm in agreement with the pundits who conclude that there was absolutely nothing new for consideration offered in Netanyahu's speech.[26] Perhaps he achieved a personal milestone by finally uttering the words "Palestinian state," but beyond this, it was a tune we've all heard before. He offered "peace negotiations immediately without prior conditions," then proceeded to spell out the all-too-familiar prior conditions that everyone knows are nonstarters for the Palestinians (i.e., Jerusalem remains the "united capital of Israel," "natural growth" of the settlements will continue, there will be no right of return for the Palestinians).

Same old, same old. For me, at least, the most interesting parts of his speech were not his tired policy pronouncements but his extended forays into historical analysis—and in particular, his repeated justifications of the Jewish people's right to the land:

> The connection of the Jewish People to the Land has been in existence for more than 3,500 years. Judea and Samaria, the places where our forefathers Abraham, Isaac, and Jacob walked, our forefathers David, Solomon, Isaiah, and Jeremiah—this is not a foreign land, this is the Land of our Forefathers.[27]

It seemed clear that Netanyahu's history lesson was a pointed rejoinder to Obama's Cairo speech, in which Obama stated that the "Jewish homeland is rooted in a tragic history that cannot be denied."[28] You may have heard that following his speech, many in the Jewish community criticized Obama for connecting Israel's right to exist to the Holocaust and failing to cite the Jewish people's historical connection to the land. Witness this livid *Jerusalem Post* editorial:

Mr. President, long before Christianity and Islam appeared on the world stage, the covenant between the people of Israel and the Land of Israel was entrenched and unwavering. Every day we prayed in our ancient tongue for our return to Zion. Every day, Mr. President. For 2,000 years.

Perhaps it's because Palestine was never sovereign under the Arabs that even moderate Palestinians cannot find it in their hearts to acknowledge the depth of the Jews' connection to Zion. Instead, they insist we are interlopers.

When Obama implies that Jewish rights are essentially predicated on the Holocaust—not once asserting they are far, far deeper and more ancient—he is dooming the prospects for peace.

For why should the Arabs reconcile themselves to the presence of a Jewish state, organic to the region, when the US president keeps insinuating that Israel was established to atone for Europe's crimes?[29]

Thus Netanyahu's pointed words yesterday:

The right of the Jewish People to a state in the Land of Israel does not arise from the series of disasters that befell the Jewish People over 2,000 years—persecutions, expulsions, pogroms, blood libels, murders, which reached its climax in the Holocaust, an unprecedented tragedy in the history of nations. . . . The right to establish our sovereign state here, in the Land of Israel, arises from one simple fact: Eretz Israel is the birthplace of the Jewish People.[30]

It's fascinating to me that Netanyahu, et al., are so threatened by the suggestion that Israel's establishment is ultimately bound to the Holocaust. After all, didn't Theodor Herzl himself found political Zionism as a response to world anti-Semitism? And whatever historical claim the Jewish people might have to the land of Israel, it's safe to say there would never have been international support for a Jewish state had it not been for the Holocaust.

Beyond this, I'm troubled by the need to continuously and defensively remind the world of the historical Jewish connection to this particular piece of land. I'm not at all sure that this is really a road we really need or want to go down.

What does it really mean for any people to have a "right" to a land? I understand that the Jewish nation, like every nation, has its historic narrative, but let's face it: Nations don't exist by right, they exist by fiat. Nations exist by virtue of military power and by their ability to maintain a system of governance that will ensure their survival as a polity. Beyond this, it's pointless to argue one's historical or moral right to a land. It seems to me that if history has proven anything, it's that might makes right—and all the rest is commentary.

The real question here is not who has a right to this land. The central issue is how its inhabitants will see fit to exist on the land. And on this point, I don't see that Netanyahu gave us anything fresh to consider.

Discussion

Rabbi Brant Rosen
Just took a closer look at the apoplectic *JPost* article. Note that it actually refers in the first paragraph to "the covenant between the people of Israel and the Land of Israel."
!!!
Actually, the traditional view holds that the covenant is between the people of Israel and *God*. (Could the *JPost* be advocating a quasi-pagan rereading of the covenant?)
Further, according to traditional covenantal theology, the Children of Israel will only have a future in the land if they uphold their covenant with God. In other words, we can only dwell in the land if we prove ourselves worthy of it.
Food for thought. . . .

Ross
Thanks for giving me another opportunity to plug the excellent essay "The Bible in Israeli Life" by Uriel Simon, which is in the Oxford *Jewish Study Bible*.[31] Simon discusses the practice of replacing God with The Land in scriptural passages.
I am no Mordecai Kaplan expert, but I believe that Kaplan was careful to use words and phrases for God that retained that idea that God has dominion over us, not the other way around.

Ethan
If we should step back for Iran and let the country sort things out even when police beat protesters, something that isn't done in Israel, then why do you feel differently about Israel? You don't think we should be outraged when there was election fraud (by the way [Iranian Supreme Leader Ayatollah Ali Khamenei] decides who gets to run in the elections, so it isn't much of an election), then why do you feel that Bibi Israel shouldn't? Even though we have a stronger connection to Israel than to Iran because we are Jews, that should give you a strong incentive to speak out against an Iranian regime funding terror through Hamas, Hezbollah, and other organizations.

Also, as God tells Abraham, Isaac, Moses, and many, many other prophets in the Torah, the Jewish people have a right to a Jewish state in Israel, just as the Muslims have a right to have Muslim states in Iran, Saudi Arabia, Somalia, and many other countries.

Rabbi Brant Rosen

I believe we should always protest against injustice whenever and wherever it occurs, including in Iran. I never wrote anywhere that we should not speak out against the beating of protesters in Iran. I did, however, write that it would be wrong for our country to meddle in their politics, which is very different. (By the way, Israel does indeed use violence against protesters—read my earlier post on the weekly nonviolent demonstration in Bil'in, for instance.)

Your Iran-Israel comparison is unhelpful and misleading. Israel is the beneficiary of billions of dollars of military aid from the US, which means I am financially implicated in its actions. Israel is also a Jewish state, and it purports to act in the name of Jews everywhere. I would say that gives American Jews the right, if not the responsibility, to urge our country to pressure Israel politically when it acts unjustly.

As for your biblical justifications: I believe you are wrong. I challenge you to find a biblical quote anywhere that says God gives the Israelites the "right" to the land of Israel. It says nothing of the kind. God tells Israel that they will have a future on the land if they are worthy of it: If they act justly, extend one law for all the inhabitants, if they do not oppress their neighbor. (If you are tempted here to cite the commandments to wipe the Canaanite inhabitants, I would only say that verses such as this represent the human voice of cruelty, not God.)

From the point of view of the Torah, no one has a "right" to any piece of land. The Torah repeatedly makes it clear that the land belongs to God. The question is not who has the right to the land, but how can we extend equal rights to all who dwell on the land?

I Can't Dance Any More[32]

June 26, 2009

I know there are those who wonder why, with all of the various injustices going on in the world, do I seem to dwell on Israel's treatment of Palestinians? It's a fair and important question. For me, it boils down to this: I've come to believe that too many of us in the Jewish community will unabashedly protest persecution anywhere in the world yet remain silent when Israel acts oppressively.

I know all too well how we actively avoid this truth. We use any number of rhetorical and political arguments to deny it, to mitigate the discomfort and pain it causes us. We engage in a kind of tortured dance of rationalization that we save for no other world issue but this one. But for me, at least, none of it really addresses the core issue at hand: However difficult it might be for us to face, Israel is unjustly oppressing Palestinians.

So what are we going to do about it?

Many of us deal with it by putting our faith and efforts into the peace process. And well we should: Although I've been honest in expressing my own doubts and concerns regarding the peace process, I understand that in the end the only true solution to this conflict will be a political one. But as the peace process enters into its latest incarnation, as the various actors involved wrangle painfully over diplomatic parameters, it is safe to say this saga will continue to take its time to unfold. And in the meantime, the real lives of real Palestinians on the ground will continue to grow increasingly intolerable.

For myself, at least, I cannot use the peace process, critical as it is, as a kind of cover to keep me from facing and protesting the oppression that is occurring in Israel/Palestine every day, even as I write these very words. Although I will do what I can to advocate for a just and peaceful political settlement to this crisis, this work does not give me a pass on speaking out. If we truly believe we must protest injustice anywhere, anytime, then it seems to me that this principle must apply to Israel/Palestine as well, no matter how painful or difficult the prospect of doing so.

Earlier this week, I was the moderator of a discussion following the showing of a powerful new documentary, *This Palestinian Life*—a film that was often unbearably painful to watch.[33] *This Palestinian Life* documents a little-seen aspect of Palestinian life: the nonviolent steadfastness (in Arabic, *sumoud*) of Palestinian villagers who live with a crushing occupation, constant settler attacks, and the deliberate, relentless annexation of their farmland.

This quote from one villager sums up the movie's essential theme:

I don't own a gun.
   I don't own any weapons and I'm not prepared to own any. . . .
   My only weapon of defense is that I won't leave this place . . .
and my hope is that the world will respond to Israel's treatment of us.[34]

As difficult as it was, I was honored to have been asked to moderate the postfilm discussion. I know there are many who would regard my participation in such a program as an act of disloyalty or at the very least an exercise in masochism. But in the end, it really came down to this: I just can't do the dance any more.

Discussion

Shlomo

I hear you! And I agree with most of what you say. I also have no faith in the peace process, which looks like a political/diplomatic game and not a real attempt to make any progress (especially with Israel's new prime minister).

You seem to feel that outside pressure on Israel (if it were effective) might allow more results, but my feeling is that Israelis (and Israeli leadership) resent pressure, and even if/when they (I should say "we" actually) succumb to it on some issues, it will always be with resentment, and an inclination to find a way to "compensate" or to "retaliate" for the sacrifice they make.

One very tangible example I can give you about this psychology is very personal: When I feel that Israel is radically or unjustly attacked (e.g., by thinkers/bloggers), my first reaction is to bring justice/balance to the discussion, and for that purpose I might lean more to the right than I normally would. As an Israeli (actually, also as any plain human), it's my natural reaction.

The only approach I see is to try to help (help, not pressure) Israelis open their eyes to the injustices, which will hopefully help the Israeli left-wing movements grow and become less marginalized—that will ultimately bring change at the top as well.

Unfortunately, in spite of the geographical proximity between Israelis and Palestinians, interaction between the two people is very limited! Rather than see each other as humans, mutually suffering from the same stalemate they created (and let's not quantify or compare the sufferings here!—does that request raise *your* objection? . . .), they see each other as enemies (and often as inhuman). How can you empathize or consider the suffering of someone you perceive as a cold-blooded, inhuman (and inhumane) enemy?

The more we do to bring people together, the more both sides will open up to seeing the other as a human and making real efforts to work toward peace.

Shirley

I wish I had a response, but all I can do is to communicate to you my intense respect for your decision. It takes so much guts to be open, when most of us aren't exactly sure where we stand.

Thanks for being who you are.

Chapter 3

The Jewish Fast for Gaza

July–September 2009

Frustrated by the Jewish community's silence over Israel's brutal blockade of Gaza, my colleague Rabbi Brian Walt and I founded the Jewish Fast for Gaza initiative in the summer of 2009. Although it was, and remains, a modest volunteer effort, it received a barrage of well-publicized criticism from the Jewish communal establishment. As of this writing, Jewish Fast for Gaza has been endorsed by nearly a hundred rabbis, cantors, and rabbinical students.

The Jewish Fast for Gaza[1]

July 10, 2009

In response to the dire humanitarian crisis in Gaza, my dear friend and colleague Rabbi Brian Walt and I have organized a new initiative, Ta'anit Tzedek—Jewish Fast for Gaza.

Here is our press release about the project, which is already attracting increasing numbers of supporters, including many rabbis:

Rabbis Announce Monthly Fast for Gaza

Seeking "to end the Jewish community's silence over Israel's collective punishment in Gaza," an ad hoc group of American rabbis has called for a communal fast. Known as Ta'anit Tzedek—Jewish Fast for Gaza, this new initiative will organize a series of monthly fasts beginning on July 16.

The project was initiated by a group of 13 rabbis representing a spectrum of American Jewish denominations. The group's website explains the religious meaning of the campaign: "In Jewish tradition a communal fast is held in times of crisis both as an expression of mourning and a call to repentance. In this spirit, Ta'anit Tzedek—Jewish Fast for Gaza is a collective act of conscience initiated by an ad hoc group of rabbis, Jews, people of faith, and all concerned with [this] ongoing crisis."

The fast has four goals: to call for a lifting of the blockade; to provide humanitarian and developmental aid to the people of Gaza; to call upon Israel, the US, and the international community to engage in negotiations with Hamas in order to end the blockade; and to encourage the American government to "vigorously engage both Israelis and Palestinians toward a just and peaceful settlement of the conflict."

The water-only fast will take place every third Thursday of the month, from sunrise to sunset. In addition to signing on to the fast statement, participants have been asked to donate the money they save on food to the Milk for Preschoolers Campaign sponsored by American Near Eastern Refugee Aid (ANERA), a relief campaign that combats malnutrition among Gazan preschool children.

Since the electoral victory of Hamas in January 2006, Israel has imposed a blockade that has severely restricted Gaza's ability to import food, fuel, and other essential materials. As a result, the Gazan economy has completely collapsed, and it suffers from high levels of unemployment and poverty and rising levels of childhood malnutrition.

"Israel's treatment of the Palestinian people in Gaza amounts to nothing less than collective punishment. While we condemn Hamas's targeting of Israeli civilians, it is immoral to punish an entire population for the actions of a few," said Rabbi Brant Rosen, who serves Jewish Reconstructionist Congregation in Evanston, IL. "This blockade has only served to further oppress an already thoroughly oppressed people. As Jews and as human beings of conscience, we cannot stand idly by."

"We've been enormously encouraged by the initial response we've received from the Jewish community thus far," said fast organizer Rabbi Brian Walt, former executive director of Rabbis for Human Rights—North America, who noted that the initiative has signed up numerous supporters prior to the launch of the project. "We truly believe this effort is giving voice to a significant number of people who been looking for a Jewish voice of conscience on this issue."

Discussion

Debbie

Where is your concern for Gilad Shalit? And why are you so concerned with supporting a population of which the majority voted in a ruling party that educates children to become suicide bombers, that doesn't follow the Geneva Conventions and resorts to firing rockets into civilian areas? The people of Gaza have to learn that they are accountable for their actions, and your way is just letting them get away with murder.

Rabbi Brant Rosen

As regards Gilad Shalit: While Gilad is part of our people and his kidnapping is a crime, so is the imprisonment by Israel, without any charges, of hundreds if not thousands of Palestinians, some of whom are children and women. I personally strongly support a deal in which Gilad is freed along with those Israel has imprisoned unjustly (likewise in violation of the Geneva Conventions).

As regards the election of Hamas, I believe your description of them is simplistic. Although I have no love lost for Hamas, the reality is that Israel will have to deal with them if any true peace will be achieved. And in truth, Israel has already dealt with Hamas through any number of channels over the years.

Most analysts agree that Hamas was elected in 2006 not because Palestinians supported their religious/political ideology but because they had a track record of delivering effective social services and because the Palestinian public was fed up with the corruption and incompetence of Fatah. Whether or not you accept this analysis, do you really believe that starving 1.5 million people as a consequence of a democratic election is morally appropriate?

You say that this blockade will teach the Palestinians to be accountable. I disagree. I believe the blockade will only increase the Gazans' misery, inflaming and radicalizing them against Israel even further. (Do you believe that the children who are suffering from malnutrition now will grow up loving the state of Israel?) The blockade will not make Israel any safer—it will only endanger its security all the more.

Lisa K

Like Shirley who responded above, I cannot participate in the fast (low blood sugar), but I fully support this initiative, and I am thinking of an alternative way for me to participate. This is a thoughtful way to attempt to bring attention to the thousands of innocent children and their families who are suffering in so many ways: malnutrition, lack of basic medical care, lack of sanitation, daily power outages intention- ally imposed by Israel (can you imagine being in the Middle East in the summer without so much as a fan?). Let us also not forget: Many of them have also been orphaned and are grieving for their family mem- bers who were killed by the IDF during the recent invasion and attack. I continue to admire your courage and your leadership in stepping up for real Jewish values. Hopefully, those in Gaza will know that the world has not forsaken them.

Avi Ben Tzvi

Folks . . . debate is fine, but let's remember to check our facts. For example, Lisa makes statements about intentional blackouts caused by Israel. The fact is that 75 percent of electrical power in Gaza comes from the Israeli electrical grid. It has not been cut off. Five percent comes from Egypt. The remaining 20 percent is generated in Gaza. Fuel for those generators is delivered weekly. By way of example, here is a summary of the crossing in and out of "blockaded" Gaza in the last two weeks alone.

Weekly summary of the Gaza crossings: 5–10 July 2009

- 422 truckloads (9,592 tons) of humanitarian aid were transferred to the Gaza Strip via the Kerem Shalom cargo terminal and the Karni conveyor belt.
- 2.192 million liters of heavy-duty diesel for the Gaza power station and 1,275 tons of gas for domestic use were delivered via Nahal Oz fuel depot.
- 214 Gaza residents entered Israel for medical and 180 for humani- tarian reasons via Erez Crossing.

All for the free exchange of ideas. Let's just not let hyperbole get the better of us.

Rabbi Brant Rosen

I took the opportunity to check into the statistics you cited, and I noticed you took them word for word from Israel's Foreign Ministry website. I hardly think this qualifies as an objective source.

As per Israel's "weekly" shipment of diesel fuel to Gaza, please read this recent report from Human Rights Watch:

Israel . . . continues to restrict supplies of industrial diesel fuel used to generate electricity, keeping Gaza's only power plant oper- ating at two-thirds capacity and exacerbating Gaza's already severe electricity shortage. Israel blocked all petrol, diesel, and cooking gas into Gaza between February 8 and 14, OCHA said. Electricity cuts contribute to widespread water access problems.[2]

Regarding food aid: The World Food Programme estimates that it would take 400 trucks of food per day in order to meet Gaza's basic nutritional needs.[3] I think this stat offers some critical context against the claims you cite. For those who are interested in less biased reports on the politics of humanitarian aid in Gaza, I also recommend the checking out the website of the International Crisis Group—and in particular their report entitled "Unfinished Business."[4]

This seems to be Israel's latest ploy in the propaganda war: not merely to defend the blockade for reasons of security but now to deny there is even a blockade at all. Please don't buy into it.

Gaza: A Rabbinical Exchange[5]

July 14, 2009

Since we launched the Jewish Fast for Gaza, we've received all kinds of feedback, some supportive, some critical, some utterly unprintable. (My personal favorite from the latter category: "You should all get severe stomach ailments.")

On occasion, however, our effort has offered us the opportunity for genuinely respectful dialogue. Below is one such exchange—an e-mail I received from a rabbinic colleague, followed by my response:

Dear Ta'anit Tzedek,

Having cares and concerns of the plight of humanity is a most noble cause. That you are willing to extend effort is most commendable. Your organization, however, is extending its efforts in a manner that is not only counterproductive but can be harmful as well.

How can you look into the face of a 12-year-old girl from Sderot who suffers from post-traumatic syndrome as for most of life she has been awakened on a nightly basis by sirens and rocket fire? What do you say to the families of victims [of] suicide bombers who killed their teenagers while they casually enjoyed a slice of pizza? What do you say to an organization whose very goal is the annihilation of our people?

You may answer, "Had we been better, they may have liked us more," or some such configuration thereof. It's not plausible. Since 1948, the goal of the Arab world has been the removal of a Jewish presence in the Middle East. Our interference with their dream of a Pan-Arabic state stretching from Morocco to Iraq is sullied by our very presence.

It would better for your organization to spend its resources on ideals that truly further the continuity of Jews and Judaism.

I await your response,
Rabbi X

Dear Rabbi X,

I want to thank you for taking the time to reach out and respond to our initiative. I'm glad to have the opportunity for this dialogue.

You ask what I would say to the 12-year-old girl from Sderot or the families of terror victims. I believe I would say that as a fellow Jew, their pain is my pain as well. I would say that I could not begin to comprehend the realities they must face. But I would also share my belief that Israel's current treatment of the people of Gaza will bring them neither safety nor security—and that the only true way out of these traumas is a lifting of the blockade and the negotiation of a settlement by all parties involved.

As regards Hamas, "whose very goal is the annihilation of our people": Although I have no love lost for Hamas, the reality is that Israel will have to deal with them if any true peace will be achieved. And in truth, Israel has already dealt with Hamas through any number of channels over the years already. Making peace is a sacrosanct Jewish value—and as difficult as it is, the truth is that we make peace with our enemies. In the past, Israel has made peace with former enemies whom we once believed sought nothing but our "annihilation." To surrender this value means to doom the people of this region to endless violence and tragedy.

Thus we do indeed believe that this effort furthers the resources of Jews and Judaism. We do not hold that the only Jewish path is the one that addresses Jews and Jewish "needs" alone. In the case of Jews and Palestinians in particular, our fates are fundamentally intertwined: We will either live together or else we will die together. The Jewish path has always been to choose life—this sacred imperative is at the core of our initiative.

Thank you again for sharing your thoughts with us. Even as we may disagree, I hope you will share my conviction that our conversation is a *"machloket l'shem shamayim"* [argument for the sake of heaven]. I also know that you join with me in prayers for peace for this tortured region that is so dear to both of us.

Best,
Rabbi Brant Rosen

Flesh of Our Flesh[6]

July 24, 2009

Learn to do good, seek justice; relieve the oppressed. Uphold the orphan's rights; take up the widow's cause. (Isaiah 1:17)

This classic verse comes from the Haftarah portion for this Shabbat. It is the final so-called "Haftarah of affliction" coming annually on the Shabbat before the festival of Tisha B'Av. Beginning next week, our prophetic [Torah] portions will offer messages of consolation, reminding us that the path of return to righteousness is always open to us. Indeed, it is this very message that will guide us into the High Holiday season itself—the season of our return.

As I read this passage this year, I was mindful of a very similar passage that will appear in the Haftarah of Yom Kippur, also from the book of Isaiah:

> No, this is the fast that I desire: to unlock fetters of wickedness and untie the cords of lawlessness; to let the oppressed go free and break off every yoke. It is to share your bread with the hungry, and to take the wretched poor into your home; to clothe when you see the naked, and never forget your own flesh (Isaiah 58:6–7).

In a way, these two similar Isaiah passages seem to represent spiritual bookends to the High Holiday season. These characteristically prophetic calls to justice and repentance guide us through our High Holiday journey, reminding us not only of our seemingly chronic hypocrisy but also of the eternally simple route to return: "learn to do good, free the oppressed, feed the hungry. . . ."

As many of you know, our recently organized Fast for Gaza has cited Isaiah 58 as a kind of spiritual proof text to our initiative. As it turns out, ever since we've launched this project, I've been in a kind of dialogue with more than one correspondent over this particular verse. Several people have already written to me that we've misinterpreted Isaiah. It appears that for some, calling a Jewish fast in support of Gazan Palestinians rather than Jewish Israelis represents a betrayal of this prophetic imperative (not to mention the Jewish people). As one writer put it, "never forget your own flesh" means "charity begins at home."

This criticism motivated me to do a bit of digging into the source material. As it turns out, the Hebrew word for "your flesh"—*b'sarcha*—can indeed refer to blood relations or kin. But interestingly, according to the

Brown, Driver, Briggs Hebrew-English Lexicon,[7] this term can also mean "all living beings" (occurring in this usage at least 13 times throughout the Bible).

So, in fact, there is good, solid linguistic evidence to reject this narrow, tribal reading of Isaiah. Now I'm certainly willing to admit that this passage might have referred only to fellow Israelites when it was originally written. But today we live in a fundamentally different time than the ancient Israelites. In our globalized, postmodern world, the Jewish community has become interdependent with others in profound and unprecedented ways. Whether we are prepared to admit it or not, our Jewish security, our Jewish destiny is now irrevocably bound up with the destiny of all peoples and nations of the world.

I am well aware that this viewpoint represents a distinctly 21st-century Torah. I also have no illusions that it will be a simple matter for the Jewish community to heed this call. Having only recently emerged from the ghetto, still living with a collective memory of anti-Semitism, still reeling from the trauma of the Holocaust, it will necessitate a radical shift in consciousness to understanding our place in the world in such a way.

It will not be easy, but I believe it will be essential. It can no longer be us against them. At the end of the day, we are all one flesh.

Discussion

YBD

Okay, let's say that to be concerned primarily with the welfare of your own people is "particularist" and "narrow," and so, according to this thinking, Jews are responsible for all the hungry and miserable in the world. But, by what stretch of the imagination does this mean worrying about the welfare of your enemy? The Arabs of Gaza are the self-declared enemies of Israel and work daily for the eradication of Israel. This is what they proudly proclaim. Egypt also has a border with Gaza. The Egyptians are brother Arabs and Muslims, and as we are always told, all Muslims are brothers and all Arabs love one another, so therefore Egypt should be happy to supply Gaza with everything they want. So why aren't they, and why is Israel responsible for providing a comfortable life (beyond mandatory humanitarian basics like food and medicine) to the Gazans who are in a state of war with Israel?

Right of Reply: Time for a Moral Reckoning[8]

September 7, 2009

By Brian Walt and Brant Rosen. Originally published in the Jerusalem Post, *September 7, 2009*[9]

The Jewish community has survived for so long and through so many horrors in no small part because we know, from our history and in our bones, that *kol yisrael arevim zeh le zeh*—all of Israel is responsible for one another.

At the same time, however, Jewish tradition also reminds us that we aren't responsible only for each other.

One of the Torah's first moral teachings is that all human beings are created in the image of God. The meaning is clear: All people are intrinsically worthy of respect and dignity. Thus, whenever we diminish the humanity of another, we tarnish the image of God in our world.

Torah regularly calls on us to care for the "other" because we know from our own experience what it means to be the "other." And on Yom Kippur, the words of Isaiah will remind us of the fast we're meant to seek: "Is this not the fast that I have chosen: to loose the bonds of wickedness, to undo the heavy burdens, to let the oppressed go free, and that you break every yoke?"

It's never easy to "undo heavy burdens" for others. It's only human to consider our own needs—particularly if the burdens in question are laid upon an enemy with whom we've been locked in violence for decades.

But that's what we, the rabbis of Ta'anit Tzedek—Jewish Fast for Gaza, are asking our fellow Jews to do. We have turned to our community to say: The yoke on Gaza—the Israeli blockade—must be broken. We have thus called for a monthly communal fast to break the silence of the Jewish community on Gaza, to call upon Israel to lift the blockade, and to vigorously pursue peace with all relevant Palestinian parties.

Indeed, Israel's blockade of Gaza has led to widespread suffering in the Gaza Strip, including the increasing malnutrition of children, denial of medical care and of basic goods and services. Numerous human rights groups have found that 60 percent of Gazans don't have continuous access to water; homes and hospitals alike face near-daily power outages, often for 10 hours at a time (while 10 percent of Gazans have no electricity whatsoever); and because Israel hasn't allowed the electric and water treatment systems to import many spare parts or enough fuel for two years, tens of millions of gallons of untreated human waste are being dumped daily into the sea—threatening the health of Israelis as well.

As Jews and rabbis who care deeply about the Jewish tradition of human decency, we feel a special responsibility to speak out against a policy that leads to suffering on this scale. We're committed to breaking the silence in the Jewish community surrounding the blockade, and we are joining together with those who have been working tirelessly to end it.

It has been suggested in the pages of this paper[10] that our concern for the suffering in Gaza indicates that we're unconcerned about Israeli suffering, particularly in the South, where hundreds of rockets have fallen. We were called anti-Israel, "borderline anti-Semitic"; we've even been accused of standing by when Jewish blood is spilled. Overall, it was claimed that we can't love Israel if we seek justice for the Palestinians.

Let us be clear: We oppose this Israeli policy, not the State of Israel. But we reject this "either-or," zero-sum view of the conflict. We believe that the denial of food and other basic necessities is not only an affront to our moral teachings, but only serves to further anger and alienate the Palestinian people, adding to a cycle of hatred that further endangers the lives of Israelis.

But beyond accusations of Jew-hatred, it was also suggested that we don't know the whole truth about the blockade.

In fact, we've examined many sources, including the reports of such important Israeli human rights organizations as B'Tselem, Gisha, and Physicians for Human Rights. Eight such organizations recently produced a video decrying the blockade, "Lift the Closure, Give Life a Chance."[11] We're happy not only to learn from but also to partner with these prominent Israeli organizations and were honored when the Association for Civil Rights in Israel chose to endorse Ta'anit Tzedek.

Those who disagree with the findings of these internationally respected Israeli organizations should argue the substance of those findings rather than question the loyalties of those who question Israeli policy.

We started the project with just a minyan of rabbis; today we're pleased that more than 70 rabbis are involved. We know that there are many more rabbis who support the cause but fear that going public could put their jobs in jeopardy.

We'll continue to break the silence and insist that the suffering caused by the blockade be addressed in our community—not by name-calling but by a serious discussion of the facts and the moral implications for us as Jews.

This is the season when Jews search their souls and engage in a *heshbon nefesh* (moral reckoning). Ta'anit Tzedek calls on our community, and all people, to do a moral reckoning about Israel's blockade of Gaza until it is finally lifted.

Chapter 4

The Goldstone Report

September–November 2009

In the fall of 2009, as Gaza's plight was fading almost completely from the media radar, the United Nations Fact Finding Mission on the Gaza Conflict released its findings to the public, creating an impact that resonates even to this day. What came to be called the Goldstone Report concluded that Israeli and Hamas forces had committed "war crimes and possible crimes against humanity" before and during Operation Cast Lead. Even more controversial was the mission's finding that Israel had engaged in a "deliberately disproportionate attack designed to punish, humiliate, and terrorize a civilian population."

The Goldstone Report's findings caused a titanic uproar in Israel and throughout the American Jewish communal establishment; the mission's leader, Judge Richard Goldstone, was the target of intense and often hateful personal attacks. Goldstone, a highly respected human-rights jurist and a lifelong Zionist, was personally branded as a traitor by many in the Jewish community, his report branded "blood libel."[1]

At the height of this uproar, Brian Walt and I interviewed Judge Goldstone on a rabbinical conference call sponsored by Jewish Fast for Gaza. Although the call took place while Goldstone was under withering public criticism, he did not back away from his mission's controversial findings regarding Israel's "intentionality." He also spoke openly about the emotional toll of ongoing personal attacks directed against him and his family.

In what many would believe was an act of "penance" to the Jewish community, Goldstone submitted a vague "reconsideration" of some of his mission's findings in a much-publicized April 2011 Washington Post op-ed.[2] The two other members of the UN fact-finding mission, Hina Jilani and Desmond Travers, continue to stand fully behind the findings contained in their report.

I continue to believe that the ongoing controversy stirred up by the Goldstone Report is the surest sign of its continuing moral power—and of the continuing need for Israel to conduct an independent, credible, and transparent investigation of its actions during Operation Cast Lead.

The UN Reports on Gaza: How Will We Respond?[3]

September 16, 2009

The long-awaited UN Human Rights Council Fact Finding Mission's report on Israel's war in Gaza[4] has finally been released, and its conclusions are breathtaking. The mission, led by Justice Richard Goldstone, has concluded that during the Gaza conflict, Israel committed serious violations of international human rights and humanitarian law, actions amounting to war crimes, and possibly crimes against humanity.

Some background: Justice Richard Goldstone, who is Jewish, is a highly respected international jurist. He is a former member of the South African Constitutional Court and former chief prosecutor of the International Criminal Tribunals for the former Yugoslavia and Rwanda. His mission compiled a 574-page report that contains detailed analysis of 36 specific incidents in Gaza as well as a number of others in the West Bank and Israel. According to the UN press release announcing the report:

> The Mission conducted 188 individual interviews, reviewed more [than] 10,000 pages of documentation, and viewed some 1,200 photographs, including satellite imagery, as well as 30 videos. The mission heard 38 testimonies during two separate public hearings held in Gaza and Geneva, which were webcast in their entirety. The decision to hear participants from Israel and the West Bank in Geneva rather than in situ was taken after Israel denied the Mission access to both locations. Israel also failed to respond to a comprehensive list of questions posed to it by the Mission. Palestinian authorities in both Gaza and the West Bank cooperated with the Mission.[5]

Here is what the Mission concluded:

> In the lead-up to the Israeli military assault on Gaza, Israel imposed a blockade amounting to collective punishment and carried out a systematic policy of progressive isolation and deprivation of the Gaza Strip. . . . Houses, factories, wells, schools, hospitals, police stations and other public buildings were destroyed. . . . More than 1,400 people were killed. . . .
>
> Significant trauma, both immediate and long-term, has been suffered by the population of Gaza. The Report notes signs of profound depression, insomnia, and effects such as bed-wetting among children. The effects on

children who witnessed killings and violence, who had thought they were facing death, and who lost family members would be long lasting. . . .

. . . The Israeli military operation was directed at the people of Gaza as a whole, in furtherance of an overall and continuing policy aimed at punishing the Gaza population, and in a deliberate policy of disproportionate force aimed at the civilian population. *The destruction of food supply installations, water sanitation systems, concrete factories, and residential houses was the result of a deliberate and systematic policy that has made the daily process of living, and dignified living, more difficult for the civilian population.* [Emphasis mine.]

The Report states that Israeli acts that deprive Palestinians in the Gaza Strip of their means of subsistence, employment, housing and water; that deny their freedom of movement and their right to leave and enter their own country; and that limit their rights to access a court of law and an effective remedy could lead a competent court to find that the crime of persecution, a crime against humanity, has been committed.[6]

According to the JTA news service, the Israeli government and the American Jewish establishment have wasted no time in pouncing on the report.[7] But from what I've read so far, none of the respondents has addressed its substance. Not surprisingly, they're only interested in attacking the UN—in particular, the UN Human Rights Council.

Israeli Knesset Speaker Reuven Rivlin said, "The same UN that allows the president of a country [Iranian president Mahmoud Ahmadinejad] to announce on a podium its aspiration to destroy the State of Israel has no right to teach us about morality."[8] According to ADL Director Abe Foxman, "This is a report born of bias. What do you do with an initiative born of bigotry?"[9]

AJC Director David Harris:

Let us not forget that this commission was a creation of the Human Rights Council, arguably the UN's most flawed body. The Council has consistently demonized Israel, while giving a free pass to some of the world's worst tyrants, from Sudan to Iran.[10]

My two cents:

It is worth noting that this "flawed, biased" commission had this to say about Palestinian human-rights abuse during the Gaza war:

The Fact-Finding Mission also found that the repeated acts of firing rockets and mortars into Southern Israel by Palestinian armed groups "constitute war crimes and may amount to crimes against humanity," by failing to distinguish between military targets and the civilian population. "The launching of rockets and mortars that cannot be aimed with sufficient precisions at military targets breaches the fundamental principle of distinction. . . . [T]hey constitute a deliberate attack against the civilian population."

The Mission concludes that the rocket and mortar attacks "have caused terror in the affected communities of southern Israel" as well as "loss of life and physical and mental injury to civilians and damage to private houses, religious buildings, and property, thereby eroding the economic and cultural life of the affected communities and severely affecting the economic and social rights of the population."

The Mission urges the Palestinian armed groups holding the Israeli soldier Gilad Shalit to release him on humanitarian grounds. . . . The Report also notes serious human-rights violations, including arbitrary arrests and extra-judicial executions of Palestinians, by the authorities in Gaza and by the Palestinian Authority in the West Bank.[11]

So much for the accusations of bias.

If Foxman, Harris, et al., have any problems with the procedural process of the Mission (with which Israel refused to cooperate), I'm interested in hearing it. And if they have any evidence that counters the findings of the report, then let them bring it. Until this happens, I'm not sure their general opinion of the UN is germane to the matter at hand.

Based upon the comments and e-mails I get on a daily basis, I know I will be considered by some to be a self-righteous simpleton at best and a traitor to my people at worst. But here goes: As a Jew, I am devastated by these findings. The moral implications of this report should challenge us to the core. And I am deeply, deeply troubled that the primary response of our Jewish communal leadership is to attack the source of the report while saying absolutely nothing about its actual content.

Yes, there are other human-rights abusers in the world. And yes, some of them are even worse than Israel. Yes, the structure and governance policy of the UN is far from perfect. And yes, nations tend to use the UN for their own self-serving ends. But do these facts give us a pass on holding Israel up to the most basic standards of human rights and international law?

On Gaza and Yom Kippur: A Call to Moral Accounting[12]

September 27, 2009

Also published on the same date as an op-ed.

On Sunday night, the Jewish community will begin our annual Yom Kippur fast.

The physical deprivation is a crucial element of the day, but, as with many faith traditions, the fasting itself isn't really the point. Going without food and water is, rather, a device intended to sharpen our senses and lead to reflection.

This reflection is notably, pointedly, not a personal pursuit. All through the Yom Kippur prayers, we're called to do *cheshbon nefesh*, a moral accounting, as a community: "We have sinned," we pray. "Forgive us."

But though the rituals are ancient, they're never far removed from modern life. Between our prayers, American Jews are sure also to discuss the current events that touch our community most deeply: the prospects for Israeli-Palestinian peace, President Barack Obama's recent meetings with the leaders of Israel and the Palestinian Authority, and the UN's recent Goldstone Report, in which Israel and the Hamas government are accused of war crimes. To my great sorrow, however, many in the Jewish community have already rejected the latter out of hand.

Rather than jointly consider Israel's acts in Gaza, carry out real *cheshbon nefesh*, and accept our communal responsibility, it has proven easier for many of us to employ communal defense mechanisms and insist that in this particular case, there's no need for reflection.

Since the report's publication, the UN and Commission Chair Judge Richard Goldstone have been vilified and disparaged by the Israeli government and American Jewish leaders. There has been little consideration of the actual findings or the fact that Israel refused to cooperate with the commission or conduct its own investigation.

As a rabbi, this grieves me deeply. For, painful as it is for us to admit, Israel's behavior in Gaza has consistently betrayed our shared Jewish ethical legacy.

This was true before the war, when the Israeli blockade denied Palestinians basic necessities; it was true during the war, when Israel responded with disproportionate force to Hamas rockets; and it has been true since the war, as Israel has deepened the blockade, preventing Gazans from rebuilding their homes. As a result of Israeli actions, some 60 percent of Gazans don't have continual access to water and face near-daily power outages of up to 10 hours at a time, while hundreds of thousands are dependent on foreign-aid agencies for food.

A humanitarian crisis of this magnitude demands a response from within the Jewish faith community—and knee-jerk rejection of any and all criticism of Israel won't change the facts. It will only distance us from a just and peaceful solution to this conflict.

I don't mean to suggest that the report is perfect. No human endeavor is. Evidence of bias in the commission's make-up is important and should be honestly addressed, as the White House has suggested. But to categorically reject the Goldstone findings—which echo the work of highly respected Israeli and international human-rights groups, such as B'Tselem and Human Rights Watch—is to thrust our heads into the sand. In the end, the report's most critical recommendation is that Israel and Hamas thoroughly and credibly investigate themselves and hold accountable any combatants or commanders who violated the law.

The actions of the Jewish State ultimately reflect upon the Jewish people throughout the world. We in the Diaspora Jewish community have long taken pride in the accomplishments of the Jewish State. As with any family, the success of some reflects a warm light on us all. But pride cannot blind us to the capacity for error on the part of the country we hold so dear. We cannot identify with the successes but refuse to see the failures.

As we approach Yom Kippur, I call on America's Jews to examine the Goldstone findings and to consider their implications. In the spirit of the season, we must consider the painful truth of Israel's behavior in Gaza and understand that we must work, together, to discover the truth—and then urge on all relevant parties in the search for peace.

Every Yom Kippur, we read the words of the prophet Isaiah: "Is such the fast I desire, a day for people to starve their bodies? . . . No, this is the fast I desire: To unlock the fetters of wickedness and untie the cords of the yoke, to let the oppressed go free."

Let this be the Yom Kippur on which American Jews choose not just to starve their bodies but also to unlock the fetters and untie the cords—let this be the Yom Kippur on which we act on the Scriptural imperative to "seek peace and pursue it," by calling ourselves and Israel to account.

Discussion

Elaine

This was brave, and I'm sure you'll get a good communal thrashing from some segments of the Jewish community who feel unable to open this door for fear of what else might enter. But if a major challenge of this High Holiday season is to lead us back to the examined life, individually and collectively, then we are compelled to find a way to confront these very complicated ethical issues. Criticizing the examinations of others does not absolve us of the task before us. I hope those who respond negatively to your opinion piece will not just attempt to explain away what happened and is happening in Gaza, as if everything is justifiable in the name of security.

David B

I've never gotten a straight answer to this question from any critic of Israel's Gaza operation, but maybe you'll be the first: If Israel's reaction to Hamas's rockets was "disproportionate," what, in your view, would a "proportionate" response be?

You could also answer this one: If Iranian rockets were to somehow fall on suburban Chicago, what would a "proportionate" US response be?

Reading Goldstone[13]

October 1, 2009

Why should we trust the Goldstone Report if it was produced by the UN Human Rights Commission—a body that has a notorious history of focusing overwhelmingly on Israel to the near exclusion of other potential human-rights abusers around the world?

I posed this very question to Fred Abrahams, senior researcher for Human Rights Watch's emergencies division, who, together with B'Tselem executive director Jessica Montell, participated in a remarkable conference call organized by Ta'anit Tzedek yesterday.[14]

Fred, who is currently in Geneva attending the UN discussion of the report, answered that there is ample reason to be concerned about the HRC's undue attention to Israel, but that this particular mission presented a very real "opportunity" for the council to prove otherwise.

In fact, Justice Richard Goldstone initially refused to chair the mission until it was agreed that Palestinian wartime behavior would be investigated in addition to Israel's. Indeed, both sides were taken to task in the report's final recommendations. It was a shame, Fred said, that Israel's abject dismissal of Goldstone might actually be thwarting the HRC in its first genuine attempt to realize its true mandate.

For her part, Jessica pointed out that B'Tselem did have some concerns about possible bias in the report—a point she also made in a recent *Jerusalem Post* article. She did add, however, that Goldstone largely confirms the findings of B'Tselem's own investigations, including the huge number of civilian casualties and the targeting of civilian neighborhoods and Gazan infrastructure with no clear military objective.

I've started reading the Goldstone report myself—all 575 pages of it—and encourage you to do the same (but recommend that, like me, you save some trees by reading it from your computer screen). My initial impression: This report is an honorable, good-faith attempt to elucidate the facts of what occurred. Quite frankly, it makes for compelling and often devastating reading. I am certainly aware that it is not a perfect document, but in the end, I cannot accept that it deserves to be dismissed without due consideration (let alone be painted as "blood libel").

And I will only add that after reading the report, I consider Richard Goldstone to be a heroic individual who should be lauded for taking on this enormously difficult task with such moral courage.

I was particularly moved by his willingness to address the critical context of this tragic crisis. Witness this excerpt from his opening statement to the UN upon presenting the report:

> The Mission found that the attack on the only remaining flour-producing factory, the destruction of a large part of the Gaza egg production, the bulldozing of huge tracts of agricultural land, and the bombing of some 200 industrial facilities could not on any basis be justified on military grounds. . . .
>
> . . . Israeli political and military leaders . . . stated in clear terms that they would hit at the "Hamas infrastructure."
>
> If "infrastructure" were to be understood in that way . . . it would completely subvert the whole purpose of international human rights law. . . . It would make civilians and civilian buildings justifiable targets.
>
> These attacks amounted to reprisals and collective punishment and constitute war crimes.
>
> The Government of Israel has a duty to protect its citizens. That in no way justifies a policy of collective punishment of a people under effective occupation, destroying their means to live a dignified life, and the trauma caused by the kind of military intervention the Israeli government called Operation Cast Lead. . . . The teaching of hate and dehumanization by each side against the other contributes to the destabilization of the whole region.[15]

A transcript of our conference call will be posted on the Ta'anit Tzedek website soon. I'm excited to report that Ta'anit Tzedek is sponsoring a conference call between Justice Goldstone and Jewish clergy on October 18. We have a great deal to learn from him, and I look forward to reporting on our conversation.

Dirty Laundry[16]

October 13, 2009

I've been getting a heap of feedback about my recent op-ed ("On Gaza and Yom Kippur: A Call to Moral Accounting"), ranging from abject excoriation to deep gratitude and pretty much everything in between. It's obviously impossible to respond to it all, but I would like to address one consistently recurrent criticism: Namely, that a statement so critical of Israel should have been kept within the Jewish community—and that it was wrong of me to publish it in a paper as prominent and public as the *Tribune*.

A few disconnected thoughts on the "dirty laundry" argument:

I'm not sure I understand what it means to keep a conversation "within the community" anymore. Whether we like it or not, we Jews are now part of an open, pluralistic society. We've long since left the ghetto, and most of us consider this to be a good thing. And part of that deal is that for better or worse, our community conversations have become transparent, and our so-called "internal debates" are now part of the public domain. (I'd say this is all the more so in the postmodern information age—in which no community conversation can truly be considered private or internal anymore.)

I've been blogging for several years now and have written my share of sharp posts on Israel. This one was relatively milder than what I generally post here, yet it really seems to have struck a chord. I'm intrigued that for all the talk about the death of print media, its reach is still significant—and the traditional op-ed page still seems to have important symbolic significance for folks.

In this day and age, which do we really think is better for the Jews: a public communal face that demonstrates a monolithic, knee-jerk defense of Israel's every action, or a Jewish community that is confident and secure enough in itself to model healthy self-reflection? In my experience, non-Jews tend to be much more alienated by the former and appreciative of the latter.

Many in the Jewish community feel that we should not be contributing to the already significant public criticism of Israel. I am not so naive to say that some of this criticism has fairly dark motivations. But I am also not so cynical to say that the "outside world" cannot tell the difference between abject prejudice and legitimate self-criticism.

If we do believe that speaking out against oppression is one of our most sacrosanct values, then we are guilty of hypocrisy if we fail to speak out when Israel acts oppressively. For me, at least, the value of pursuing justice ultimately trumps the fears that arise when we publicly call our community to account.

I know it is painful and complicated when we do so. I know this firsthand. I realize that such a step comes with difficult consequences—but at the very least we should be willing to honestly face the consequences of keeping silent.

I welcome your (respectful) feedback.

Discussion

David

Shortly after the Gaza siege, I wrote an article in our local paper. The reaction by members of the clergy in my community was very much like you've described. One rabbi, who asked me to come visit his office, was friendly but concerned that criticisms of Israel had strayed outside the Jewish community and could give anti-Semites fodder. Indeed, I might even be guilty of anti-Semitism. He even recited some religious parable: the "dirty laundry" of the time. But the sad fact remains that the actions of our cousins in Israel are an American foreign-policy and foreign-aid problem as well as a Jewish issue. And that puts it squarely in the public sphere.

Shirley

There are ample examples of our being "in the open." It is hard even to imagine lines around the Jewish community that would allow our dirty laundry to remain in the basement. Although it hadn't entered my mind before, it seems absolutely logical that we accept that we are now on an open field, vulnerable to assault but also capable of thinking and speaking.

Don't stop. Maybe we need to help do the wash.

Lisa

I think the point though, Brant, is that your criticism of Israel can be measured in loaves, and your criticism of Hamas, Hezbollah, the PA, et al., and, dare I say it, support for Israel in trying times can be measured in crumbs.

Rabbi Brant Rosen

You make a valid point, Lisa. I grant that the majority of the criticism on my blog is focused on Israel. I suppose this reflects my own anguish, as a Jew, that such acts are being perpetrated by the Jewish state—and my own desire for Israel to live up to its own articulated ethical Jewish values—values that I also consider sacred.

Although you might not see this or accept this, my criticism comes from a deep love for Israel—and from a growing fear that the course Israel is currently on will lead to its extinction and not its survival.

I personally believe Palestinian attacks against Israeli civilians—Qassam rockets on Sderot, suicide bombings in pizzerias, etc.—are morally disgusting. I don't hesitate to say so here and regret if my focus on Israel's actions creates the impression that I condone them in any way. The attempt to even rationalize this form of violence is reprehensible.

A final thought: When I wrote that we Jews must be willing to speak out against all oppression—including Israel's—I was referring to the organized Jewish community's pointedly knee-jerk defense of any criticism leveled against Israel. I believe there are many in the "outside world" who justifiably see hypocrisy in our willingness to protest any number of persecutions around the world except Israel's persecution of Palestinians.

I know that my own activism, taken on its own, might appear unfairly imbalanced—especially to those who don't know me and my personal feelings for Israel. For my part, I am trying to do my part to redress a larger Jewish communal imbalance on this issue.

I know that there are many more rabbis who feel as I do but are intimidated into staying silent. I do believe that if more Jewish leaders could find the wherewithal to speak out when they believe Israel is acting wrongly, we would have a more vital and balanced Jewish communal voice. And in the end, I think that would be a good thing.

Elaine

Actually, Lisa, I would say that the American Jewish community's unwillingness to own the fact that there are serious wrongs being committed in Israel, which is disproportionately the more powerful entity in the conflict, is what can be measured in loaves. I strongly believe the efforts by Brant, *J Street*, Brit Tzedek, and others to open the dialogue to greater balance is a long-overdue adjustment to the distortions in this conversation. It may not suit your personal views, but it is deeply welcomed by many of us who have felt shut out by the American Jewish community's reflexive defense of Israeli policy. I am very grateful that I attend the type of synagogue that is willing to put these complicated moral questions squarely in front of us and will not let us walk away from them. I certainly prefer that to attending one that would put an IDF bulletproof vest in its lobby, as one well-known shul in Chicago apparently did. That sort of Judaism makes me sick to my stomach.

YBD

I think it is incorrect to categorize the Gaza War/Goldstone controversy as "dirty laundry." A good example of a "dirty laundry" type of thing would be to go to a non-Jewish newspaper and write something like, "We Jews should be collectively ashamed that Bernie Madoff is one of us."

The Gaza War is a totally different matter. Israelis, by and large, supported the war, think it was justified and oppose Goldstone. It is not "dirty laundry" in that it is something to be ashamed of.

What those who go to non-Jewish media and excoriate Israel are doing is admitting that they have lost the political battle in Israel. That, of course, is where the battle has to be fought, and the "progressives" lost it. This also applies to the so-called "peace process" in general, which most Israelis have long ago lost faith in. Those who oppose these consensus positions of the Israeli public now feel their only alternative is to go to some outside power to convince them to impose their views on Israel *against Israel's will, against Israel's interests, and against Israel's security.* The question that these who are doing these things must ask themselves is, "By what right are they bypassing the Israeli public in trying to get outside forces to use punitive measures to get the Israeli public to capitulate to policies they have rejected?"

Now, I know the answer will come back, "The US grants aid to Israel and I, as an American taxpayer, have a right to weigh in on where my tax dollars are going." But this is no longer a "Jewish matter," and so those who do so *must not speak in the name of the Jewish community* or even a part (e.g., the "progressive" part). This is the fatal mistake *J Street* is making. . . . They want to break with policies of the elected Israeli government, they want the US to impose the policies they want, and yet they are speaking as Jews against what the Jewish community of Israel and much of what the American Jewish community support. This is why they will fail. They can't have it both ways.

Thomas

A just person is a good person. Justice, real justice, not legal justice, is based on moral and ethics. Killing a person is immoral and can only be defended in the specific case of defending yourself. By the way: This expression makes it already clear that no killing can be taken lightly, as the person who kills another one in self-defense has also to defend himself afterward.

The State of Israel is not accused of defending Israel or for doing this by killing persons who attacked innocent Israelis. The State of Israel is accused that, in its name, more innocent people have died than were necessary to defend Israel; that these victims have died under circumstances that are in principle forbidden by international law and conventions to which Israel—as a civilized country—adheres; and that Israel does not investigate by its own these cases in which possibly murder occurred. This last point is the most important: If Israel takes serious legal action to prosecute those persons who committed these odious crimes, no international action will take place. If Israel flatly and willingly ignores that these crimes have been committed— and here we are at the "dirty laundry"—the Goldstone Report calls for deferral to the ICJ [International Court of Justice]. By the way, the Goldstone Report asks the same from Hamas.

"Dirty laundry" is to me nothing else than "double standard." It is like saying: "There was a crime, but since it has been perpetrated by persons of my people, I close my eyes, and it is no longer a crime." This is the definition of hubris. It is interesting to note what Wikipedia says about hubris: "In ancient Greece, hubris referred to actions which, intentionally or not, shamed and humiliated the victim. . . . Hubris, though not specifically defined, was a legal term and was considered a crime in classical Athens." It was considered a crime, for it undermined the order of the world, in this case the social tissue.

Two thousand years later, we live in a world of the Universal Declaration of Human Rights; the first words of it read: "Recognition of the inherent dignity and of the equal and inalienable rights of all members of the human family is the foundation of freedom, justice, and peace in the world." Bluntly said: All humans are equal, and no one is worth more than any other.

Invoking "dirty laundry" to avoid the discussion of committed crimes is a direct action against this Declaration of Human Rights and makes those who want to escape the discussion co-responsible for these crimes.

Your blog, Rabbi, is so important to me, because you call "oppression" what it is—namely, "oppression"—and you say it publicly. Yours is one of the voices who keep my faith up in mankind: "I believe that people are really good at heart." Your honesty makes me believe that Israel will survive and one day will live in peace with its neighbors.

Marge

YBD: In my opinion, you tend to speak for large populations rather than for yourself personally.

As an Israeli/American Jew, I know many, many people who do not fit into your mass assumptions of what either Israelis or American Jews want. Those I speak of want the freedom to speak out strongly against our governments' policies when we believe they are wrong. For me, that was Iraq in America, where one couldn't even disagree without being considered traitorous, and now, in Israel, where the use of overly massive force has caused poverty, destruction, unemployment, and hatred toward the Israelis we all love. And where those of us who love the country are called anti-Semitic and anti-Israel. What we want, and I hasten to add I speak for myself and for those I know, is for a peace process to proceed, and quickly, one that will require both sides to make compromises and sacrifices, to overcome centuries of hatred and distrust, to come to the understanding that we must learn to live as brothers or we are all lost. My many years of living in Israel taught me how much the Arabs and Israelis have in common. This is not a struggle for "capitulation" or "winning," it is a struggle for the survival of both peoples.

My HR 867 Postmortem[17]

November 13, 2009

Last week, the US House of Representatives passed Resolution 867 by the whopping margin of 344 to 36.[18] For all you non–House watchers, HR 867 was the one that called upon

> the President and the Secretary of State to oppose unequivocally any endorsement or further consideration of the "Report of the United Nations Fact Finding Mission on the Gaza Conflict" in multilateral fora.[19]

In plain English, this means that the US Congress has, for all intents and purposes, quashed the Goldstone report.

A few thoughts postmortem:

In this age of nonpartisan Congressional gridlock, what do we make of the eye-popping rapidity with which this resolution was crafted, brought to the floor, and passed in an overwhelmingly bipartisan manner? For me, at least, it proves only this: Walt and Mearshimer [authors of *The Israel Lobby and US Foreign Policy*] are right. (If you haven't read their book[20] yet, check it out—I believe it's becoming more relevant by the day.)

During the House debate, Goldstone wrote a letter to the sponsors, addressing the resolution point by point and identifying numerous factual inaccuracies. Even though the vote is now history, I encourage you to read it. I wonder how many of the 344 yea voters actually took the time to do so—or if it would have made a difference if they had.

I commend to you this powerful *Huffington Post* article, written by Fred Abrahams of Human Rights Watch. An excerpt:

> The resolution succumbs to predictable American politics, in which criticisms of Israeli actions are rejected as delegitimizing attacks on Israel, and even as anti-Semitism. It misses a chance to break the impunity on all sides that has dogged the conflict and impeded efforts at peace. And, most significant for US foreign policy, it gives abusive governments around the world a handy excuse to deflect US criticism of their own unlawful conduct.[21]

Chapter 5

Beyond Tribalism

October 2009–February 2010

Many of my blog posts have explored the challenges presented by Jewish tribalism in the globalized 21st-century world. It is ironic indeed that while our global village is fast creating connections between peoples and nations, Israel has become an increasingly militarized Jewish garrison state that builds bigger and higher walls between itself and the outside. This is one poignant tragedy of Zionism: Although it was founded to "normalize" the Jewish condition, there is today a palpable and widespread "us against the world" mentality inherent in Israeli culture.

In the meantime, it has been well-documented that young American Jews—a generation that largely embraces the new global mentality and does not view the outside world with fear—are feeling largely disconnected from the state of Israel. Thus, in my writing and my activism, I'm increasingly compelled to ask: Is this the kind of Judaism we seek to espouse? To pass to our children? Do we truly believe it points the way to a better Jewish future?

On Jewish Hearts and Minds[1]

October 23, 2009

Just read Rabbi Daniel Gordis's recent op-ed in the *Jerusalem Post*,[2] one of several articles that have given some free publicity to Ta'anit Tzedek. But it wasn't Gordis's offhand slam on Ta'anit Tzedek that really bothered me: It was the decidedly patronizing way he analyzed the gulf between the

American Jewish community and Israel—or, as he termed it, American Jewry's "growing abandonment of Israel."

Gordis's main premise: American Jewry's newest generation is essentially self-centered (tainted "with the 'I' at the core of American sensibilities") and simply cannot relate to the national sense of duty embodied by Israel:

> In America, the narratives of immigrant groups are eroded, year by year, generation after generation. In America, we are oriented to the future, not to the past, and if we cling to some larger grouping, it is to a human collective whole rather than to some "narrow" ethnic clan. . . .
>
> . . . Similarly, the recreation of the State of Israel is truly powerful only against a backdrop of centuries of Jewish experience and is spine-tingling only if my sense of self is inseparable from my belonging to a nation with a past and a people with a purpose.
>
> In today's individualistic America, the drama of the rebirth of the Jewish people creates no goose bumps and evokes no sense of duty or obligation. Add the issue of Palestinian suffering, and Israel seems worse than irrelevant—it's actually a source of shame.[3]

It's not clear to me if Gordis is interested in winning over the hearts and minds of young American Jews, but if he is, I'd suggest that talking down to them from an Israeli ivory tower is not the way to do it. I'm afraid that record just doesn't play anymore.

Gordis is correct when he posits that the old narratives simply aren't working on American Jews the way they used to. But that's only because a new, more complex narrative is now being written by the current generation. It's compelling in its own right, although this may be difficult to understand when viewed from the conventional Israeli vantage point.

I work with a great number of American Jews—particularly the 35-and-younger demographic that Gordis cites—and from where I sit, they look nothing like the narcissistic, self-obsessed Americans he describes. On the contrary, most are engaged, seriously seeking Jews. Yes, it's true that unlike previous generations, they don't necessarily understand their Judaism in traditionally tribal terms anymore. But that doesn't make them self-centered. Rather, they are increasingly viewing their Jewishness against a larger, more universal global reality. In short, to be a Jew and a global citizen is what gives them "goose bumps."

If, as Gordis suggests, American Jews are abandoning Israel, I'd suggest it's not due to the lack of a sense of Jewish "duty or obligation"—I believe it's because they are left cold by an Israeli national culture that appears to them to be overly tribal and collectively self-centered.

Indeed, while most young people today seem to be interested in breaking down walls between peoples and nations, Israel often appears determined to build higher and higher walls between itself and the outside world. It's a poignant irony of Jewish history: While Zionism was ostensibly founded to normalize the status of Jewish people in the world, the Jewish state it spawned seems to view itself as all alone, increasingly victimized by the international community.

Gordis himself exemplifies this "it's us Jews against the rest of the world" ethos in the opening paragraphs of his article:

> About one thing, at least, the world seems to be in agreement: Israel is the primary culprit in the Middle East conflict, the cause of relentless Palestinian suffering and the primary obstacle blocking the way to regional peace.
>
> The international chorus of opprobrium is growing by the day. . . . It's relentless, this ganging up, but it's also not terribly new. The momentum has been building for years, and though we may not like it, we cannot honestly claim to be surprised.[4]

Although I understand the psychology of this worldview, I don't think it helps make Israel's case for young Jews today—nor do I think it promotes a particularly healthy Jewish identity. It seems to me to be the product of self-pity more than pride—a victim mentality that's not likely to get us anywhere with newer generations of Jews, who feel increasingly comfortable with the "outside world" and who don't particularly identify with the claim that when push comes to shove, the whole world really does just hate the Jews.

I will also predict that Gordis's two cynical references to "Palestinian suffering" will not resonate for growing numbers of Jews who are legitimately troubled by Israel's treatment of Palestinians. I understand full well that our criticism sounds galling to most Israeli ears. And no, I don't believe that we American Jews can even begin to understand how Israelis feel—on so many levels. But whether Israelis like it or not, there is a steadily growing demographic in the American Jewish community: proud, committed Jews who are deeply troubled when Israel acts oppressively, who feel implicated as Americans and as Jews in these actions, and who are galled at being labeled as traitors when they choose to speak out.

At the very least, I hope that Gordis will understand that if American Jews are identifying with organizations that protest Israel's oppressive policies (such organizations as Ta'anit Tzedek, yes), their affiliation does not come from a shame-filled desire to "bash" Israel. It comes from a deeper and much more Jewishly authentic place than that.

I realize that all this may be too much to ask for. It's long been clear that the American Jewish and Israeli Jewish communities are two very different animals with two decidedly different ways of understanding what it means to be a Jew in a rapidly changing world. (Sociologists Steven Cohen and Charles Liebman pointed this out with great insight 20 years ago in their book *Two Worlds of Judaism.*[5])

But it seems to me if we truly want to facilitate the Jewish future, we're going to have to do it together. And to do that, we'll need to meet one another with openness and understanding, not dismissal and judgment.

Discussion

Rebecca

It doesn't seem to me at all helpful to try to postulate a simplified or stereotyped American Jewish character. Clearly there are Jews for whom the state of Israel is a central part of their identity. There are also Jews who don't particularly give a damn, and there are Jews, like me, who identify as human beings first (how does this make me selfish, exactly?) and feel that there are moral imperatives that override cultural, ethnic, and political concerns. I am grateful that my American sons are growing up in a culture where they are side by side with Muslims, Hindus, Buddhists, Christians, and different kinds of Jews. I am hopeful that they will have the strength of character, rooted in Jewish values and identity, to demand justice and to deplore oppression and, yes, suffering in their own community and everywhere.

Debbie

Although it is always useful to engage in self-reflection, both individual and communal, as American Jews, I must point out that increasing generations of Israeli Jews also find themselves farther removed from the immigrant narrative and have cultivated a decided emphasis on "future" rather than "past." I realize his point is about spotlighting American Jews (I actually don't find as much inaccuracy in some of what he concludes), but I, for one, am not comfortable with the implicit statement that parallel processes are not taking place among Israelis.

Eric

The phenomena Gordis describes in America—the focus on the future, the melting-pot aversion to an identity focused on "some 'narrow' ethnic clan," the individualism balanced by xenophilia—strike me as truly powerful things, spine-tingling, even.

That's because my own sense of self is, as the rabbi says, "inseparable from my belonging to a nation with a past and a people with a purpose."

That would be, of course, the American past and the American people. Much of which has been shaped, at the level of idea, by Jews. (Ask Emma Lazarus.)

In fact, I think what we have here isn't an argument between a Jewish identity (which can only be truly realized in Israel) and an American one.

Rather, it's between two versions of Jewish identity: a Zionist one, which emerged from Europe, and a diasporist one, which flourished here, insinuating itself into the American mainstream.

Gordis thinks his is better, which is why he lives in Israel. I live here, and raise my children here, for exactly the same reason.

Dan

I think that American Jews, living in the relative safety of their homes, have no right to dictate Israeli policy as to whether to lift the blockade in Gaza. Only Israelis will be subject to a barrage of rockets, if the decision to lift the blockade is a wrong one. Therefore, it doesn't behoove American Jews to interfere with military policy that is deemed to be a deterrent to terror and to increase the security of its inhabitants. When American Jews make *aliyah* and their sons will be called up to army duty, then, by all means, make your voice heard. But, while living in America, [where] the greatest decision one has to face is which television channel to watch that evening, it is best not to interfere with Israeli government policy.

Elliot

So now there are preconditions on us even expressing our opinion? If you in fact think American Jews have no right to weigh in on Israeli government policy until we have made *aliyah* and sent our children to serve in the IDF, will you similarly not object when we urge the US government to reduce the amount of our tax dollars spent on aid to Israel? It strikes me that Israeli Jews cannot have it both ways. If you want the support of us American Jews—political, moral, monetary, or otherwise—it behooves you to engage in a dialogue with us in which all parties actually listen to what their interlocutors are saying. Crying foul when we express criticism (whatever you think our motivation may be) while at the same time expecting continued support regardless of your own actions doesn't really work. A more productive approach would be addressing the substance of criticisms of Israeli actions raised by American Jews rather than attacking our presumably comfortable life, our motivation, or our right to express our concerns and opinions.

Shai

It was hard for me to get to the end of the Gordis article, because I found the intro's "The world is ganging up against us, so what is new" approach to be so flawed.

According to Israeli Army numbers, more than 1,100 Gazans were killed in Operation Cast Lead. What kind of a world would we be living in if people weren't asking questions?

Kenneth

If I said that I really loved my wife, and I would show it if only she did this and said that and looked like Bar Refaeli, then it would be reasonable to say that I really don't love my wife.

Israel is a real country, which is to say that it is populated with real people, some of whom are jerks, bigots, and crooks. Israel is also in a war for survival, fighting against enemies who hide behind civilians. Wars are not nice, wars for survival are particularly unpleasant, and wars fought amidst civilians are even more so. This is reality, and if you can't support the real Israel, then just admit it. Because the real Israel will never conform to your fantasies of a Jewish utopia.

In the real world, we make choices, and we define ourselves by our choices. If you really can't deal with the real and imperfect Israel, then you are deciding to be neutral in the fight between Israel and its enemies, to include Saudi Arabia, Syria, Iran, Sudan, Fatah, Hamas, Islamic Jihad, Hezbollah, al-Qaeda. If that's your choice, then please don't annoy us with your sanctimonious talk about human rights. It's not my side, right or wrong. It's my side, imperfect but vastly better than the alternative.

Lori

Kenneth, I am sad when I read your comment. It resembles the viewpoint of so many of our community who have given way to the threat of *broiges* [breaking up the family] because of disagreements. This is most unfortunate for the Jews of Diaspora, I think.

If I love my husband, and my husband gets drunk at bars and beats people up, when I give my husband a hug and some cash, I am not expressing my love. I am enabling him to continue behavior that threatens other people, himself, and my whole family.

You may or may not agree with this metaphor, but I hope you understand that your viewpoint is not the only one that is valid. There are others—viewpoints with which you may feel free to disagree—held by people who consider themselves lifelong Zionists and whose lives have been committed to the Jewish people. Disagree, but please do not stoop so low as to smear other members of your community in order to win your point.

Kenneth

Lori: Israel is a democracy with fair elections, a free press, an independent judiciary, and a diverse population. The idea that you or I can explain to them how to run their country or fight their battles is either condescending or foolish. There probably is a reason why Israelis (or at least Jewish Israelis) have decisively rejected the Left, and those who would preach to Israelis should probably understand that reason. What friends of Israel can do is support Israel, even when they disagree with the positions of its elected government. Probably a good start to supporting Israel would be to refrain from comparing it to a drunkard who beats people up. A good example of how to support Israel was provided by my evangelical Christian friends, who certainly opposed the withdrawal from Gaza and regarded PM Ehud Olmert as a doofus at best yet still strongly supported Israel.

With regard to Israel, I am uninterested in your self-assessment of your Zionism and Jewish identity. What interests me is your willingness to support Israel in word, deed, and through your associations. In particular, I am interested in what you are doing to prevent Israel from being isolated, terrorized, and overrun by murderous savages or obliterated with nuclear weapons by genocidal fanatics. To me, that is the bottom line for supporters of Israel.

I am not a blind supporter of Israel. I am keenly aware that Israel is not a utopia and not populated by saints. I would like it to be better (as I define "better," of course), but as a Zionist, I respect the choices of the Israeli people, because they have a lot more "skin in the game" than I do.

Elliot: You are certainly within your rights as an American to "urge the US government to reduce the amount of our tax dollars spent on aid to Israel." There are any number of reasons to advocate such a course of action, some of which are not animated by animosity to Israel. But if you do so with the intent or effect of coercing Israel to do actions that its elected government thinks are detrimental to its security, then honesty demands that you cease to refer to yourself as pro-Israel or Zionist.

Elliot

I think you are saying that encouraging Israel to undertake actions that its elected government does not currently favor cannot be pro-Israel or Zionist. That strikes me as simplistic. What if a substantial segment of the Israeli voting public feels the way I do, even if their view is not espoused by the ruling coalition? Are they unpatriotic? The history of Zionism is one of multiple opinions, of numerous and sometimes opposing agendas and philosophies. Israel continues to enjoy vigorous and multifaceted political discourse. Why should Jews outside Israel who agree with the current Israeli government be considered Zionist and pro-Israel, while those of us who agree with Israeli minority opinions are not so considered? . . . If we both agree that whichever party leads the Israeli government, the minority is by and large the loyal opposition, why should the diversity of political thinking end at Israel's borders? It does a disservice to the rich history of Zionism to boil it down to a Bush-ian "you're either for us or against us." . . .

. . . Separately, a better-fitting metaphor . . . might be as follows: My father has failing eyesight and gets into repeated small fender benders. I tell him he should stop driving before anyone is more seriously injured, my brother thinks it is disrespectful and demeaning to say so, and my father worries about his independence. We can all be in the same family, love one another, and share many of the same concerns, but we each have different assessments of which concern outweighs another. Similarly, why should your focus on Israel's security be more (or less) valid than my focus on its respect for human rights? We can each express our concerns to our Israeli cousins and take those actions dictated by our respective consciences while acknowledging the validity of each other's concerns and of our shared concern for Israel's future.

Exchanges of blog comments like these are not the ideal vehicle for respectful and candid discussion, particularly on as sensitive a subject as the relationship between American Jews and Israel. That discussion is taking place face to face in my community, with an emphasis on listening to and respecting one another. I hope it is taking place in yours and many other American Jewish communities as well.

Jack

So what you are really saying is that Americans should have a right to weigh in on policies of any country that receives American aid, no matter how big or how small, right? . . .

. . . Has Israel made mistakes? Yes. Should Israel be criticized? Yes, but it needs to be balanced.

We need to take into account things like Hamas's charter, which calls for the destruction of Israel. We need to account for discrepancies in number of civilians killed. They don't wear uniforms. It is intentional so that when the dead are counted, the numbers are skewed.

It is a known fact that not all of those who were killed in Gaza were civilians. It is a known fact that the rocket fire that was launched from Gaza rained down upon land that wasn't in dispute, wasn't considered occupied by anyone who accepts the State of Israel.

It is a known fact that Abbas and Hamas do not see eye to eye. How do you intend to negotiate with someone who doesn't have the ability to speak or represent all?

I am not suggesting that peace talks should forever be suspended, but we need to be real. It feels uncomfortable to see some of the things that we have seen, but they do not operate off the same value system we do.

Are there good Palestinians? Undoubtedly, they are people. But again, the leadership makes it quite difficult to try to negotiate terms

There are better ways to try to effect change than the critics of Israel are engaging in.

Lori

The great supporters of Israel, Bush-Cheney, and their American-Jewish loyalists are responsible for putting Hamas in power in Gaza and letting the peace process end up in rigor mortis over the past decade. We won't go into whether they are also responsible for dragging Israel's world popularity down to its lowest low—I think so. To me, Zionism isn't about waving the flag and cursing the Arabs. It's about finding a practical way to ensure Israel's survival. George Mitchell managed to make it happen in Ireland, which has been at war for longer than Israel. But the will to find a way has got to be there, rather than the impulse to cave in to fear. There is no way to win by force in this case. All the Americans' horses and men can't defend Israel from the Muslim world in which it dwells. The only chance to live to see the Zionist dream into the next century is to find a way to live among them. The major Arab countries of the region have proposed ways to make that happen. If we let every extremist with a bomb derail that process, how will we ever go forward?

"Cursed Be He That Keepeth Back His Sword from Blood"[6]

November 16, 2009

From yesterday's *Ha'aretz*:

> The Israel Defense Forces' chief rabbi told students in a pre-army yeshiva program last week that soldiers who "show mercy" toward the enemy in wartime will be "damned."
>
> Brig. Gen. Avichai Rontzki also told the yeshiva students that religious individuals made better combat troops. Speaking Thursday at the Hesder yeshiva in the West Bank settlement of Karnei Shomron, Rontzki referred to Maimonides' discourse on the laws of war. That text quotes a passage from the Book of Jeremiah stating: "Cursed be he that doeth the work of the Lord with a slack hand, and cursed be he that keepeth back his sword from blood."
>
> In Rontzki's words, "In times of war, whoever doesn't fight with all his heart and soul is damned—if he keeps his sword from bloodshed, if he shows mercy toward his enemy when no mercy should be shown."[7]

Whatever else we might think about Maimonides' (or Jeremiah's) words, we are certainly free to debate their academic meaning. But when they are uttered by the chief rabbi of the IDF to future Israeli soldiers, such words as these are much, much more than merely academic.

You may remember that Rabbi Rontzki was in the news following Israel's military operation in Gaza, when soldiers alleged that he gave them a religious booklet entitled *Go Fight My Fight*.[8] This publication includes extensive quotes by Rabbi Shlomo Aviner, head of the Ateret Cohanim yeshiva in Jerusalem, who ruled that Palestinians were the equivalent of the biblical Philistines and that cruelty can sometimes be a "good attribute."

You may also remember that Israeli soldiers from the organization Shovrim Shtika ("Breaking the Silence") brought this issue to light following the war in Gaza.[9] Although they have been attacked mercilessly by the Israeli political establishment, these young soldiers have continued to speak out. Last September, Gal Einav and Shamir Yeger, two reserve infantry soldiers who fought in Gaza, wrote a powerful editorial in the Israeli press about what they considered to be an unwelcome "messianic" religious influence into the IDF:

> There is a problem with the growing tendency to provide religious elements with a monopoly on values and fighting spirit, and particularly with the

legitimacy granted to organizations with a missionary and messianic character to operate amongst the soldiers. Most of the commanders in our division are religious, yet up until the last war there was complete separation between their private world and their military position.

If we fail to clearly draw the line right now, in a few years we shall find ourselves shifting from wars of choice or no-choice to holy wars.[10]

In a September BBC report, Reserve General Nehemia Dagan had this to say about the issue:

We [soldiers] used to be able to put aside our own ideas in order to do what we had to do. It didn't matter if we were religious or from a kibbutz. But that's not the case anymore.

The morals of the battlefield cannot come from a religious authority. Once it does, it's Jihad. I know people will not like that word but that's what it is, Holy War. And once it's Holy War there are no limits.[11]

What explains the growth of this right-wing religious influence in the IDF? I tend to agree with blogger Zachary Goelman, who points out a larger demographic trend in Israeli society:

With conscription rates dropping annually, especially among secular Jews, and a simultaneous increase in the country's religious population, Yeger and Einav are part of a shrinking minority. No doubt they know many who ducked their conscription call. If they have draft-age children, they've certainly heard them discuss the myriad ways of obtaining a deferral.

This trend is reversed in the *dati-le'umi* sector, the category of Israeli Jews broadly classified as "national religious." In one way or another the men and women woven from this cloth see military and national service as a form of religious duty, and their ranks in uniform and civil society will increase in the coming decades. Coupled with the consistent growth of ultra-orthodox families, secular Israel may be in the final throes of its *götterdämmerung.*[12]

Whatever the explanation, I personally find the implications of this trend to be beyond troubling. How will we, as Jews, respond to the potential growth of Jewish Holy War ideology within the ranks of the Israeli military? How do we feel about Israeli military generals holding forth on the religious laws of warfare? Most Americans would likely agree that in general, mixing religion and war is a profoundly perilous endeavor. Should we really be so surprised that things are now coming to this?

I do not ask these questions out of a desire to be inflammatory. I ask them only because I believe we need to discuss them honestly and openly—

and because these kinds of painful questions have for too long been dismissed and marginalized by the "mainstream" Jewish establishment.

For myself at least—as a Jew and as a rabbi—I will take this opportunity to register my personal offense at statements such as those made last week by Rabbi Rontzki.

Discussion

YBD

Einav and Yeger fear that, because of the large number of religious soldiers in the IDF, the IDF will soon be fighting "holy wars." Apparently they don't understand that in Israel, like all other democracies, the army doesn't decide what wars to fight, but rather the government does. All armies, with religious or secular soldiers, tell them in wars to fight to win.

Even secular countries give religious encouragement to their soldiers. In the movie *The Longest Day* . . . a British paratrooper sees someone bobbing up and down in the water of a stream. He inquires what is going on, and it turns out that it is the Catholic chaplain of his unit who lost his communion set. The paratrooper helps him find it, and when they do, the chaplain says, "Okay lad, let's go do the Lord's work." In other words, the chaplain believed and told the paratrooper that the Lord wanted them to fight the Germans and defeat them. And this is in the secular British Army. He *didn't* say, "Well, you know that we have our narrative, and the Germans have theirs, who's to say which is right, there is no such thing as an absolute truth . . . blah, blah, blah."

If Einav and Yeger think there are too many religious combat soldiers in the IDF, then I suggest that they encourage their secular friends to sign up for combat units and not try to avoid conscription or get cushy "jobnik" desk jobs. Everyone admits religious soldiers are good soldiers, very disciplined and *less* likely to commit breaches of discipline that could lead to atrocities. General Dagan says that in a holy war, "there are no limits." I could say the opposite—with secular people, there are no limits. Who says Dagan has a monopoly on morality? In fact, secular officers want religious soldiers in their units.

So I don't think there are any grounds to be worried.

Mike

As we approach Hanukkah, it is worth noting how the narrative of the festival is told. Namely, the last part where the Maccabees did not hold back their swords is greatly downplayed and not traditionally endorsed by the rabbinate. One reason for this relates to zealotry. Zealotry presumes you know the true voice of the Almighty, and He has directed you to show no mercy. This was deemed an anathema, because who among us can claim to know the absolute truth that allows one to take a life of an individual (or multitudes) created in the image of the Almighty? Many zealots, including the Taliban, also claim this knowledge.

We must also remember that Israel is a political state whose policies are set by humans with imperfect knowledge.

Ross

I think Jeremiah 48 is referring to the Babylonians attacking Moab. In the prophet's worldview, when a nation does wrong to Israel, God can take vengeance through another nation's army (which in turn gets slaughtered by another nation for its sins and so on . . .). But for Israel to fight would be idolatry, because it means placing our faith in human hands instead of in God's salvation.

There is a midrash (Genesis Rabbah 68:14) that conveys a related idea of Israel standing aside from the nations when it comes to war. Rabbi Kalonymos Kalmish Shapira refers to it in his *Torah Commentary*, written in the Warsaw ghetto on November 18, 1939:

> The angels who were going up and down on the ladder in Jacob's dream were lords representing the nations of the world, who rise and fall. When there is war between these lords, one rising and trying to push the other down and vice versa, then the Jew stands in the greatest need of the mercy of heaven.[13]

The Judaization of Jerusalem: What Is Our Response?[14]

December 2, 2009

Are these the actions of a country interested in negotiating in good faith for a Palestinian state alongside it, with East Jerusalem as its capital?

Ha'aretz announced today that

> 2008 set an all-time record for the number of Arab residents of East Jerusalem who were stripped of residency rights by the Interior Ministry. Altogether, the

ministry revoked the residency of 4,577 East Jerusalemites in 2008—21 times the average of the previous 40 years.[15]

Also from today's *Ha'aretz*:

Clashes erupted yesterday in the Sheikh Jarrah neighborhood of East Jerusalem between demonstrators and counter-demonstrators, after a group of Jews announced their intention to move into a house in the neighborhood. The entry of the Jews into the home follows a court order ruling that the Arab al-Kurd family, which lives in a portion of the house, had no right to occupy an addition that they had built onto the house.[16]

This situation has been unfolding for some time. In a nutshell: Palestinian families in Sheikh Jarrah have been evicted from their homes so that their land can be turned over to a settler organization that seeks to build a Jewish settlement called Shimon Ha Tzadik.

According to the Jerusalem NGO Ir Amim, this settlement

constitutes one of a series of plans that seek to penetrate and surround Sheikh Jarrah with Israeli settlements, yeshivas, and other institutions as well as national park land, and complement government efforts to ring the Old City with Jewish development and effectively cut it off from Palestinian areas.[17]

Meanwhile, since their eviction, the Palestinian families (55 people in total) have been sleeping on mattresses in the street "and spend the day sitting in the shade watching settlers walk in and out of their front doors."[18]

And in another part of East Jerusalem:

The World Likud movement held a cornerstone-laying ceremony yesterday for the expansion of the neighborhood of Nof Zion, despite—or possibly because of—American pressure against building in East Jerusalem. The Jewish settlement is in the middle of the Arab village of Jabal Mukkaber. Meanwhile, the Jerusalem municipality razed two Palestinian homes in East Jerusalem yesterday.

The plan is to add to Nof Zion 105 new apartments to the 90 ones that are already there, most of which are already occupied. The neighborhood is considered "prestigious," but the developers ran into trouble a few years ago after they failed to sell the apartments to Jews from overseas. About a year ago the developers changed their marketing strategy to target the local national-religious market—and the apartments began selling quickly. The developers expect the same for the new part of the neighborhood. . . .

Yesterday the Jerusalem municipality razed two Palestinian homes in East Jerusalem, one in Isawiyah and one in Silwan. In both cases, local residents battled security forces.[19]

It does not take a great deal of insight to connect these dots. These are not simply random municipal disputes: We are witnessing the systematic Judaization of Jerusalem.

International protesters refer to these actions as "ethnic cleansing."[20] If that seems like too incendiary a term, what do we prefer to call it? And more critically, what are we going to do about it?

Discussion

YBD

It is certainly novel to hear a rabbi complaining about the "Judaization of Jerusalem." Wasn't the idea of Zionism to "Judaize Eretz Israel"? Wasn't it "Judaization" to build the "progressive" Tel Aviv University on the land that belonged to the Arab village of Sheikh Munis but whose residents fled during the War of Independence?

On the other hand, is it "Arabization" when Arabs move into Jewish areas in Lod, Akko, or Nazeret Ilit, or when they take illegally over state lands in the Negev, as happens every day?

Rabbi Brant Rosen

As a rabbi, I have no trouble saying that the Judaization of Jerusalem is immoral. Jerusalem is certainly significant to Jews, but it is also a city with a population of multiethnic, multireligious peoples who also consider it to be their home. If "Judaization" means that this city (or the land as a whole) should only be inhabited by Jews—and all others must be removed or otherwise stripped of their rights—then I will oppose this as a rabbi, as a Jew, and as a person of conscience.

Further, I do indeed consider it to be a moral issue that Tel Aviv University is built on the top of Arab village. I disagree with your analysis that the residents of al-Shaykh Muwannis simply "fled" in 1948. According to Israeli historian Benny Morris, the depopulation of this village was prompted when the Irgun kidnapped five village leaders at the end of March 1948.[21] "Coerced fleeing" by any other name would be called "expulsion," and I think we should be at least able to own it for what it was.

I'm intrigued by your term "Arabization." Lod and Akko were both originally Arab-majority cities that were depopulated in 1948. It is well documented that in Lod, Arab residents were forcibly expelled by Israeli forces (you can read Rabin's autobiography[22] or *The Lemon Tree*[23] for the specifics). In the case of Akko, the Haganah besieged the city, and its inhabitants fled (yes, fled) in every direction, including into the sea. Nazareth Illit was created largely out of expropriated land from the Arab city of Nazareth.

What do we make of this history? It's certainly not a simple answer. But I do believe that recognizing it, owning it, and talking about it would be a good first step. And if we are troubled by this history, I think a good second step would be to protest when we see it repeated in our own time, in Sheikh Jarrah and elsewhere.

YBD

So, is Zionism, i.e., the "Judaization" of Eretz Israel, legitimate or not?

Rabbi Brant Rosen

If Zionism means ethnic cleansing, inequity, and transfer of indigenous peoples without some form of justice or repatriation, then no, I do not consider it to be legitimate.

I believe the only way Zionism can be "legitimate" is if it finds a way to coexist with basic tenets of human rights, civil rights, democracy, and equality without regard to religion or ethnicity (values that I assume many of us purport to hold dear).

Gilad Shalit and the Sorrows of Tribalism[24]

December 15, 2009

Not long ago, I was asked by a friend: Why are Israelis and Jews so fixated on the kidnapping of Gilad Shalit? With all the crises and injustices being committed in the world, why is there such a hue and cry over this one particular man?

I answered that, like all nations, Israel takes this kind of thing personally. I also experienced Hamas's abduction of Gilad Shalit as an injustice committed against one of my own. Even as a Jew living in the comfort of my Evanston home, I felt a visceral sense of pain three years ago when I first heard the news of Shalit's kidnapping. Over time, my pain turned to anger as Hamas denied him Red Cross visits and refused to confirm (until only recently) whether he was even dead or alive.

I went on to compare Israel's trauma to the feeling of collective trauma we felt in our country in 1979, when Iranian militants took American embassy workers hostage: how violated our nation felt, how personally we identified with the hostages, how deeply we experienced the injustice of their imprisonment.

On a less tribal level, of course, I do understand that there was a deeper context to the hostage crisis. Underneath our feelings of personal violation were more challenging questions—questions few of us were prepared to ask out loud. Why, for instance, did we have so much concern over 53 fellow Americans but not for countless other political prisoners around the world, many of them incarcerated by regimes actively supported by our nation?

In just the same way, I believe too few Jews even know—let alone protest—that while Hamas unjustly imprisons Shalit, Israel holds hundreds of Palestinians taken in operations that at best must be considered ethically dubious. While Israel defends its actions legally by terming these prisoners "enemy combatants," the hard truth remains that for decades Israel's security services have rounded up scores of Palestinians without charge and have imprisoned them indefinitely—in many cases for years.

Yes, many of the prisoners are undoubtedly guilty of plotting or carrying out violent acts against Israelis. Many of these incarcerations can surely be defended on grounds of security. But it has become impossible to ignore that Israel has also incarcerated considerable numbers of Palestinians who by any reasonable definition must be considered political prisoners.

One recent case in point: Many Jews are familiar with the case of Gilad Shalit, but I'm sure that far fewer know about Abdallah Abu Rahmah, a Palestinian high school teacher and coordinator of the nonviolent campaign in the West Bank village of Bil'in, who was arrested last week by the Israeli military.[25] According to eyewitness accounts, Abu Rahmah was taken from his bed at two in the morning in the presence of his wife and children.[26]

And so, beyond the emotions of tribalism, the question remains: Will we ever be able to see past our own loyalties and find equal value in the lives of others—human beings who are just as eminently worthy of fair treatment, justice, and dignity? And even more challenging: Will we ever be ready to admit that the acts of violence committed against us are often inspired in no small way by the injustices we ourselves have committed—and continue to commit?

To return to the Iranian hostage example: Back in 1979, few Americans cared to even ask why their Iranian captors might have been so motivated to commit this act. Most of us were ignorant to the powerful significance of the American embassy for Iranians—that from this very same embassy, our nation had plotted the overthrow of Iran's democratically elected government in 1953. As it turned out, the regime we subsequently installed would persecute and unjustly imprison countless Iranian citizens over the next two decades.

So too in the case of Gilad Shalit. Few of us in the Jewish community are truly ready to examine the source of Gazans' fury toward Israel—a fury that has been building since long before Hamas even existed. Few of us are willing to face the history of Israel's oppressive policies in Gaza or the fact that Gazans have been living under intolerable occupation for decades.

And even fewer of us know that the overwhelming majority of the 1.5 million who live in Gaza belong to families that originally came from outside Gaza—from towns and villages like Ashkelon and Beersheba—and were expelled from their homes by the Israeli military in 1948. Indeed, when I think of Gazan rage in 2009, I can't help but think of these chilling words by Moshe Dayan back in 1956:

> Who are we that we should bewail their mighty hatred of us? [They] sit in refugee camps in Gaza, and opposite their gaze we appropriate for ourselves as our own portion the land and the villages in which they and their fathers dwelled.[27]

The history of Gaza is indeed tragic—and yes, Israel's oppression of its population is a critical part of this tragedy. Unless we take the time to understand this history and our part in it, I don't believe we can even begin to pretend there is a way out of this conflict.

To be clear: Understanding the source of Gazans' feelings toward Israel does not mean condoning their actions. Hamas's imprisonment of Gilad Shalit is barbaric. As a fellow Jew, I grieve for Shalit, and I pray for his safe return. But at the same time, I cannot look away from the more painful realities that led to his capture in the first place, and I truly believe that until we make an honest effort to face and address these realities, there will invariably be more Gilad Shalits in Israel's future.

After Israel's military campaign in Lebanon in the summer of 2006, journalist Amira Hass wrote these powerful words in *Ha'aretz*. I believe she presents us with a profound model of an Israeli who is able to hold her own concern for her people together with a willingness to face the truth of the injustices perpetrated by her nation. Her words are doubly tragic as we now approach the one-year anniversary of Israel's military campaign in Gaza:

> We are justly concerned about the welfare of northern residents, proud of their fortitude, understand those who leave, are shocked by the death of each person

and by every rocket hit, and identify with those suffering from anxiety. Take what the northern residents have been going through for a month, multiply it by 1,000, add an economic blockade, power and water cuts, and no wages. This is how the Palestinians in the Gaza Strip have been "living" for the past six years.

The Israelis allow their army to continue destroying, trampling, and killing in the Palestinian territories . . . ignoring the extent of our uninhibited, unrestrained devastation and their amazing power of human endurance. This is why Israel has delusions of "victories." If the homemade rockets are still being fired at Sderot despite the Palestinians' extensive suffering, it is because they have concluded, correctly, that Israel's destructive power is not intended to stop Qassam rockets—or to free Gilad Shalit. It is intended to force them to accept a surrender arrangement, which they reject not with military victories but with their power of endurance.[28]

Discussion

David

Good post. One aspect that I think needs clarification after reading some of the replies is the tendency for us to place a greater importance on "our own" than on the "other." Is it not normal to love our family and friends more than the stranger? Doesn't this fact allow for the family unit and our communal identity as Jews? If everyone loved each other equally, there would be a breakdown in society as we know it (perhaps this is how peace on earth would look). But is this actually what we are contemplating here? Do we really mean to love the stranger (i.e., Palestinians) as we'd love our family?

I would argue that the family unit, and the concentric social circles that extend outward from it, including friends and then other Jews, is the mechanism that allows us to learn *how* to love and because of it gives us the ability to extend that to the stranger, not in spite of it. We should not denigrate this fact but hope that our connections with these circles allows us to develop the required empathy those strangers deserve.

Eric

I'm not as fond as Brant of scripture-based arguments, but here's one where the Torah offers a bit of guidance.

David asks, "Do we really mean to love the stranger as we'd love our family?" The imperative comes from Deuteronomy 10:19, but the reasoning—and the "as," the equivalent, the point of comparison—is somewhat different: "Love the stranger, for you were once strangers in the land of Egypt."

It's not that we should love the stranger as we'd love our family, then. (Which can be a vexed, love/hate kind of relationship, Lord knows.) Rather, we should love the stranger as we wish we had, ourselves, been loved when we were in his or her shoes.

Which is not, perhaps, "normal," but it might be helpful.

Tel Aviv: "One of Your Own Kind, Stick to Your Own Kind . . ."[29]

February 24, 2010

In past posts, I've raised questions about the implications inherent in the establishment of a Jewish state—and the problems that invariably seem to arise in relations with Israel's non-Jewish citizens and residents.

How do we American Jews react, for instance, when we read that Israel is concerned about a "demographic threat" to the Jewish state?[30] (That is to say, what would we say if our president raised questions about the "demographic threat" of a particular minority group to the "American character" of our country?)

And now: What would we say if an American city funded a campaign to discourage girls from dating or marrying boys from another ethnic group?

From *Coteret* (an Israeli news/media aggregator):

> Maariv reported on February 23 that the Tel Aviv municipality launched a "counselling program" to "help" Jewish girls who date and/or marry Arab boys.
>
> Grassroots and governmental campaigning against interfaith mingling is nothing new in Israel. . . . But this is the first time officially sanctioned racism, funded by taxpayers, has come to Tel Aviv, Israel's liberal heartland.[31]

I'm not asking these questions to "bash Israel." I'm genuinely concerned by certain realities that seem intrinsic to ethnocracies. If we truly do cherish values inherent to American civil democracy, how do we react to such news as this? Do we simply put these values on the shelf out of our desire for a Jewish state? Or can we understand these kinds of measures in a way that is consonant with our most essential civic beliefs

(beliefs, by the way, that have been quite kind to the American Jewish community)?

And if not, then how will we respond?

Discussion

Eric

Brant, you talk about "American civic democracy," but of course, this particular issue hasn't always been easy here in the US, either. Antimiscegenation laws were on the books until they were declared unconstitutional 40 years ago—and when Zangwill's hymn to Jewish exogamy, "The Melting Pot," became a US hit in 1908, he had to scramble to explain that of course he didn't mean that whites should marry blacks!

I sometimes wonder whether this notion of America as the place where people can marry and mix isn't, in part, a particularly Jewish gift to American culture, just as the notion of America as a "Mother of Exiles" was.

On an unrelated note, why are they only worried about Jewish women dating and marrying Arab men? If Jewish men date or marry Arab women, is that okay?

Lori

I also see it from the standpoint of those who derive their perspective not from the very recent phenomenon of American and European mixed-race marriages but from the vantage point of the thousand years or so of Jews keeping the Jewish people alive in *galut* [exile] by attempting to avoid mingling and dissolving into the surrounding culture.

It has been a survival skill for so long that a myriad of cultural associations have grown up around it—sharing similar family history with the *mechutonim* ["in-laws"], reexperiencing holidays and low points in Jewish history as one educates one's family, etc. One has to comprehend and commiserate with this vantage point, I think, in order to be able to communicate one's own different viewpoint going forward, along with the assurance that one truly believes that intermarriage will not put an end to the Jewish people.

Why is the problem, I wonder, Jewish-Arab intermarriages? Not Jewish-Christian?

Shirin

I'm not sure why you make a distinction between Arabs and Christians, given that they are far from mutually exclusive, especially in the

Levant, and notably in Palestine, where many Palestinians are descended from the original Christians. Perhaps you meant Arabs versus European Christians?

I also think it should be obvious why the problem is with Arabs. Anti-Arab racism is endemic in Israel and goes back as far as political Zionism does. Anti-Arab racism in Israel has always included even Jews of Arab background, let alone Arab Christians and Muslims.

YBD

In Islam it is permitted for Muslim men to marry non-Muslim women, but it is absolutely forbidden for Muslim women to marry non-Muslim men. The all-too-common "family honor killings" that happen in Israel and the rest of the Arab world usually occur because the family discovers that one of its girls is interested in a non-Muslim (or even someone from a socially "inferior" family that is Muslim). Thus, there is no need for Jews to warn Jewish men about Muslim women: Her own family will "take care" of the problem. Thus, if you think Israel is "racist" for discouraging intermarriage, then so is Muslim society.

I don't understand what is puzzling everyone here. Judaism prohibits intermarriage. So what if America has different values? In America, the view is "sleep with anyone you want, anyone, anytime, anywhere." Who says that is right? Who says that is the overriding value? Judaism has survived for thousands of years, often in the most difficult circumstances. It has the secret of success, and I don't see why it should arbitrarily be held up and criticized in the light of some other passing values.

And do *not* claim that the Jewish prohibition to intermarriage is "racist"—because anyone can convert to Judaism, if they are sincere.

Eric

I'm glad to see that Judaism and Islam have come to an agreement here: Control the women! Patriarchy has survived for thousands of years, and clearly it has the secret of success. Why, after all, should it arbitrarily be held up and criticized in the light of some other passing values?

More seriously, when you ask who says that the value of loving and marrying across ethnic lines (and within gender lines, for LGBTQ folks) should trump the value of community cohesion, I'm happy to answer that in the first person: I do. I don't consider this to be a "passing value" but a "rising" or "emerging" one, and it's one that I find morally just and beautiful, not just a matter of sexual convenience. So do an awful lot of American Jews.

In the long run, perhaps you're right: Maybe this will turn out to be a passing fad, and American Jewry will simply melt away. I doubt that, but there's only one way to find out. In the meantime, I note that there are still plenty of people who believe that secular democracy is a passing fad. I'm not willing to write off either of them; indeed, I see them as deeply linked with one another.

As for whether the prohibition on intermarriage is racist—no, not inherently. But I have no doubt that it exacerbates the inherent human (or at least Western) tendency to racism and more generally the impulse to think that one's own group, whether racially or otherwise defined, is inherently superior. But then, maybe I just have a *goyishe kop*.

Shirin

Not accurate. It is not "absolutely" forbidden. That is not the language, nor is it how it works out in the real world.

1. While I would agree with you that there are too many so-called honor killings—even one is too many—you are incorrect to suggest that they are common. So-called honor killings are actually very uncommon.

2. So-called honor killings are by no means limited to Muslims. They happen among Christians, Yezidis, and other non-Muslims, and it would not surprise me to learn that they are not unknown among Jews as well.

3. They do not "usually" occur because a girl is interested in a non-Muslim—not at all. In fact, only a small minority of so-called honor killings are related to "interest" in a non-Muslim. These crimes are most often committed not because a girl or woman shows interest in a non-Muslim *or* a Muslim but because a girl or woman is suspected of "illicit" sexual activity with a male, period. The religion or social status of the alleged partner is beside the point, but the great majority of the alleged "illicit" behavior involves Muslim, not non-Muslim males.

[With regard to the Muslim woman's family "taking care" of the problem,] this is beginning to sound uncomfortably close to Muslim bashing.

There is nothing "racist" about people of faith preferring to marry within their religion, or people whose culture is deeply important to them preferring to marry within their culture. It is a wise impulse, because shared faith and shared culture certainly improve the odds of a successful marriage, not only of two individuals but of two families. In addition, virtually all religions seek to preserve or to increase their numbers, and one of the ways they do that is to forbid or to at least strongly discourage intermarriage, and deeply religious people will be obedient to their religions' demands.

Without taking a position on the question of whether Israel is racist for discouraging intermarriage in the way it does, I would point out that your opening statement contradicts your conclusion. Muslim society, as you pointed out, accepts intermarriage between Muslim men and any "believing" woman, which includes, according to the Qur'an, Christians, Jews, and Sabaeans, and by tradition also includes Zoroastrians. In addition, the Qur'an allows Muslim men to marry nonbelieving women who are of good character. Further, racism is the incorrect term in the case of Muslims, because, unlike Jews, Muslims do not claim to be a race or an ethnicity or even a distinct culture but are adherents to a religion who come from many different races, ethnicities, and cultures. So, it is contrary to the facts to suggest that racism is involved in Muslims discouraging marriage outside the religion.

Muslim society is more able to deal with women marrying non-Muslim men than you would like to think. First, if the man will convert to Islam, it is 100 percent acceptable. If he will not convert, then it can be tough indeed if her family is very religious and may even result in her estrangement from some of the family, although usually not as severe or final as, for example, a Jewish family sitting shiva for someone who marries out. As with any group of humans, the less educated the family is, the more likely they are to have a strong negative reaction, and there is a tiny minority at the extreme who will commit criminal and un-Islamic acts, but this is, as I said, far rarer than you seem to believe.

". . . anyone can convert to Judaism, if they are sincere."

And anyone can also convert to Islam if they are sincere. In fact, unlike Judaism, Islam actively encourages conversion.

PS: I should also explain why Islam permits men but does not permit women to marry outside the faith. As with Judaism and Christianity, which came before it and upon which it is largely modeled, Islam is a patriarchal religion. Children take the religion of their father. Therefore, when Muslim men marry outside the faith, their children are still Muslims, and the result is a maintenance of or increase in the number of Muslims. When Muslim women marry outside the faith, their children take the faith of their father and so do not contribute to the maintenance or increase. Religions, especially new ones, need to grow, or at least maintain their numbers, so as a practical matter, Muslim women were instructed in the Qur'an to marry only Muslims.

Steve

Rabbi, you may be too kind. You've pointed out an obvious problem that should help us question the whole premise of a Jewish state. Is this state one of the last vestiges of mid-1900s thinking, a time when it seemed to be okay for whites to say they were different than blacks, a time when it seemed to Germans that it was okay to want to keep their race pure? How different are we when it seems to be okay for us to try to stop miscegenation?

When we consider that we founded a Jewish state by expelling hundreds of thousands of non-Jews (Muslims and Christians) from their homes and villages, we should come to realize that we've gone about this wrong. It's time to invite our non-Jewish Palestinian brothers and sisters back, to rebuild their homes and villages together.

Yisrael

Do you not comprehend the difference between Galut Jewry and Jewry of the Land of Israel? Of course there's a difference in how we react to problems like demography.

You simply move from the Lower East Side to Queens to Nassau to Florida. The Jews of Malmö, Sweden, have now begun a trek out due to Muslim demography.

We don't have that luxury, Rabbi.

Rabbi Brant Rosen

Are you suggesting that Israel doesn't have the luxury to respect basic human rights? Jews more than anyone should understand the tragic results of viewing another demographic group as a "threat":

> *A new king arose over Egypt who did not know Joseph. And he said to his people, "Look, the Israelite people are much too numerous for us. Let us deal shrewdly with them, so that they may not increase; otherwise in the event of war they may join our enemies in fighting against us and rise from the ground." So they set taskmasters over them to oppress them with forced labor; and they built garrison cities for Pharaoh: Pithom and Ramses. But the more they were oppressed, the more they increased and spread out, so that the (Egyptians) came to dread the Israelites. (Exodus 1:8–9)

Or more apropos to the season:

Haman then said to King Ahasuerus, "There is a certain people, scattered and dispersed among other peoples in all the provinces of your realm, whose laws are different from those of any other people and who do not obey the king's laws; and it is not in Your Majesty's interest to tolerate them. If it please Your Majesty, let an edict be drawn for their destruction." (Esther 3:8–9)

Dave

If American Jews are so accepting of exogamy, then how do you explain the success of JDate?

Shirin

How about:

- Some American Jews are not accepting of exogamy.
- Some American Jews are accepting of exogamy in a general sense but do not choose it for themselves.
- Some American Jews who are accepting of exogamy are under significant pressure from their families only to date and marry Jews, and JDate is a good way to meet a variety of eligible Jewish potential partners.
- Some American Jews who are accepting of exogamy for others and for themselves would nevertheless prefer to marry a Jew if they found the right person, and JDate is a good way to meet a variety of Jewish potential partners.
- Some American Jews who are accepting of exogamy for others and for themselves use a variety of methods to meet potential partners, and JDate is one of them.

All five of the above added together, plus some I probably have not thought of, could explain the success of JDate in a country in which Jews are generally accepting of exogamy.

Chapter 6

Boycott from Within

December 2009–May 2010

When these blog posts were written, the 2005 Palestinian civil society call for Boycott, Divestment, and Sanctions (BDS) against Israel was not yet firmly on the radar screen of the American Jewish community. When I first wrote about BDS in 2009, however, I was convinced that we were greatly mistaken to simply dismiss this movement as the work of "delegitimizers" or anti-Semites. I believed—and continue to assert—that BDS is a time-honored nonviolent tactic used by disempowered peoples to leverage public support for social change.

Although the Israeli government and the American Jewish establishment invest enormous amounts of energy, resources, and finances in combating BDS, the movement continues to gain support. It remains my hope that my community will yet find the wherewithal to discuss the significance of BDS openly and honestly.

I'd like to think that these posts and comments provide one modest step in that direction.

Gaza One Year Later: Beyond the Complications[1]

December 28, 2009

It was exactly one year ago that I read the first news accounts of Israel's military assault in Gaza:

Waves of Israeli airstrikes destroyed Hamas security facilities in Gaza on Saturday in a crushing response to the group's rocket fire, killing more than 225—the highest one-day toll in the Israeli-Palestinian conflict in decades. . . .

. . . [There] was a shocking quality to Saturday's attacks, which began in broad daylight as police cadets were graduating, women were shopping at the outdoor market, and children were emerging from school. The center of Gaza City was a scene of chaotic horror, with rubble everywhere, sirens wailing, and women shrieking as dozens of mutilated bodies were laid out on the pavement and in the lobby of Shifa Hospital so that family members could identify them. The dead included civilians, including several construction workers and at least two children in school uniforms.

By afternoon, shops were shuttered, funerals began, and mourning tents were visible on nearly every major street of this densely populated city.[2]

Previously, whenever I'd hear this kind of news out of Israel/Palestine, my shock and anguish would quickly be tempered by a familiar voice telling me to calm down, don't overreact, don't forget how terribly "complicated" the situation is. (Indeed, I distinctly recall hearing that voice three years earlier when the IDF responded to Hezbollah rocket attacks with a similarly massive military onslaught.)

This time, though, it was different. This time I didn't hear the voice. Somehow, it just didn't seem all that complicated to me anymore.

Ideologically speaking, I've regarded Zionism with great pride as the "national liberation movement of the Jewish people." Of course I didn't deny that this rebirth had come at the expense of another people. Of course I recognized that Israel's creation was bound up with the suffering of the Palestinians. The situation was—well, it was "complicated."

Last year, however, I reacted differently. I read of Apache helicopters dropping hundreds of tons of bombs on 1.5 million people crowded into a 140-square-mile patch of land with nowhere to run. In the coming days, I would read about the bombing of schools, whole families being blown to bits, children literally burned to the bone with white phosphorous. Somehow, it didn't seem complicated at all anymore. At long last, I felt as if I were viewing the conflict with something approaching clarity.

Of course I think we'd all agree that the Israeli-Palestinian conflict is technically complicated. But at the end of the day, there is nothing complicated about persecution. The political situation in Darfur, for instance, is enormously complicated—but these complications certainly haven't stopped scores of Jews across North America from protesting the human-rights injustices being committed there. We do so because we know that underneath all the geopolitical complexities, oppression is oppression. And as Jews, we know instinctively that our sacred tradition and our own tragic history require us to speak out against all oppression committed in our midst.

I'd suggest that if there is anything complicated for us here, it is in possibility that we might in fact have become oppressors ourselves. That is painfully complicated. After all, our Jewish identity has been bound up with the memory of our own persecution for centuries. How on earth can we comprehend, let alone respond to, the suggestion that we've become our own worst nightmare?

More than anything else, what I was trying to say in that anguished, emotional blog post one year ago was: Is this what it has come to? Have we come to the point where Israel can wipe out hundreds of people, whole families, whole neighborhoods, and our response as Jews will be to simply rationalize it away? At the very least, will we be able to stop and question what has brought us to this terrifying point? Have we become unable to recognize persecution for what it really and truly is?

Those who know me (or read my blog) surely know that it has been a painfully challenging year for me. My own relationship to Israel is changing in ways I never could have predicted. Since I started raising questions like those above, I've lost some friends—and, yes, my congregation has lost some members. If Zionism is the unofficial religion of the contemporary Jewish community, then I'm sure there are many who consider me something of an apostate.

But at the same time, I've been surprised and encouraged by the large number of people I've met who've been able to engage with these questions openly and honestly, even if they don't always agree with me. I suppose this is what I decided to do one year ago: to put my faith in our ability to stand down the paralyzing "complexities," however painful the prospect.

One year later, I still hold tight to this faith.

Discussion

Sandra

I am so heartened to read what you have written here. As a Jew raised on Leon Uris's *Exodus* and other stories of the Holocaust, I have long been horrified to find that my own people have become the oppressors in the name of "never again." It makes sense psychologically. (I'm a psychologist.) I have compassion on us for getting lost in this way. But I am horrified to see us losing so much of what has made our culture unique in the name of preserving it. . . . So many otherwise wise and compassionate Jews seem to have a blind spot when it comes to Israel. So I am heartened. . . . Thank you.

Cotton

Like Sandra, I'm a psychologist, [and] also an Episcopal priest. What strikes me is our common capacity to lose our way . . . and later to wonder how on earth we could have been so blind. As many Christians review our own history, we wonder how we could ever have used our own Good News to justify our oppression of others. It's most humbling. Many thanks, Brant, for your willingness to struggle publicly with this terrible situation. You give many of us courage to struggle with our own culpability.

Sydney

Although I make no claim to understand the historical, geographic, and political complexity of the occupation, my heart is quite clear. Kill someone's child, and you make an enemy for generations—perhaps for as many generations as you've wiped out by killing that child. When the killing is done in my name and by my people, I'm not entirely sure how to manage my own culpability. Your complex (!) understanding of the relationship between Israel and Palestine and your clear comments about oppression make me a proud (and better-educated) member of JRC.

Lesley

Thanks for coming over to the dark side, Brant. We need you, we've been waiting for you, and you've made it easier for many of us to speak up. Thanks for reminding us that belief in Zionism is not the same as belief in Judaism.

Palestinian Christians: "The Occupation Is a Sin"[3]

December 18, 2009

Last week, a group of Palestinian Christians representing a variety of churches and church-related organizations issued a powerful, prayerful call for an end to the Israeli occupation. My friend Rabbi Brian Walt was present at the meeting in Bethlehem in which the statement, known as "The Kairos Palestine Document,"[4] was released. Upon his return, he described to me his profound, often painful conversations with Palestinian Christians and told me that as a Jew, he considered the Kairos Document to be an enormously important spiritual/political statement. I must say that I agree wholeheartedly.

Palestinian Christian liberation theologians, such as Naim Ateek of the Sabeel Institute, have been doing important work for decades, and I believe their ideas present important spiritual challenges to the Jewish community. Many Jews point to the more radical incarnations of these theologies—and although I share some of these concerns, I believe that we make a profound mistake by dismissing Palestinian Christian theology wholesale. (Frankly, I am much more troubled by the "End of Days" theologies of fundamentalist Zionist Christians, such as Pastor John Hagee, than I am by Naim Ateek and the authors of the Kairos Document.)

My friend and colleague Father Cotton Fite, of St. Luke's Church in Evanston, tells me he hopes that American Christians will study the Kairos Document carefully. I hope Jews will read it as well. In fact, I think we should create opportunities to read it together. Despite our differences, I believe it offers both of our communities an ideal place to begin meaningful dialogue over the spiritual implications of this conflict.

One of the more important and challenging passages:

> Our presence in this land, as Christian and Muslim Palestinians, is not accidental but rather deeply rooted in the history and geography of this land, resonant with the connectedness of any other people to the land it lives in. It was an injustice when we were driven out. The West sought to make amends for what Jews had endured in the countries of Europe, but it made amends on our account and in our land. They tried to correct an injustice and the result was a new injustice.

I can already predict that many Jews will bristle that this passage does not specifically reference the Jewish connection to the land as well. To this I would say: How deeply do we Jews ever honor the reality that we are not the only people who are "deeply rooted in the history and geography of this land"? How deeply do we ever face the true injustice that was committed when a people with deep roots in the land was driven out and not allowed to return?

Another sobering passage in the document describes the occupation as no less than a "sin":

> We also declare that the Israeli occupation of Palestinian land is a sin against God and humanity because it deprives the Palestinians of their basic human rights, bestowed by God. It distorts the image of God in the Israeli who has

become an occupier just as it distorts this image in the Palestinian living under occupation. We declare that any theology, seemingly based on the Bible or on faith or on history, that legitimizes the occupation, is far from Christian teachings, because it calls for violence and holy war in the name of God Almighty, subordinating God to temporary human interests, and distorting the divine image in the human beings living under both political and theological injustice.

Many of us view the occupation as a political problem to be solved. But indeed, as Jews, we must admit that basic human rights are rooted in our religious tradition. Like Christians, we believe that all human beings are created in the image of God. We also believe that when the basic dignity of anyone's humanity is diminished, the Divine Image is diminished as well. How then can we fail to understand that the occupation is not only a geopolitical problem but a spiritual and moral problem as well?

This conclusion leads to a logical next step:

Love is seeing the face of God in every human being. Every person is my brother or my sister. However, seeing the face of God in everyone does not mean accepting evil or aggression on their part. Rather, this love seeks to correct the evil and stop the aggression.

The injustice against the Palestinian people which is the Israeli occupation is an evil that must be resisted. It is an evil and a sin that must be resisted and removed. Primary responsibility for this rests with the Palestinians themselves suffering occupation. Christian love invites us to resist it. However, love puts an end to evil by walking in the ways of justice. Responsibility lies also with the international community, because international law regulates relations between peoples today. Finally responsibility lies with the perpetrators of the injustice; they must liberate themselves from the evil that is in them and the injustice they have imposed on others.

Again, the occupation is viewed not as a diplomatic issue to be negotiated but a spiritual evil to be resisted.

I have no illusions that for many Jews, such suggestions as these will present daunting and painful challenges. So will many of the ultimate political ramifications of the Kairos Document. All I can hope for is that political disagreements will not keep us from honestly facing the profound spiritual dimensions of this conflict. Speaking for myself, I do believe this statement was written in good faith, genuine love, and true religious conviction:

Our message to the Jews tells them: Even though we have fought one another in the recent past and still struggle today, we are able to love and live together.

We can organize our political life, with all its complexity, according to the logic of this love and its power, after ending the occupation and establishing justice.

What can I say to this except "Amen"?

Discussion

David
I have not read the document yet, but I assume "resistance" to the occupation is meant as a peaceful and nonviolent one?

Rabbi Brant Rosen
Yes, the document specifically advocates resistance in the form of non-violent direct action:

> Palestinian civil organizations, as well as international organizations, NGOs, and certain religious institutions call on individuals, companies, and states to engage in divestment and in an economic and commercial boycott of everything produced by the occupation. We understand this to integrate the logic of peaceful resistance. These advocacy campaigns must be carried out with courage, openly [and] sincerely proclaiming that their object is not revenge but rather to put an end to the existing evil, liberating both the perpetrators and the victims of injustice. The aim is to free both peoples from extremist positions of the different Israeli governments, bringing both to justice and reconciliation. In this spirit and with this dedication, we will eventually reach the longed-for resolution to our problems, as indeed happened in South Africa and with many other liberation movements in the world.[5]

As I've written before,[6] I know that advocacy for Boycott, Divestment, and Sanctions is a nonstarter for many Jews—and I understand why this is so. At the very least, however, I think it's important that we understand that it is a form of grassroots nonviolent resistance on the part of the Palestinian people. (Worth thinking about the next time you hear someone ask, "Where are the Palestinian Gandhis?")

Ken
This all seems so wrong to me. I see nothing in the document to say "Amen" to. The document only continues the kind of misinformation that, rather than moving us toward a responsible peace, supports a vision that will only lead to continued conflict.

The occupation is not a sin. After surviving the Arab war of genocide in 1948 and losing 1 percent of its population, the new Israel
found itself surrounded by hostile Arab countries. Israel was attacked
again in 1967 from the Jordanian-annexed West Bank. Israel's victory
led to the legal occupation of the West Bank territory, and [Israel]
was bound legally to administer it. One can discuss whether Israelis or
Israeli governments sinned in their administration of the territories,
but occupation in itself is not a sin.

The document ignores the invasion of 1948 and Arab and Palestinian
violence against Israel prior to the occupation.

The document ignores the right of Jews to live and to exercise their
right to self-determination in their homeland by ignoring the continuous history of Jews in Palestine and throughout the Middle East.

The document wrongly implies that the Arabs of Palestine were driv-
en out by the Jews. This is not supported by the old histories, nor the
new histories, and not even by reputable Arab histories of the conflict.
The general thrust of the history is no other than an exodus of Arabs
from Israel due to an Arab invasion led by foreign Arab forces and
local Arab mafia families. Examples of extreme Jewish acts of violence
cannot be used to whitewash the actual cause of the refugee problem.
Understanding this may enlighten you to the same conclusion today—
namely, foreign Arab powers and local mafia families are preventing
any chance for real peace.

The document does not self-reflect in any way as to Arab responsibility for any aspect of the current condition of the Palestinians. It
sees no "sin" in Arab and Palestinian actions against Israel and Jews.

It is foolish to expect peace while ignoring those responsible for
the problem: the invading Arab armies of the Arab states and the local
power brokers of the Palestinians. They must be held accountable for
the 60-plus years of conflict that followed. It is those countries who
should be held responsible for solving the refugee problem. Examples:
Close down your refugee camps and let the Palestinians become citizens
in your countries; pony up $$$$$ for the new Palestinian state.

This document only confuses any hope for clarity. The first real step
toward real peace will be a Palestinian movement that seeks reconciliation by acknowledging its own responsibility for the situation, just
as so many Israeli movements, leaders, and activists have done for
decades.

Finally, I am very confused by a rabbi who sees Boycott, Divestment,
and Sanctions as a nonstarter for other Jews but not himself. Israel
has the right to exist, to defend herself, to be the Jewish homeland,
to flourish, and, yes, to make peace, too. This document will only push

the needed peace partner further away from the self-reflective, responsible partner that is required.

Rabbi Brant Rosen

It's not clear to me how you differentiate between Israel's occupation
and its "administration" of its occupation. Either way, the occupation
has been a corrupt and corrupting enterprise. Israel was not "legally
bound" to begin colonizing the West Bank immediately after capturing
it in 1967. Israel has not been "legally bound" to settle and to expand
these colonies steadily over the past 40 years. Nor has it been legally
bound to extend one form of law to Jewish settler residents and another for the Palestinian population.

I take exception to many of your historical claims—and although
I'm tempted to address each of them in turn, I don't think it would
accomplish anything to engage in rhetorical Ping-Pong. I will only say
that your comment reads more like "Israel Myths and Facts" than an
honest response to a heartfelt theological statement.

I'm astonished that you find no "self-reflection" in this document. I
find it suffused throughout with such a spirit. Such statements as "we
cannot resist evil with evil" and "we do not resist with death but rather
through respect of life" are not only direct references to Palestinian
violence—they are important spiritual imperatives.

I understand that you disagree with the statement, but I'm saddened by
your cynicism toward it. As I wrote in my post, I believe it makes an important starting point for interreligious dialogue. Dialogue does not begin with
total agreement but with a good-faith attempt at engagement. Hardened
attitudes such as yours do nothing to further this critical conversation.

A BDS Wake-Up Call?[7]

March 1, 2010

A recent report from the *Jewish Daily Forward*:

> With anti-Israel boycott, divestment, and sanctions efforts gaining visibility,
> the Jewish community's main public-policy coordinating body is for the first
> time confronting the BDS movement as a specific and stated priority [that]
> should now "be regarded with the utmost seriousness and urgency."

"This is a very serious matter," JCPA's executive director, Rabbi Steve Gutow, told the *Forward*. "We need to wake up, whether we are on the right, left, or center.". . . JCPA member groups are planning to create a permanent body that would respond to the activities of the BDS movement.[8]

My two cents: Creating a permanent body to combat the "negative branding" caused by BDS is a waste of Jewish communal resources. I just don't believe that the old counterattack tactics will work anymore (if they ever did). I'd suggest that if the Jewish community really wants to "wake up" to the challenge presented by BDS, then we need to honestly confront the fundamental reasons for its growth in the first place.

The BDS movement was founded in 2005 by a coalition of Palestinian groups who sought to fight Israel's human-rights violations through nonviolent direct action. It arose out of their frustration over Israel's continued refusal to comply with international law on any number of critical issues—and the oppressive manner in which it has occupied and ruled over Palestinians. I can't help but think that by treating BDS simply as a public relations threat to be fought, we're utterly misunderstanding the essentials of the point (and strength) of this movement.

By all accounts, this campaign is rapidly gaining support.[9] It's not a stretch to assume that the longer this oppressive status quo is allowed to continue, the longer Palestinians will resist—and the longer they will seek international support for their resistance. One year ago, I predicted as much on this blog: BDS will grow as long as very real injustices remain unaddressed.

When will we wake up to this painful reality?

Four More Questions for Pesach[10]

March 25, 2010

For those of you who believe that Jewish liberation and Palestinian liberation are inextricably intertwined, here are "Four More Questions for Pesach," a seder supplement I've written for Jewish Voice for Peace.

1. Magid: Telling the Tale

> *A new king arose over Egypt who did not know Joseph. And he said to his people, "Look, the Israelite people are much too numerous for us. Let us deal shrewdly with them, so that they many not increase; otherwise in the event of war they may join our enemies in fighting against us and rise from the ground." So they set*

taskmasters over them to oppress them with forced labor; and they built garrison cities for Pharaoh: Pithom and Ramses. But the more they were oppressed, the more they increased and spread out, so that the (Egyptians) came to dread the Israelites. (Exodus 1:8–11)

As we begin the Exodus story, we read that the oppression of the Israelites resulted from Pharaoh's fear that their growth would somehow overwhelm the Egyptian nation. These verses certainly have an ominous resonance for the Jewish people. Indeed, any member of a minority faith or ethnic group knows all too well the tragedy that can ensue when a nation views their demographic growth as a "threat."

Today it is all too common to hear Israel's leaders and supporters suggest that the "Jewish character" of Israel is threatened by the demographic growth of the Palestinian people. How should we react to the suggestion that the mere fact of this group's growth necessarily poses a national threat to Israel? As Jews living in the Diaspora, how would we respond if our leaders raised questions about the "demographic threat" of a particular minority group to the "national character" of our country? In a multiethnic society, can a state's identity ever be predicated upon the primacy of one ethnic group without the oppression of another?

2. Zayit—Olive

Olives are distributed to seder participants, and the following is recited:

> *Zayit: Al shum mah?*
> This olive: Why do we eat it?

The olive tree is one of the first plants mentioned in the Torah and remains among the oldest species in Israel/Palestine. It has become a universal symbol of peace and hope, as it is written in Psalm 52: "I am like a thriving olive tree in God's house, I trust in God's loyal kindness forever and ever."

We add this olive to our seder plate as a reminder that we must all be God's bearers of peace and hope in the world. At the same time, we eat this olive in sorrow, mindful that olive trees, the source of livelihood for Palestinian farmers, are regularly chopped down, burned, and uprooted by Israeli settlers and the Israeli authorities. As we look on, Israel pursues systematic policies that increasingly deny Palestinians access to olive orchards that have belonged to them for generations.

As we eat now, we ask one another: How will we, as Jews, bear witness to the unjust actions committed in our names? Will these olives inspire us to be bearers of peace and hope for Palestinians—and for all who are oppressed?

3. Barech: Blessing after the Meal

When God returns Zion from captivity, it will be as in our dream; our mouths will be filled with laughter, our tongues with songs of joy. (Psalm 126:1–2)

We begin the blessing after the meal with the image of return: a vision that has always been central to our collective Jewish "dream." Today, of course, this Jewish ideal has been realized by means of political nationalism. Zionism has succeeded in "returning" the Jewish people to sovereignty in its historic homeland.

The founding of the Jewish state, however, has tragically created a nightmare for another people. The creation of Israel in 1948 displaced 700,000 indigenous inhabitants from their land. As a result, more than 4 million Palestinian refugees now yearn passionately to return to their homes.

And so we ask: What has the Jewish "return" to Zion wrought? How do we understand a Jewish "right of return" to Israel that grants automatic citizenship to any Jew anywhere in the world while denying that same right to the very people who actually lived on this land not long ago? Can any "return" truly be complete as long as it denies that right to others? Could there possibly be a way that both peoples might realize their respective dreams of return?

4. Nirtzah: "Next Year in Jerusalem!"

We now end our seder meal once again with the proclamation "Next Year in Jerusalem!" And so we ask: What will we do to ensure that Jerusalem lives up to its name as a City of Peace? How will we respond as the Jewish state increasingly implements policies that claim this holy city in the name of one people only? Do we dare to dream of a city divided or a city truly united for all its inhabitants?

. . . And if we do believe that Jerusalem must be, once and for all, a true City of Peace, what are we willing to do to make it so?

Next year in Jerusalem! Next year in al-Quds! Next year in a City of Peace!

Next Year in a Jerusalem for All Its Citizens[11]

March 31, 2010

The words "Next year in Jerusalem" seriously stuck in my throat at seder this year.

I know that these words are largely a spiritual metaphor. I know that for centuries of Jewish history, these words referred to a messianic vision of the future and not literal immigration. Still, given the political realities of the day, it's just so very difficult to separate spiritual metaphor from literal facts on the ground.

It was enormously difficult for me to proclaim "Next year in Jerusalem!" together with Jews the world over, knowing that right now in *Yerushalayim Shel Mata* ("earthly Jerusalem"), non-Jewish residents are being evicted from their homes,[12] and the construction of Jewish residences is increasing with utter impunity.[13] By any other name this would be called "ethnic cleansing," and I have no trouble saying so.

Many will claim that Jews have a right to build houses anywhere they please. That is not the issue. The issue, of course, is that Palestinians in Israel do not. Others will say that the government is only building in parts of Jerusalem that "everyone knows" will be always be part of Israel anyway. This is, in fact, exactly what Netanyahu claimed in his address at the recent AIPAC Policy Conference:

> Everyone knows that these neighborhoods will be part of Israel in any peace settlement. Therefore, building them in no way precludes the possibility of a two-state solution.[14]

This claim is hogwash. If you would like to know why, please read this article by Danny Seidemann and Lara Friedman, who understand the recent history and politics of Jerusalem better than just about anyone:

> What Netanyahu really means is that East Jerusalem land falls into two categories: areas that "everybody knows" Israel will keep and where it can therefore act with impunity, and areas that Israel hopes it can keep, by dint of changing so many facts on the ground before a peace agreement is reached that they move into the first category.
>
> It is an approach that can be summed up as: "what's mine is mine, and what you think is yours will hopefully be mine, too.". . . The notion that Israel can be taken seriously as a peace partner while acting this way is farcical. And the notion that the United States can be a credible steward of peace efforts while tolerating such behavior is laughable.[15]

Next year in a Jerusalem for all of its citizens. . . .

Discussion

Rabbi Brian

What a great post! Just returned today from a tour of East Jerusalem
with Ir Amim. The tour was in Hebrew, so it was mostly for Israelis.
We saw the huge Jewish neighborhoods (Pisgat Zeev, Ramot, Maaleh
Admumim) and smaller neighborhoods like Ramat Shlomo, Neve Yaakov,
Givon, all built between Palestinian areas. We saw the roads that Jews
use and the roads used by local villagers. All this was not new for me.
What was new was that there is one new Palestinian neighborhood
(I thought there was none) built by the Waqf, the Islamic Religious
Council, with the approval of Israel. This neighborhood, one of only
two new Palestinian neighborhoods, still does not have the infrastruc-
ture from Israel (water, electricity, etc.) that is supplied to all the
Jewish settlements. The second neighborhood also doesn't have the
infrastructure.

At the end of the tour, the participants asked the tour guide what
is the solution to this mess. I was stunned that most people on the
bus argued for a settlement imposed by the US. Their argument was
that there was no way that Israel was about to solve this issue and like
any "failing family business," to use the metaphor suggested by one
participant, someone has to step in to save it before it goes completely
broke!

Is America up to this task?

Israel

I think it is really unfortunate to see the "ethnic cleansing" charge
tossed around so easily. It does a real disservice to those who have
really suffered from ethnic cleansing in this violent world. You may not
be happy with all of Israel's policies, but that is no excuse for using
such charged rhetoric. Jews were actually ethnically cleansed from the
West Bank in 1948. During that war, the invading Arab armies attacked
the civilian centers of the Jewish communities throughout Israel with
the real goal of ethnically cleansing Palestine of its Jewish population.
Today, after years of war and conflict, Israel continues to exist as a
multiethnic democracy. In Jerusalem, Jews and Arabs live together; I
know because I lived there, alongside Arabs. It should also be noted
that Arabs have reached very high positions in Israeli society and are
contributing in all fields. As one Israeli Arab said, "In Israel an Arab

doctor gets paid the same as a Jewish doctor." He said this in defense of his Israeli Arab identity. Charged rhetoric that seeks to demonize Israel does nothing for peace and makes it harder for Jews and Arabs to live together.

I must also say that I find this blog very sad, as it seems to have nothing positive or uplifting to say about Israel and all that it achieves on so many levels all while facing the constant pressure of existential threats and potential war.

Maybe I misunderstand: Maybe you don't believe Israel has a right to exist as a Jewish state.

Rabbi Brant Rosen

You will not be surprised to learn I take exception to your version of history. After the UN passed its Partition Plan in 1947, well before Arab countries mobilized their military operations, the Jewish Yishuv embarked upon a systematic campaign of expulsion of Palestinian Arabs from their villages. These actions largely took place in areas that were designated as part of the new Arab state, according to the UN plan.

This is well-documented history but, of course, is notably absent from the Zionist narrative of Israel's founding. Even if you do not accept this narrative, I don't see how anyone could possibly excuse current Israeli policy that is forcibly removing Palestinians from their homes in order that these areas can be populated by Jewish residents.

I also take exception to your rosy picture of the status of "Israeli Arabs" in Jerusalem. Anyone who has visited both West and East Jerusalem cannot help but note there is a significant disparity in the standard of living between the Jewish and Arab populations. There is also a significant disparity in legal status. You can visit the Ir Amim website to get the full picture.

Yes, I am consistently critical of Israel on my blog. This is partly because I want to provide an antidote to the widespread unwillingness of the American Jewish community to address Israel's ongoing persecution of Palestinians. I simply cannot subscribe to the view that Israel is a stable and wonderful democracy that has a few "blemishes." I believe that Israel's oppression of its non-Jewish population is fundamental and systematic—and it's high time we Jews owned the policies of the Jewish state for what they really and truly are.

YBD

Rabbi Brant, because you are anti-Israel and because you oppose its existence as a Jewish state, could you then please explain to us why you support J Street, which claims to be "pro-Israel"? Because I view

J Street also as an anti-Israel organization (and by anti-Israel, I mean it supports policies, particularly in the security realm, that are opposed by the vast majority of the Jewish Israeli population, including the Zionist Left), is it that you are attempting to subtly redefine what being "pro-Israel" means in order to lure in unsuspecting and unknowledgeable American Jews by throwing the word "peace" around?

By the way, I reject your assertion that Israel started some sort of unprovoked attacks on Arab villages after the UN Partition Plan Resolution was passed on November 29, 1947. Recall the Jews accepted partition, the Arabs rejected it and *immediately* attacked Jewish *yishuvim* and particularly transportation arteries as a result of this rejection, which included express intentions, publicly stated, to "throw the Jews into the sea." The attacks by the Haganah, Etzel, and Lehi on the Arab villages you referred to were designed to secure the *yishuvim* the roads connecting them.

I also *vehemently* reject your use of the loaded statement that Israel *persecutes* the Palestinians. This is an outrageous statement, and I suggest you retract it if you intend to have any place in public Jewish discourse.

Rabbi Brant Rosen

I'm "anti-Israel," and you don't understand why I support J Street, which is also "anti-Israel"? The only way I can possibly understand this calculus is to assume you believe anyone who doesn't share your views to be "anti-Israel."

Please show me real, actual evidence for your claim that J Street supports policies that are opposed by "the vast majority of the Jewish Israeli population." That sounds suspiciously like a sweepingly false statement to me.

Again, I find your historical claims re 1948 to be sweepingly false. You cite the Arab states' rhetoric to "throw Jews into the sea," but you conveniently leave out a myriad of Zionist statements that made their ultimate intentions clear well before 1947. Just one of many examples: "If there are other inhabitants there, they must be transferred to some other place. We must take over the land." —Menachem Usshiskin, chairman of the Jewish National Fund, speaking in 1930.[16] I can come up with a myriad of other such statements if you like.

Bottom line: By late 1947, it was clear to the Palestinian Arab community that the Jewish Yishuv intended to "cleanse" as many Arab population centers as possible in order to create a new reality on the ground—and this included many villages that would be part of the new Jewish state, according to the UN Partition Plan. Again, there is plenty of historical documentation to support this—most of which has been presented to us by Israeli historians.

You also leave out important context: Palestinian Arabs opposed the UN Partition Plan, because it was an unfair and inequitable solution. In 1947, Jews were a clear minority in terms of population and land ownership in Palestine. Palestinian Arabs constituted more than two-thirds of the population and were a majority in all but one of its subdistricts. By comparison, Jews owned just over 6 percent of the total land of Palestine.

In spite of these demographic realities, the UN Plan handed over 55.5 percent of Palestine to the proposed Jewish state. Palestinian Arabs would make up almost half the population of the new Jewish state (territory that included the Negev, which was then 1 percent Jewish.) It also included the prime agricultural land and 40 percent of existing Palestinian industry.

In short: Palestinians did not oppose partition because they wanted to "throw Jews into the sea." They opposed partition because they opposed officially sanctioned Jewish takeover of their land and resources.

You take exception to my claim that Israel persecutes Palestinians? This is controversial? Look carefully at what Israel is doing to Palestinians in Gaza and the Occupied West Bank. By any other definition, this would be considered oppression pure and simple—and I have no trouble making this claim "in public Jewish discourse."

And with all due respect, it is not for you to determine what can or cannot have any place in public Jewish discourse. That is up to the Jewish public.

Why I Support the Berkeley Student Divestment Resolution[17]

April 14, 2010

I'm sure many of you have been following the huge communal dust-up that has been swirling around a resolution recently passed by the Associated Students of UC Berkeley. Known as SB118, it calls for the ASUC to divest its holdings in General Electric and United Technologies because of "their military support of the occupation of the Palestinian territories."

The bill further resolves that:

The ASUC will further examine its assets and UC assets for funds being invested in companies that a) provide military support for or weaponry to support the occupation of the Palestinian territories or b) facilitate the building or maintenance of the illegal wall or the demolition of Palestinian homes, or c) facilitate the building, maintenance, or economic development of illegal Israeli settlements on occupied Palestinian territories . . .

. . . [and] the ASUC will divest, and will advocate that the UC divests, all stocks, securities, or other obligations from such sources with the goal of maintaining the divestment, in the case of said companies, until they cease such practices. Moreover, the ASUC will not make further investments, and will advocate that the UC not make further investments, in any companies materially supporting or profiting from Israel's occupation in the above mentioned ways.[18]

On March 18, after eight hours of dialogue and deliberation, the resolution passed by a vote of 16 to 4. After a barrage of criticism from Jewish community and Israel advocacy groups, the resolution was vetoed by the president of the ASUC on March 24. As things currently stand, the veto can be overridden by 14 votes. The final decision will be made on Wednesday, April 14, at 7:00 p.m. (PST).[19]

The most prominent Jewish statement of condemnation against the resolution came in the form of a letter cosigned by a wide consortium of Jewish organizations[20] that called the bill "anti-Israel," "dishonest," and "misleading." Supporters of the resolution have mobilized as well: Jewish Voice for Peace recently responded to the consortium's letter with a strong public statement, and other prominent public figures, including Archbishop Desmond Tutu[21] and Naomi Klein,[22] have voiced their support of the Berkeley resolution.

As I've written in the past,[23] I do believe that the longer Israel's intolerable occupation continues, the more we will inevitably hear an increase in calls for boycott, divestment, and sanctions (BDS). I'm certainly mindful of what these kinds of calls mean to us in the Jewish community—and I know all too well how the issue of the boycott pushes our deepest Jewish fear buttons in so many ways. Despite these fears, however, I personally support the ASUC resolution.

Although I understand the painful historic resonance that boycotts have for the Jewish community, I truly believe this bill was composed and presented in good faith—and I am troubled that so many Jewish community organizations have responded in knee-jerk fashion, without even attempting to address the actual content of the resolution.

It is also unfair and untrue to say that this resolution is "anti-Israel." The bill makes it clear that it is condemning a crushing and illegal occupation, not Israel as a nation. The wording of the resolution leaves no doubt that its purpose is to divest from specific companies that aid and abet the occupation, not to "demonize" Israel itself. If a group of students oppose the occupation as unjust, then why should we be threatened if they ask their own organization to divest funds that directly support it? This is not demonization—this is simply ethically responsible investment policy.

Why, many critics ask, are the Berkeley students singling out Israel when there are so many other worse human-rights abusers around the world? To answer this, I think we need to look at the origins of the BDS movement itself. This campaign was not hatched by the Berkeley students, or even by international human-rights activists. It was founded in 2005 by a wide coalition of groups from Palestinian civil society who sought to resist the occupation through nonviolent direct action.

In other words, BDS is a liberation campaign waged by the Palestinian people themselves—one for which they are seeking international support. By submitting this divestment resolution, the Berkeley students are not seeking to single out Israel as the world's worst human-rights offender— they are responding to a call from Palestinians to support their struggle against very real oppression.

The JVP statement makes this point very powerfully:

Choosing to do something about Israel's human-rights violations does not require turning a blind eye to other injustices in the world as these groups suggest; but refusing to take action because of other examples would indeed turn a blind eye to this one. Now is the time to support Palestinian freedom and human rights. Berkeley students have done the right thing. Others should follow suit and divest from the occupation, as part of their general commitment to ethical investment policies.[24]

I believe that the actions of these Berkeley students represent an important challenge to those of us who believe that Israel's occupation equals oppression. Quite simply, we cannot stay silent forever. Sooner or later, we will have to ask ourselves: When will we be willing to name this for what it really and truly is? When will we find the wherewithal to say out loud that this policy of home demolitions, checkpoints, evictions, increased Jewish settlements, and land expropriations is inhumane and indefensible? At the very least, will we be ready to put our money where our moral conscience is?

I know that this debate is enormously painful. And I respect that there are members of the Jewish community who disagree with this campaign. But I must say I am truly dismayed when I witness the organized Jewish community responding to initiatives such as these by simply crying "anti-Semitism." For better or worse, we are going to have to find a better way to have these conversations. Because whatever happens with the ASUC resolution tomorrow, we haven't heard the end of this movement by a long shot.

This summer, in fact, the Presbyterian Church General Assembly will be taking up a number of resolutions related to Israel/Palestine, including one that recommends divestment from Caterpillar because it knowingly supplies Israel with bulldozers that are used for illegal (and deadly) home demolitions in the West Bank and Gaza. I'm sad to see that the organized Jewish community is already gearing up for another major confrontation.

Discussion

Lynn

Thank you, Brant, for bringing this issue to your readers and giving them an opportunity to speak out in favor of the growing nonviolent tool of BDS. If Israel meets nonviolent protests by Palestinians with violence, scorns truce offers, and continues to build settlements and steal Palestinian land, what else can Palestinians do to end the occupation other than call on the world to support them with BDS? What will make Israel give up its foolhardy course and begin to negotiate in good faith? Surely not just finger-wagging by the US. BDS may just be the only way forward to a peaceful future for Israelis and Palestinians.

YBD

This piece is simply more proof of my assertion that you have placed yourself outside the realm of public Jewish discourse.

First of all, you claim that this BDS move is not "anti-Israel." As you well know, there is a move to delegitimize Israel around the world on all fronts. *You yourself* say Israel was created immorally and illegally. So why should you and the others who oppose Israel simply stop with Israel's conduct in the territories? This is the first step toward wider boycotts and delegitimization. Please don't use Orwellian laundering of terms that are anti-Israel and then try to call them "pro-Israel."

Secondly, you claim this only is directed at means for "military support for the occupation." Does that include guns? Tractors? Jeeps? Food for the soldiers serving there (some of which is made in the US)? How do you draw the line?

Third, you can jump [up] and down all you want talking about the "illegality" of the settlements in Judea/Samaria. Again, because you oppose Zionism, how are these settlements more "illegal" than those built after the 1948 War, which you claim involved "ethnic cleansing" (e.g., Tel Aviv University sitting on the land of the pre-1948 Arab village of Sheikh Munis)? Maybe those should be boycotted too? In any event, the Israeli government doesn't recognize them as being illegal, and many international law scholars say the same, so the matter is in dispute and *not* as clearly one-sided as you indicate.

Fourth, as a congregational rabbi, you can't simply say that these are your "private" opinions. Do you represent your congregation in these views? Do you speak for them? Do you speak for the Reconstructionist movement (which I had thought was pro-Zionist dating from the time of Mordecai Kaplan)? What do they think of one or more of their rabbis declaring war on Israel and much of world Jewry, which vehemently oppose this move? (For heaven's sake, J Street opposes this!)

Rabbi Brant Rosen

As I wrote to you earlier, it is not up to you to define what is in the "realm of public Jewish discourse." I would also point out that you and I and many others are having this very conversation publicly, as Jews. In fact, the main reason I started this blog was to widen what we consider to be the realm of "public Jewish discourse." I'm glad that you are part of this conversation.

To answer your first issue: Yes, there are indeed some who are seeking a wider BDS campaign—but even here I would disagree with you that "delegitimization" of Israel its ultimate goal. Those mobilizing the campaign would likely say that Israel is delegitimizing itself through its oppressive policies toward its non-Jewish population. The point, as I've already written, is to mobilize a nonviolent action campaign to resist this very real oppression.

At any rate, your reference to wider BDS campaigns is really just a red herring, because that is not at all what we are talking about here. The Berkeley resolution recommends selective divestment from two specific companies that manufacture weapons that Israel uses against civilians, causing grievous injury and death on a massive scale.

This is where the Berkeley students are drawing the line: against two companies that profit from weapons that have been used in war crimes, as has been documented by numerous human-rights organizations. Not food, not Jeeps, not guns, but immensely powerful high-tech weaponry that certain Berkeley students have determined they do not want to subsidize with their school tuition. Any other campaign(s) outside this are simply not germane to this debate.

Yes, these are my personal views. Everything I write here reflects my own personal views, and I make this very clear on my home page. My posts do not represent the corporate views of my congregation. There is a diversity of views at JRC—some members agree with me, some partly agree with me, some disagree with me, and there are many more who are frankly unsure where they stand on this issue.

The same goes for the Reconstructionist movement: There are rabbis who share my views, and there are those who do not. I will say, however, that they all respect my right to air my opinions whether they personally agree with me or not. I have always been proud that we have a wide and inclusive ideological tent in the Reconstructionist movement. And I know for a fact that we give voice to many Jews out there who feel marginalized because the "official" Jewish community too often takes it upon itself to define what is "acceptable public Jewish discourse."

Dan

I am a member of Rabbi Rosen's congregation, and I am glad he is having this discussion. I find it quite informative. You claim he is "outside the realm of public Jewish discourse." If this is true, then it reflects poorly on the Jewish community, because I believe he is expressing a legitimate and informed point of view that should be part of the discussion.

Eric

You would like to declare certain ideas outside the realm of "public Jewish discourse"—which is to say, I suppose, that we can think such things in private, but we'd all better shut up and toe the party line in public.

That strikes me as a cowardly, bullying request. So does your attempt to use professional pressure to get Brant to shut up in public about his views. I know rabbis who have lost their jobs because of such pressure, and I'm sure Brant does as well; many have been cowed into silence for a very long time. If that silence is now breaking, that's a very good thing, and like Dan, I'm very proud to have my congregation's rabbi as part of that return of honesty to Jewish communal discussion.

I'm sure you're motivated by love of your country and fear for the lives of its citizens, both of which are worthy values. But to say that Brant's support for this measure amounts to "declaring war on Israel and much of world Jewry"? I'm sorry, but that's contemptible. And, let me add, unconvincing.

> I haven't been a supporter of BDS in the past, but your post is turning me into one.

My Lunch with Yonatan Shapira[25]

May 5, 2010

I had the pleasure of meeting Yonatan Shapira for lunch in Evanston yesterday. If you've never heard of him, Yonatan was an officer in the Israeli Air Force who flew hundreds of missions over the territories in a Blackhawk helicopter squadron during the course of his 11-year career. After a targeted bomb assassination of a Hamas leader killed 14 civilians in Gaza, he became a prominent Israeli "refusenik," authoring the "Pilots' Letter,"[26] a 2003 statement signed by 27 Israeli pilots who publicly refused to fly missions over the Occupied Territories.

Since that time, Yonatan has gone on to cofound Combatants for Peace, a prominent organization in the growing Israeli refusenik movement. A few years ago, he gained some more notoriety for writing and performing "Numu, Numu," a powerful protest song written in the form of an ironic "Lullaby to Pilots."

I knew of Yonatan's refusenik activism, but during our lunch conversation I was surprised to learn that he is also very active in supporting nonviolent Palestinian actions in Sheikh Jarrah, Bil'in, and throughout the Occupied Territories. (He was, in fact, arrested last January at a demonstration in Sheikh Jarrah.) He told me that this work has been transformative for him, explaining that as an IDF officer—and even as a leader in the Israeli peace movement—he has always been socialized to step forward and lead the way. He said he's come to realize that the most important way he can serve now is to "stand behind" Palestinians in their nonviolent campaign for liberation.

He told me several stories about his experiences at demonstrations. He mentioned that the IDF is increasing their crackdown on protesters, that they hire infiltrators to throw stones at the army to give the soldiers a pretext to open fire. None of it succeeds, of course: quite the opposite. The Palestinian nonviolence movement is growing steadily—a "White Intifada" that Yonatan believes has already begun. As an IDF officer himself, he explained the Israeli military mentality: Army commanders truly believe they have the power to "outlaw" these protests through the sheer force of their military might.

I assumed that Yonatan would be made a pariah for his public stands. He replied that, as a military man, he understands how soldiers think. He knows how to engage them in dialogue even when they strongly disagree with him. His family is supportive of his work: His father "is not quite there yet" but respects his activism, and his mother is "the most active of them all."

Yonatan also mentioned that as part of his support of nonviolent Palestinian activism, he has also signed on to the internal Israeli BDS movement, known as "Boycott from Within." Now *that* is the new definition of bravery: A high-ranking Israeli Air Force veteran who comes from a military family (his father was a fighter pilot during the Six-Day War) has now firmly put himself on the front lines of a global nonviolence campaign initiated by the very people he himself was trained to attack.

Discussion

Miriam

Thank you for posting this. It's so great to read about how Israelis are involved in the peace movement. So often in America, we American Jews have been painted the picture of soldiers as the strong and tough *sabra*. Certainly Yonatan is incredibly strong and tough but has chosen to follow his heart for truth and justice. He is another example of someone who is leading and modeling Jewish values of peace and justice. Hopefully the Israeli government will someday follow his lead.

Chapter 7

Jewish Conscience, Jewish Shame

April–May 2010

This chapter features my public dialogue with a dear friend who moved to Israel in the late 1980s. My friendship with David goes back to our under-graduate days at UCLA, where our mutual connection to Israel was always an important aspect of our relationship. Despite the long distance and the passage of time, our families have remained close. When he wrote to tell me that he was very troubled by my blog posts, I asked if he would be willing to engage in an online conversation about these issues with me. I was immensely grateful when he agreed. Our dialogue resulted in some of my favorite posts to date.

Jewish Conscience, Jewish Shame[1]

April 22, 2010

A few days ago, a longtime friend of mine who has been living in a small community village in the Upper Galilee for the past 20 years sent me this comment:

> Hi Brant. How about writing something positive about Israel for a change? Israel must mean something to you other than one large injustice to the Palestinian people. How about balancing your blogs with items that can help your readers find pride in Israel and its accomplishments, despite all the real problems that you primarily focus on?

It's a fair and important comment—and it's been put to me more than once. Invariably, some of them are presented in a much less tactful manner. One commenter recently complained that "the level of Israel bashing [on this blog] is sickening."

It gives me a strange, queasy feeling to be called an "Israel basher." It's an odd switch. It wasn't that long ago that I felt the same way about Jews who seemed to regard Israel as little more than a source of shame.

For many years, Israel and Zionism have been central to my Jewish identity. I too had a hard time abiding those Jews who viewed Israel as, as my friend put it, "one large injustice to the Palestinian people." Although I certainly didn't deny many of these injustices (and would often protest them), I also had an unabashed Jewish pride in Israel— and in Zionism itself as the "national liberation movement of the Jewish people." In my most cynical moments, it often felt that those who chronically "bashed" Israel were motivated by Jewish self-hatred more than anything else.

Those who read my blog must certainly know that my relationship to Israel is being painfully challenged—particularly since Israel's military assault on Gaza last year. I'm well aware that I often address these painful issues head-on and sometimes with uncensored candor. And I'm certainly not unmindful that the cumulative effect of these posts may well come off as unduly harsh, unbalanced, and, yes, to some, "Israel bashing."

Those who know me well know how deeply I feel about Israel. I continue to identify deeply with many aspects of Israeli life—particularly with the new Jewish cultural spirit that is being created and re-created there. I will always love the Hebrew language, literature, and poetry as well as the powerful rhythms of Jewish life that a Jew experiences when living in Israel. However . . .

However, as a Jew, I am growing increasingly heartsick that this culture has been and continues to be created on the backs of others. I am having an increasingly difficult time getting past the fact that our Jewish national rebirth has come at the expense of the Palestinians. And I am even more painfully considering whether these problems are not mere "blemishes" on an otherwise noble national project but rather something fundamentally problematic with the Zionist enterprise itself.

I know that Israel has accomplished a great deal against all odds. And I certainly know that many feel I should "balance" my blog posts by drawing attention to these achievements. But for better or worse, I can no longer regard the Israel-Palestine reality as a balanced equation. I'm coming to believe that the moral challenges Israel faces are so critical that they fundamentally threaten the very real accomplishments Israel has achieved in its short and remarkable life.

I understand that there will be those who will never accept this—and that some people will never experience my writing as anything other than hatred for the Jewish state. Even more painfully, I am all too aware of how my words may affect my many dear friends in Israel, people who have chosen to make their lives and raise their families there and who continue to mean a great deal to me.

All I can hope is that they might somehow understand that I do not seek to "bash" Israel. Quite the opposite. My words have always and will always be motivated by Jewish conscience—not by Jewish shame.

Discussion

Julie

There was time when I might have agreed with your general premise, Brant, that the victory that comes from another's loss is tarnished, to say the least. However, two years ago a horrible event happened that changed my views in a radical way. An Arab terrorist infiltrated the library of the Mercaz Harav Yeshivah and brutally murdered eight young men before being gunned down himself. At this point, I became painfully aware of how much we, as Jews, are hated. This hatred doesn't lessen when our enemies have jobs, housing, a comfortable family life, or basic freedoms (and this terrorist had all of these things). The truth is, I admire your ability to still feel for the Palestinian people after they willfully trample on you time and again. Your sensitivity surpasses mine and that of many of the Jewish people. However, I humbly caution you against alienating your very own brothers and sisters for the sake of people who have not given a second thought to the most cruel acts imaginable and who will not stand by you as partners in peace.

Matt

Julie, it sounds like you experienced a personal loss in this incident, so I don't want to come across as insensitive or disrespectful. However, in emotional times, sometimes our logic gets put on hold, and I believe you have understandably formed a false syllogism.

I believe it's never a good idea to judge an entire people by the actions of individuals. Nor would we want to be so judged. But I believe it is such thinking that leads to the hatred of the terrorist you described. It could never be right to judge all Jews by the actions of Baruch Goldstein, or the Irgun, or the faceless pilots of F-16s with Stars of David on them destroying one's home. But people are human. They see these things, and it causes the same revulsion that you feel.

All the tanks and guns in the world could never stop anyone from hating us. And there will always be people who hate Jews (and blacks, and Arabs, and Roma, and . . .) for any reason other than who we/they are. We can't change anyone but ourselves. But we do have that power. And Brant is one of many who are working for such a change. And there are many people that some would call enemies who are passionately working for change on the other side of the line.

I firmly believe there is still hope.

Lisa K

Julie, I feel that my true brothers and sisters are those who are committed to working as partners for a just peace. Many of these people are my Palestinian friends who have experienced horrific personal losses at the hands of the IDF or individual settlers who perpetrate almost daily pogroms on Palestinians and their villages. Yet they do not hate Jews or Israelis, as a group or as individuals.

I recommend you check out the website for the Parents Circle Families Forum.[2] This is a group of Israelis and Palestinians who have lost close family members to the violence of the conflict. They come together, share their stories, and have a mission of reconciliation. You can also rent the documentary DVD *Encounter Point* to learn more about what they do and how they heal.

You sound like you are in pain, and I hope this helps.

Julie

I thank you all for the sensitivity of your replies. I often comment with a dissenting or controversial opinion on blogs like this and find that the response is almost entirely negative and dismissive, if not downright insulting. Whatever the "peace process" may be, whether between Israelis and Arabs or between factions within those groups, the ability to give others the benefit of the doubt and respond to them in a kind and measured way will be key. I still strongly feel that a situation can come to a point where measures must be taken to avoid major loss, but I think our more pressing concern is mending fences within our own communities and returning to our shared core values of wisdom and peace.

Rabbi Brant Rosen

Your comment means a great deal to me, Julie. I'm so very gratified that you've found a sensitive reception on this blog, especially from people with whom you might disagree. I agree with your feeling that blog conversations too often are nasty and insulting—but it doesn't have to be that way.

I also agree with you that the way out of these conflicts lies with our ability to empathize and to give others the benefit of the doubt. On this we must all agree, no matter where we stand, no matter how painful the issue.

BF

Arab refugees were *intentionally* not absorbed or integrated into the Arab lands to which they fled, despite the vast Arab territory. Out of the 100 million refugees since World War II, theirs is the only refugee group in the world that has never been absorbed or integrated into their own people's lands. Jewish refugees were completely absorbed into Israel, a country no larger than the state of New Jersey. Genocide is a real possibility in the 21st century. The world stood by as one-third of its Jews were murdered in the mid–20th century. Does it not follow that Jews need to take extraordinary measures to protect themselves from genocide?

Let the Jews take care of their own. Let the world take care of the few remaining refugees from World War II.

We Jews need to cut ourselves a break and let the other 6 billion take care of the Palestinian refugees.

I am heartsick that we would sacrifice the safety and security of the Jewish people for those who would not lift a finger to help themselves except by taking from us.

Rabbi Brant Rosen

Yes, Palestinians were not absorbed into Lebanon, Jordan, etc. But your reference to these countries as "vast Arab territory" is a huge generalization and suggests that all Arab nations somehow constitute one monolithic Arab country. The Palestinians' culture, heritage, and history were and are rooted in Palestine. And they did not "flee" from their homes there—they were expelled.

Of course genocide is a real possibility in the 21st century, as Darfur has already demonstrated. And of course Jews need to protect themselves from genocide—but I simply can't see how Israel's oppressive policies toward Palestinians do much to ensure Jewish security. Needless to say, I disagree strongly with your final comments. Whether we like it or not, Israel has culpability for the Palestinian refugee situation—and Israel will have to be a major part of its solution. This is not only an issue of human rights for Palestinians—it is ultimately a matter of "safety and security" for the Jewish people as well.

A Conversation with an Israeli-American Friend[3]

April 27, 2010

Dear Brant,

As an old friend of yours, I certainly know that you do not "hate Israel" and you are not an "Israel basher" with intent to harm Israel.

Nonetheless, I am very saddened to hear that you no longer have "Jewish pride in Israel and in Zionism itself." This is very evident in your writings.

I can't agree with you more in terms of the human suffering the Palestinians have endured and continue to endure. It is good that you have raised awareness in the Jewish community to this real tragedy on the ground.

But I don't accept your premise that Zionism and the creation of our national state bear the moral responsibility for the Palestinian suffering and that there is "something fundamentally problematic with the Zionist enterprise itself."

Had Arab states accepted Israel's creation in 1948 rather than attacking with the goal of destroying her, history would have played out differently, both for Israel and the Palestinians. Israel was not established based on the ideology of disenfranchising the Palestinian people. Yes, Israel conducted immoral acts during the war, such as driving many Palestinians out of their villages. But do not forget that this was a war of survival that was forced on her. Israel never had the goal of conquering and occupying the West Bank and Gaza. The Six-Day War was also a war of survival.

Oppression of the Palestinian people is not part of the Zionist dream. I have no doubt that Israelis would overwhelmingly support a Palestinian state in the West Bank and Gaza if Palestinian leadership would recognize Israel and agree to live peacefully by her side. Israel has made peace with Egypt and Jordan, to the credit of its brave leaders Sadat and Hussein. If only the Palestinian leadership would show such courage. This situation in Gaza would change overnight if Hamas would recognize Israel, agree to cease all hostilities and terrorism, and return Gilad Shalit.

The Israeli government and military apparently believes the blockade of Gaza is needed to ensure Israeli security. Tactically, this may prove to be a wrong decision in terms of Israeli security, and to your credit, I am becoming a believer that it is also morally wrong to cause such extreme hardships for the entire population in Gaza.

But again, I believe what motivates Israel's actions in Gaza is not its desire to cause suffering, but its desire to protect its citizens. I'm also sure the army could have done more to reduce innocent casualties in last year's incursion into Gaza to stop the incessant rocket fire; this is not because the military guidelines were to harm innocent people, but to the contrary. I know there are stories as well where soldiers put themselves in greater danger in order to prevent possible harm to innocent civilians.

Just yesterday I read that Israel evacuated a Palestinian in Gaza who needed medical treatment in an Israel hospital, while Hamas released a cruel video showing Noam Shalit wandering in Gaza until he finds his son Gilad in a coffin.

I support your right, and indeed obligation, to speak openly and honestly about Israel, even when it means criticizing Israeli government policy. Israel is a very open democracy. As you often find and cite in your blogs, there is plenty of open criticism of our government policy here in Israel.

Brant, what I find lacking in your blog is the larger context to the situation. Israel faces two very hostile entities whose main goal is to harm Israel: Hezbollah in the Lebanon and Hamas in Gaza. Both are radical Islamic entities sponsored by Iran who do not seek compromise or any kind of peaceful coexistence with Israel.

What I think we can agree on is that Israel should strive to find ways to reduce the suffering in Gaza without sacrificing its security.

Furthermore, I think with a little effort, you can find stories of things happening in Israel that do provide you with a source of Jewish and Israeli pride. Such stories would provide a welcome positive addition to your very thought-provoking criticisms of Israeli policy.

Still your friend,
David

Dear David,

Thank you so much for your generous and thoughtful comments. Given the sensitive nature of the issues I'm raising, the respect and friendship inherent in your words mean a great deal to me. I'm also all too aware that anything regarding Israel has directly personal significance for you and your family.

It's obvious that my own feelings have recently been going through something of a transformation—but as I tried to express in my last post, there are many, many things about Israel that will always fill me with pride. I suppose the reason that I don't seem to exude love for Israel in my writings lately is that my anguish over Israel's oppressive treatment of Palestinians has come to eclipse that pride. It's not easy for me to write that, but it's really the only way I know how to put it.

I was so glad to read that we are largely in agreement about the tragedy of Palestinian suffering. I was especially gratified—and moved—to read that you are coming to believe that Israel's current actions in Gaza are "morally wrong." I know you don't admit these things lightly. It's obvious to me, however, that we disagree over the essential background of this tragedy.

You and I were both raised with the conventional Zionist narrative of Israel's founding. Indeed, I have long accepted the version of these events in way you describe them. But to make a long story short, I've come to question this particular narrative. I'm just not sure any more that it's as simple a matter as "if only the Arab states had accepted Israel's creation in 1948." I don't think we Jews can so blithely discount the Palestinian narrative (which, I will grant, has its own mythic simplicities as well).

The conventional Zionist narrative holds that Palestinians were purely and simply rejectionist because they could not abide a Jewish presence in their land. But I'm no longer sure that it's really that straightforward. I'm becoming increasingly less dismissive of the original Palestinian concern over the Zionist settlement of Palestine. After all, as the Arab inhabitants saw it, the essential goal of the Zionist movement was to extend Jewish sovereign control over as much of historic Palestine as possible. (I'm especially mindful of what this must have meant to an indigenous Palestinian community that had endured a succession of empires—and was finally given the promise of self-determination by the British following the defeat of the Ottomans at the end of WWI).

Although according to our narrative, the 1947 UN Partition plan was eminently fair and equitable, I'm now trying to understand how this plan must have been experienced by the Arab residents of Palestine. Despite the fact that Jews were a clear minority in terms of population and owned only 6 percent of the land, the UN plan gave 55.5 percent of Palestine to the proposed Jewish state (which would have contained 400 Arab villages within its new borders). Given that indigenous Palestinians, without their consultation, were set to lose more than half their land to a minority settler population that sought political control over it, I can certainly understand the reasons behind Palestinian resistance to partition.

In reading the work of the new Israeli historians, the revelation that continues to affect me the most—and one that was *never* part of my Zionist education—was that between the date of the partition vote in November 1947 and the declaration of the State of Israel (and the exit of British troops from Palestine) in May 1948, a civil war was fought between the Yishuv forces and Palestinian military irregulars. It was during this time that Jewish forces began to forcibly expel Palestinian resident from their villages—including large swaths of territory that were intended to be part of the new Palestinian state, according to the Partition Plan. The Arab states did not join the fight until May 1948, at which time the Yishuv forces had already begun to gain the upper hand (and the Palestinian refugee problem was well under way).

Without going into more historical detail, here's the long and short of it: I'm not so sure that this war was, as you put it, a "war of survival that was forced on Israel." (I'm also not sure it was that simple in the case of 1967, either, but let's save that one for another conversation, if we're up for it.)

David, I do agree with you that "oppression of the Palestinian people is not part of the Zionist dream." I don't think that oppression of another people could ever have been the essential design of Israel's founders. But I now wonder: Was it an inevitable by-product? I can't help but question whether or not it was ever possible to establish an exclusively Jewish state in a country as historically multicultural and multireligious as Israel/ Palestine without engendering conflict. And I'm no longer sure whether it's possible under the circumstances for the Jewish state to maintain political dominion over this land without increasingly wielding its power oppressively toward its non-Jewish inhabitants.

Given what I'm coming to accept about the circumstances of Israel's founding, I've become increasingly more sensitive to the impact of these circumstances upon Israeli society—the increasing militarization, the all-encompassing emphasis on national security, and the increasing need to demonstrate Israel's overwhelming might in order to "ensure" her security.

The war in Gaza last year was something of a turning point for me in this regard. I read and watched the news obsessively as the IDF used devastating military force toward 1.5 million inhabitants squeezed into a tiny 140-square-mile strip of land. I'm sure that, as you point out, there were individual examples of humanitarian efforts by Israeli soldiers, but I also believe that these actions took place in a larger and more oppressive context.

When I asked myself why Israel was using such disproportionate force (and why the IDF was repeatedly targeting schools, factories, and essential parts of Gazan infrastructure that had nothing to do with the firing of Qassams), the only answer I could think of was that Israel's strategy was simply to beat the enemy into submission. To bring Hamas (and the citizens who elected it) to its knees through the sheer power of greater military might.

If this is indeed the case—if this is Israel's essential strategy—then I don't believe she will ever find the safety and security she so desperately seeks. It will only cause greater and greater humanitarian misery for Palestinians while further alienating Israel from the outside world. And this, as you say, was never, ever part of the Zionist dream.

At any rate, these are kinds of questions I've been asking myself these days. And while I might not have many solid answers, I feel compelled to continue to ask them. I realize that those who know me only from what they read on my blog must think I have precious little love in my heart for Israel. But I have to tell you, David, it means a great deal to me that you know me well enough to know better.

I can only hope that I can find a way to ask these questions in such a way that makes it clear they truly come from a place of Jewish love and Jewish conscience.

Your friend,

Brant

Discussion

Miriam

It saddens me to read that David is still more committed to the myth that Israel was a victim in 1948 and again in 1967. It also saddens me that David will not look at the truth that Israel has always wanted to conquer the West Bank and Gaza; indeed, even founding Israeli leaders have admitted to this. I understand how painful this is for David. If he were to look critically and consciously at the disparity between what Israel has said and what Israel has done, it might shatter his world and force him to rethink the narrative. I understand this pain, because I have gone through it.

Cotton

Thanks to both David and Brant for opening their conversation for all of us to hear and for the respectful way it is carried on. It is in marked contrast to so many conversations carried on—or suppressed—in both religious and secular circles, certainly in American society and, although probably less so, in Israeli and Palestinian societies. The critical components in Brant's and David's conversation are their willingness to listen, to allow their positions to be challenged, and the suggestion that assumptions that have been taken as dogma are being examined. We could do well with a lot more of that.

On the Right to Jewish Statehood[4]

May 1, 2010

Dear Brant,

Although we do have some agreement in regard to the dire need to improve the desperate humanitarian condition in Gaza, it appears that we indeed have some very large gaps in our understanding of the fundamental issues.

Historically, as you stated, it is easy to understand the position of the Palestinian community and why they opposed Jewish settlement and the Zionist goal of establishing a sovereign national Jewish homeland. (I would add that some parts of the Palestinian leadership went beyond this basic opposition to the establishment of a Jewish state, as demonstrated by Haj Amin al-Husseini, the mufti of Jerusalem, who was anti-Semitic and aligned with Nazi Germany.)

While you clearly empathize with the motivating factors for Palestinian/Arab resistance to a sovereign national Jewish homeland, it is less clear that you identify with:

1) The basic right of the Jewish people to a national homeland in Israel that is on par with the Palestinian right for statehood; and

2) The extremely desperate situation that existed for the Jewish people and the Yishuv during this period, given the need to provide a home for tens of thousands of Holocaust survivors from Europe.

Although the 1947 UN partition plan was problematic from the Yishuv perspective due to its lack of territorial continuity, nonetheless the Yishuv rejoiced and accepted the plan as the best course to lead to the establishment of a Jewish state. The Arab/Palestinian side flatly rejected it. After the UN partition plan was approved, violence ensued, initiated by both sides. Although some outright atrocities were committed by Jews, such as Deir Yassin, it is important to note that these acts were condemned by the mainstream Jewish leadership. After Ben Gurion declared the independence of the state of Israel on May 14, 1948, the armies of Egypt, Iraq, Jordan, Lebanon, and Syria invaded Israel.

Was the postpartition violence and subsequent War of Independence a war of survival for the Jewish state, as I claimed, or could it have been avoided, as you questioned? Given the extreme Palestinian/Arab opposition to a Jewish state, short of abandoning the immediate goal of creating a Jewish state, I don't see how it could have been avoided.

But I'm not a historian, and I'm sure you have "facts" to counter my "facts." But Brant, what really disturbs me is that I sense you are questioning whether the creation of a Jewish state in a territory with an indigenous

Palestinian population is justified, given that inevitably, conflict would ensue.

My response is a resounding "yes." We, the Jewish people, also have a historic, religious, and cultural attachment to the land and a right to our national homeland. Israel has absorbed Jews seeking to return to their homeland from the ashes of Europe, from Arab countries, Ethiopia, the former Soviet Union, America, etc. This is why Lori and I have chosen to make *aliyah,* and why we send our children to serve in the army to defend our right to live here.

I recommend reading Saul Singer's article "Stop Palestinian Denial of Jewish Peoplehood."[5] I agree with his contention that a fundamental obstacle to resolving the Israeli-Palestinian conflict today "is not just the glorification of terrorism on the Palestinian side, it is the denial of Jewish peoplehood, of Jewish history and of any legitimate Jewish connection to any part of Israel."

Now this does not mean I support disproportionate force in Gaza causing unnecessary suffering, discrimination against Israeli Palestinians, Jewish settlement in the Territories, etc. We need to constantly work toward an accommodation with the Palestinians, which I hope will some-day lead toward the establishment of an independent Palestinian state living peacefully by our side. As I wrote in my previous letter, there is a consensus in Israel for a two-state solution. But this dream must be shared by both sides to become a reality.

In friendship,
David

Discussion

Patsact

There is no basic right of any people to a piece of real estate. A state is about taking and holding territory by the successful use of violence. Perhaps a few Inuit or Patagonian Amerindians are exceptions to this—there may not be many people who have ever wanted to wrest these territories away. Otherwise, states last as long as the slingshots/ arrows/swords/ordinance/rockets hold out (and people to use them, of course). Many, many peoples/nations in the world are not in charge of states. Many of them have associations with lands that go back as far as memory goes. Do they have a right to take up arms and retake con-trol? What of people who have lived there in the interim? If an Arapaho knocks on my door and says it's time for her to come back and me to go, do I have to? What if a majority of UN members say I have to go?

Do I have to? The old/newcomers will always have an old national myth to be invoked—are some of these legitimate and others not? On what basis?

YBD

The points you are making are totally irrelevant today. The Balfour Declaration was issued, lots of Jews immigrated to the country, the UN said a Jewish state could be established, and one was. What is the point you are trying to make? Do you think it can be retroactively be negated? Do you think the Jews of Israel will do this even if you think it is "right"?

Patsact

David speaks to conditions at the time the state was formed, so I did. He also spoke to the "right" of Jews in Israel/Palestine to a state that is the equal of the Palestinians' rights. I think it is more on the mark to speak of Jews' power to have a state, which is considerable right now—hence, Jews have a state. I don't think Palestinians have any more or less right to a state than Jews; plainly, they do not, on their own, have the power to create and to maintain a state right now.

I think Jews will have a state longer, and have a better state, if some of the power that maintains the State of Israel is used to create and to maintain a State of Palestine, as well as more distributive justice for Israeli Arabs. In other words, I believe the Jewish majority in Israel/Palestine, the majority of whom are now as native as many Palestinians (i.e., born there), should use power more wisely.

Would it be useful if Palestinians behaved more wisely? Well, sure, there's never a wisdom surplus. But they have little power to back whatever wisdom they come up with. For there to be peace, they will need to deal with losing, at least for now. Those with more power can make that easier or harder on those with less. We have much Jewish wisdom on how to help others save face, and we need to use it, exactly because the power balance is in our favor right now.

Dana

Is the creation of a Jewish state in a territory with an indigenous Palestinian population justified, given that, inevitably, conflict would ensue?

My answer is yes. But in answering yes, I believe that Israel, as a Jewish state, now has an obligation to do everything in its power to help the Palestinian population, to ease its poverty, homelessness, and powerlessness with real solutions that choose sympathy even over

safety. Until we choose a path of real sympathy, doing everything
in our power as we would for sisters and brothers, we will not have
peace. It's as though you think Israel was earned with the blood of the
Holocaust. The right of Israel is earned through our historic actions to
be kind. In the former, everyone becomes our enemy. With the latter,
everyone becomes our sisters and brothers in understanding the misery
in being powerless.

A Debate for the Sake of Heaven[6]

May 3, 2010

Dear David,

Yes, it does indeed seem that the crux of our disagreement comes down
to the historical issues surrounding the establishment of a Jewish state.
Although I'm not a historian either, I am becoming increasingly sensitive
to the ways in which we relate to our own history and how these perspectives affect our reality today.

So yes, we do have very different views of the history of Israel's founding—and, as you put it, I am tempted to "counter your facts with my
facts," but I'll refrain for now, except to say that those of us who have been
raised on the Zionist narrative of events would do well to open our minds
and our hearts to the reality of the Palestinian narrative as well. Otherwise
I just don't see how we will ever find a measure of justice for Palestinians—
or peace for Jews.

On the most fundamental disagreement between us, you wrote:

> But Brant, what really disturbs me is that I sense you are questioning whether
> the creation of a Jewish state in a territory with an indigenous Palestinian
> population is justified, given that, inevitably, conflict would ensue.

Believe me, I'm disturbed by this as well. It has been a deeply painful
experience to question the idea of Israel that has been so central to my
Jewish identity for so long. But this is what it's come to: I've reached a
point where I can't help but question.

To be clear, I don't disagree that the Jewish people have maintained a
centuries-old attachment to this land—and I don't disagree at all that we
Jews should have a right to live in this land that we've long considered to

be our ancient homeland. But I don't believe that all this necessarily gives the Jewish people the "right" to have political sovereign control over it.

In this regard, I disagree strongly with Saul Singer when he writes about the Jewish people's "legitimate claim to sovereignty." What gives any people a "right" to sovereignty in a land? Let's face it, when it comes to these kinds of political claims, history has shown that might makes "right." Although I don't think anyone can legitimately deny the Jewish claim to Israel as its ancestral homeland, it simply doesn't follow that this religious/cultural connection ipso facto gives us the right of sovereign political control over it.

So yes, I am questioning whether by attaching 19th-century European ethno-nationalism to Judaism, the Zionist movement was setting itself up for inevitable conflict. That's invariably what nationalism does. You point out that there was "extreme Palestinian/Arab opposition to a Jewish state," and I certainly agree. But do we ever stop to consider why this might have been so?

Arab nations in general and Palestinians in particular had endured colonial control over the lands in which they lived for centuries. Following WWI, Britain and France extended the promise of decolonization to Arab nations—while at the very same time, the Zionist movement was increasing its own colonization of Palestine. How could Palestinian Arabs regard this with anything but alarm, especially since political Zionism was predicated upon the buildup of a Jewish majority in Palestine?

I see I'm slipping back into historical argumentation. So I'll just end with this: Where does all this leave us today? As I now see it, our insistence upon the "Jewish right" to Palestine will only prolong this 60-plus-year-old conflict. For me the important question is not "does Israel have the right to exist?" (Or even, really, "does a Palestinian state have the right to exist?") I believe the real question is: "How can we find a way to extend civil rights, human rights, equality, and security for all inhabitants of Israel/Palestine?"

Like you, I hope against hope that this question can be sufficiently addressed through the peace process, culminating in a true and viable two-state solution. But I admit to growing cynicism on this front—and I truly fear the choice we will face should the peace process fail. For even if we disagree on the root causes of this conflict, I think we both agree that it would be beyond painful if we were forced to choose between a Jewish apartheid state ruled by a Jewish minority over a Palestinian majority or one secular democratic state of all its citizens.

So you see, David, these are the things that keep me up nights. But despite the painful issues involved, I've really appreciated this conversation. Please know that I've considered it, as they say in Pirke Avot, a *machloket l'shem shamayim*—a "debate for the sake of heaven." I can only hope that it might, in some small way, inspire similar dialogues throughout our community.

    In friendship,

    Brant

Discussion

Dana

The dialogue, this listening and responding, this is what we need to have. Thank you for providing this. There is so much name calling, so much emotion, so much personal nationalism in our conversation that we have ceased to listen to each other. I can only hope and pray that we will find a way to understand each other, and in understanding find peace. Thanks again for starting the real process.

Our Dialogue Concludes[7]

May 8, 2010

Dear Brant,

    I don't think the "crux of our disagreement comes down to historical issues," as you stated. Indeed, I've grown up with the "Zionist narrative," but I'm not blind to the Palestinian narrative. I acknowledge and sympathize with the depth of the Palestinian Nakba and all the events that led up to the establishment of the State of Israel and its aftermath. Furthermore, I acknowledge that the Jews contributed to the Nakba tragedy.

    But your entire perspective of the conflict today is through the prism of the Palestinian Nakba. Although you acknowledge that the "Jewish people have maintained a centuries-old attachment to this land," you don't express any identification with the tragic history of the Jewish people, culminating in the Holocaust, and in the desperate need to establish an independent Jewish state during that period. Prior to the war, no country would accept the Jews seeking to flee Europe before it was too late. Even after the war, the British severely limited the Jewish refugees seeking to start a new life. After the creation of the state, nearly 1 million Jews from Arab countries fled their native homes (many forcibly, others due to increased persecution), most of whom found refuge in Israel.

So for me, there is no question that the establishment of Israel was not only the realization of the historic aspiration for the Jewish people to return to their homeland but a historic imperative given the dire circumstances of the Jewish people at this time. The fact that the creation of the Jewish state was in conflict with the aspirations of the Palestinians and against the desire of neighboring Arab states does not delegitimize it.

Since the creation of the state, Israel has had some success in coming to peaceful terms with its Arab neighbors Egypt and Jordan. But the situation today with the Palestinians is indeed a test for Israel's morals and values. On one hand, most Israelis want Israel to remain a democratic Jewish state and avoid the nightmare of becoming an apartheid state. On the other hand, Israelis fear the nightmare of a hostile terrorist state in the West Bank and Gaza. Nonetheless, Israel is facing its fears and realizes that a two-state solution is the only option for a better future for both Jews and Palestinians.

The Palestinians have not been able to accept past Israeli proposals for a two-state solution. Nonetheless, Israel must make every effort to strengthen moderate Palestinian leadership, stop Jewish settlement in the territories, and remove unnecessary security restrictions. In this area, I indeed join in your criticism of current and past Israeli policy. Israel must be creative in its thinking and open to difficult compromises, even in the area of Jerusalem. However, the Palestinians must also make painful compromises, such as the Palestinian "right of return," as no Israeli government would accept this—as it would dissolve the Jewish character of the state.

The notion of "one secular democratic state for all its citizens" has been used for decades by Israel detractors and by Palestinian terror organizations. This is basically a call for the end of a Jewish state. I honestly hope this was not your intention.

The reason for not achieving a two-state solution up until now can't be blamed solely on Israel. Although the Palestinian Authority supports the notion of a two-state solution, Hamas is ideologically committed to continuing the conflict with Israel and is not looking for compromise, coexistence, or peaceful borders with Israel. Read the deep hatred toward Israel in Ashley Bates's interview with Jamila al-Shanti, a member of the Palestinian parliament in the Hamas government:

Bates: Do you support a two-state solution?
Al-Shanti: No. I will never allow two states. No way. This is my land. They should go away. But we have another tactical approach that we would accept a state on 1967 borders with the capital of Jerusalem for a temporary period until the whole issue has been solved. The Israelis should know that I cannot recognize a state for them. The next generations will come to fight and kill them.[8]

Brant, you stated that you don't think anyone can legitimately deny the Jewish claim to Israel as its ancestral homeland. This is certainly the view of Hamas, I believe this is the prevalent view among Palestinians, and this was my point in referring to Saul Singer's article in my previous letter.

So to conclude my response and our open dialogue, I want to say that although I can agree with many of your criticisms of Israeli policy and human-rights issues regarding the Palestinians, it rings unfair and unbalanced in light of your lack of criticism of the Palestinian side and little sympathy of the Israeli Jewish position. It is not surprising some readers of your blog consider you an "Israel basher."

Today the Jewish State of Israel is a fact and is our national homeland. Israel is central to the Jewish world, and nearly half of world Jewry lives in Israel. In our short history, we've built a modern country and absorbed millions of Jews from around the world. The Nakba is also sadly a fact, and peace with the Palestinians still eludes us. We must continue to strive to keep our high moral values and help the Palestinians realize their dream while continuing to realize our dream of a Jewish state.

L'hitraot,
David

Discussion

Bo
The problem with selectively quoting from Ashley Bates's interview with Jamila al-Shanti is that the context is lost. Without understanding the deep pain and loss of the Palestinians that Ms. al-Shanti describes, one cannot understand the context of what David describes as her "deep hatred of Israel." And without understanding the pain of the other, one can fail to recognize the humanity of the other, even when it is expressed in ways with which one doesn't agree. For a better understanding of Ms. al-Shanti's words, I urge everyone to read Ashley Bates's interview in full.

Mark
Reading Bo's comment speaks my mind. David's quote from Ashley's interview is "out of context" in a very profound way (I know Ashley and her work, and one should go to her website and see the whole piece). By that I mean that the "context" is not the entire interview. The context, as Bo points out, is the experience of the occupation itself, and even more broadly the history of the dispossession and ongoing oppression of the Palestinian people. It is sad, so sad,

that we have to sound like this—a broken record of witness to this crime—in our work to bring peace to both Jews and Palestinians. But that is the way it is. I wonder if David has been there and seen what there is to be seen, up close. If I am right and he has not, then what I have to say to him is: Before I saw it, I felt and sounded a lot like you do.

So I understand what you feel, David, and I know it's not comfortable. It's not comfortable to feel what I feel, either. But this is better than the uneasy feeling of holding on to a dream that is not sustainable, that is built—to say the least—on a tragically incomplete narrative. Our story—the Jewish story—includes the Palestinian Nakba. It must. And that, only that, will take us to what is next.

Cotton

In a speech Condoleezza Rice made three years ago in Jerusalem, she expressed an important insight: "The prolonged experience of deprivation and humiliation can radicalize even normal people." Both Jews and Palestinians have been the victims of deprivation, humiliation, and terrible violence. Many have been radicalized and bear a deep hatred for the other. There are Israeli Jews as well as Palestinians who justify terrible violence against the other. I understand their hatred and their will to violence, but I do not condone it.

I believe David is mistaken in his belief that Hamas's denial of the Jewish claim to Israel as its ancestral homeland is also the prevalent view of Palestinians. If the Jewish claim is an exclusive claim, denying that it is also the ancestral homeland of Palestinians, then he is probably right. Denying the history of either people in this land is a form of verbal violence.

David's focus on Palestinians who have been radicalized by their experience, and by those who have manipulated their resentment, misses the point. There are so many more Palestinians whose remarkable patience in the face of this terrible occupation, nonviolent resistance to their oppression, and readiness to live peacefully with Israeli Jews never claim the headlines.

Israel Gershon

Bravo, David!

And thank you, Rabbi, for allowing this exchange.

I am one who finds your demonizing of Israel to be of disservice to Israel, the Jewish people, and the cause of peace. Your blog creates a distortion by focusing on the perhaps real and/or perceived faults of Israel, while ignoring Palestinian actions and those of the

Arab world. Peace will never be established if the demonizing continues. Balance and wisdom is something I seek from a rabbi, not rhetoric. Understanding the emotions, drives, desires, and needs of the Palestinians does not require ignoring the same of your own people. Millions of Jews live today in Israel. They face existential threats, and it would be morally wrong to turn away from them. A two-state solution will only be realized when both peoples recognize each other's right to self-determination. That can only come through a balanced approach that recognizes the past but insists on moving forward.

It is my opinion that the Jewish people always remember the past but always keep moving forward with optimism and hope. On the other hand, the Palestinians seem to only remember the past at the expense of the future. I hope and pray that this may one day change.

Miriam

I am surprised by how many people continue to label Brant and others as "Israel-bashing" when such "bashers" are simply disagreeing with decisions Israel has made. When will it ever be acceptable for an American Jew to speak out about injustices that come from Israel and are directed toward the Palestinians (and paid for by us US citizens!)? When will it be acceptable for one to criticize Israel but to love being Jewish? As Mark said, it is extremely uncomfortable. It is uncomfortable for both David (and I admire David's courage and willingness to speak in such an open forum like this for the past few weeks) and people like me to speak out. It has been extremely painful for me to realize that Israel is not the utopian, idealistic place I was raised to believe it was. I lived in Israel for many years, and, like many of us, I believed that Israel was intrinsically, politically, and philosophically connected to my being a Jew. But like a child realizing that an adult was not honest with her, I have had to come to terms with this, and I struggle with the pain every day. So let us all develop some compassion for all complete narratives—Israeli, Palestinian, tax-paying US citizens, and yes, the supposed "Israel-bashers"—on our road to peace and justice.

Chapter 8

The Freedom Flotilla and Gaza's Humanitarian Crisis

May–August 2010

Like the Goldstone Report before it, Israel's tragic military raid against Gaza flotilla activists brought Gaza's plight firmly back into the media spotlight once more. On May 31, 2010, Israeli commandos attacked six boats of the Gaza Freedom Flotilla, boarding from sea and air, as they sailed through international waters bringing humanitarian relief to the Palestinians of Gaza. Following an onboard firefight on the Turkish ship Mavi Marmara, *nine peace activists were shot and killed, and dozens were injured. The 700 passengers were arrested, transported to detention centers in Israel, and finally deported. Although Israel accused the flotilla activists of being terrorists harboring weapons, it has never produced any independent evidence to prove its claim that the* Mavi Marmara *was carrying anything other than humanitarian cargo.*

The legacy of the Mavi Marmara *tragedy has been profound, particularly its emboldening impact upon the international Palestinian solidarity movement. The Freedom Flotillas have helped focus international attention on human rights in Gaza. They continue to garner support from prominent individuals, such as writer Alice Walker and Nobel Peace Prize Laureate Máiread Corrigan Maguire.*

The Freedom Flotilla Tragedy: Where Is the Soul-Searching?[1]

May 31, 2010

In the wake of Israel's military attack against Gaza flotilla activists,[2] I've been scouring the Israeli press to find any semblance of soul-searching over how things could have come to this.

To my sorrow, all I'm finding are analyses of the "tactical mistakes" made by the IDF[3] and the public-relations fallout[4] of this tragic attack. In the meantime, there's the same old defensive posturing from the government. Israeli Navy commander Vice Admiral Eliezer Marom described the attacking IDF soldiers as acting with "perseverance and bravery"; Deputy Foreign Minister Danny Ayalon told the *Jerusalem Post* that the flotilla "was an armada of hate and violence."[5]

I have no doubt that the reaction of the American Jewish community will be just as defensive, if not more so. As for me, I'll be hoping against hope that we'll start to hear different kinds of reactions: that the Freedom Flotilla was not simply a movement of provocateurs seeking to "delegitimize" Israel but a group of activists mounting an act of civil disobedience to bring attention to 1.5 million Palestinian citizens who are suffering under a crushing blockade. That mounting a military operation against civilian activists in international waters was bound to be futile, illegal, and, yes, even immoral. That for all our concern over an organized "delegitimization campaign" against Israel,[6] it may well be that Israel is actually delegitimizing itself through oppressive acts such as this.

Discussion

Mike

So the official Israel response (the *Ynet* news article cited above) is they have some right to board a Turkish ship in international waters. If then they meet with hostilities from weapons like knives and sticks (these are the weapons that Israel finds surprising aboard a ship), they can retaliate with live fire. I would think that somewhere deep down, there would be some Israel military commander wondering what war it is they are fighting.

Open the Gates: A Rabbinical Response to the Gaza Freedom Flotilla Tragedy[7]

May 31, 2010

For a full, updated list of rabbinical signatories to this letter, visit the Jewish Fast for Gaza blog.[8]

Dear Friends,

In the wake of the Gaza Freedom Flotilla tragedy, we once again feel the need to raise our voices as rabbis in the Jewish community.

According to press reports, we now know that at least 9 people have been killed and many more have been injured when Israeli Navy Seals boarded a boat that held 600 people in the middle of the night—conducting a military operation against civilian activists in the midst of international waters.

We also know that the essential aim of the Freedom Flotilla was to carry humanitarian aid to those who have been severely suffering under the effects of Israel's crushing blockade of Gaza. We call upon our community not to turn away in denial or blame those of goodwill and good purpose who risked their lives to relieve the beleaguered people of the Gaza strip.

We lift up our voices and call upon Israel to conduct an independent, transparent, and credible investigation of this incident. We also call upon the government of Israel to open the gates of compassion and allow these ships to dock so that they may deliver humanitarian aid to the 1.5 million citizens of Gaza. In so doing, we note the overall context of oppression in which this incident has occurred and call upon the Government of Israel to turn away from the policies of occupation, siege, and indifference to international law.

Our silence now is an act of betrayal to the values we purport to live by and to the words of the prophet we read every Yom Kippur:

> Is this the fast I desire? A day for people to starve
> their bodies? Or bow their heads like a bulrush
> or wear sackcloth and smear oneself with ashes . . .
> No! This is the fast the Lord desires:
> Unlock the fetters of oppression
> Untie the cords of the yoke
> Let the exploited go free, break off every chain.
> Share your bread with the hungry,
> shelter the poor in your own house,
> clothe the naked and do not ignore your own kin.

As rabbis, we believe all human beings are our kin. We cannot abide the suffering inflicted upon the people of Gaza.

We lift up our voices and say: Unlock the fetters of oppression. Untie the cords of the yoke. Open the gates.

Discussion

Raviv

It is claimed that Israel conducted a military operation against "civilian activists" and that the latter's "essential aim . . . was to carry humanitarian aid." In the accounts and filmed footage that have emerged during the subsequent days, these claims ring hollow at best. I too have major reservations about not only the decisions made by Israel's (military and political) leaders but with the very decision-making process as well. Nevertheless, what is today indisputable is that these activists were neither "nonviolent" nor motivated primarily to provide humanitarian aid.

Statements like yours therefore obscure the complex circumstances under which this incident took place and, in so doing, contribute little to the attempts of (genuine) peace-loving people to transform the troubling reality here in the Middle East.

Rabbi Brant Rosen

Our statement does not claim that the activists were "nonviolent." Were there some odious types aboard the flotilla? Absolutely. Were they prepared to fight back if they were attacked? Clearly. But I think it's simplistic and unfair to say that it is "indisputable" that they were not motivated by humanitarian aims.

The Freedom Flotilla represents an act of civil disobedience motivated by an unjust blockade of goods and services to Gaza. Yes, historically, acts of civil disobedience are experienced as acts of provocation by the objects of this disobedience—but this does not mitigate the essential justice of their cause.

Whatever else you might think about the organizers of the flotilla, they are attempting to bring desperately needed supplies to a beleaguered population who are suffering as a direct result of Israel's policies. I believe those who support these goals (like me) are quite "genuine" in their desire for peace and justice in the Middle East.

Shirin

Rabbi, with great respect, I ask you on what basis you state absolutely that there were some "odious types" aboard the flotilla. It may be that you know something I do not know, and if so, please share this information. Otherwise I must seriously question why you would make such a strong negative characterization of a group of people who appear to have been defending their lives against a deadly attack.

Based on the eyewitness accounts so far from people who were on board the *Marmara* (including several journalists, who are trained to be very observant) and others who witnessed the events from nearby boats, the Israeli commandos began firing at the people on board the Marmara from the air and from the sea before they boarded the ship. So far every eyewitness has reported seeing and/or hearing stun grenades and gunshots before the Israelis boarded the ship. One person who witnessed the attack from a nearby boat reported that she is not sure whether the Israelis were shooting so-called "rubber bullets" (which we know are really metal pellets with a coating of rubber and are potentially quite deadly) or live ammunition. Witnesses who were on the *Marmara* reported live ammunition from the air and sea before the Israelis came on board.

At least two people were killed from the air before the Israelis came on board, one by a gunshot to the top of his head. A journalist has reported seeing them both fall. The Israelis wounded three others in those early moments and then denied them any attention until they died of their wounds. One eyewitness reported watching people bleed to death after pleas to the Israelis to evacuate them were denied.

Activists on other vessels report very brutal and contemptuous treatment from the Israelis despite the fact that they did not resist or resisted without the use of violence. Any and all recording and communication equipment was confiscated by the Israelis and has not been, and probably will not ever be, returned. Journalists' recording devices, recordings, and notes were also confiscated, of course. Are the Israelis afraid of what those recordings will reveal?

Based on the information I have so far, what there were on board that ship were not "odious types," but human beings who found themselves under a terrifying brutal and deadly attack and who followed the imperative for self-preservation that is present in all living beings. In my world it is not odious to use whatever means I can to defend myself against heavily armed thugs who have invaded my space and are shooting at me and my comrades.

Based on the information I have so far, the only odious thing was the actions of the Israelis. Do you have information that will help me to change that view?

Rabbi Brant Rosen

I used the word "odious" because I saw the Al-Jazeera video of some flotilla participants chanting radical Islamic anti-Jewish slogans as they waited to board the ships.[9] I realize they did not represent all the activists, but I also take these news accounts very seriously.

To be fair, the folks aboard the flotilla are a mixed multitude. It is cosponsored by different organizations with different agendas and approaches. For instance, the International Solidarity Movement (an organization for which I personally have high regard) is strictly nonviolent in its approach. The Turkish Islamic charity IHH is not.

I think it would be wrong to describe all the flotilla participants as Jew-hating "Islamists," but I would also say it is highly naive to claim that they are all uniformly pure of motive. At the end of the day, this is the bottom line as I see it: Regardless of what we might think about individual participants, the Freedom Flotilla is an honorable act of civil disobedience against the unjust and illegal blockade of Gaza by Israel.

What are the sources you cite for your claims, Shirin?

Shirin

Thank you for your response, Rabbi. . . . If they were indeed chanting "radical Islamic anti-Jewish" garbage, that is very disappointing indeed, and the term odious is appropriate, both from an Islamic point of view and from a human point of view.

There is nothing in Islam and nothing in the Qur'an to justify hatred of Jews—quite the contrary, in fact—and it is extremely distressing that there are people who can turn any religion into a vehicle for hatred.

As for my sources, they are video, audio, and print interviews with a variety of eyewitnesses. Huwaida Arraf, whom I am sure you are acquainted with, is one of them. She witnessed what happened on the *Marmara* from the deck of her boat. Several people who were on the *Marmara* have been interviewed as well as Huwaida, Edward Peck, Ann Wright, and a number of less well-known people who were on other vessels. As more and more people who were on the *Marmara* are interviewed, we should be able to piece together a reasonably accurate picture of what happened. For now, though, it seems absurd to suggest that the violence was instigated not by the party that attacked and forcibly boarded the ship but by the people who were subjected to the attack.

Rabbi Brant Rosen

I realize the Al-Jazeera clip was posted on YouTube by the extremely partisan Palestinian Media Watch—and that they composed the subtitles. I was nonetheless disturbed by the content, and I'd love to know what you make of it. I would love even more to be proven wrong.

Shirin

I wish I could prove you wrong, Rabbi, but I cannot. Assuming the people chanting in the video were in fact participants in the flotilla (which seems probable, but not absolutely certain), the translation was accurate. I have heard this chant before and do not like it at all, although I do not interpret it in quite the same way most Jews are liable to.

It is a historical reference to the military defeat of some Jews who worked against the Muslims (some Jews were considered friends and allies, some were neutral and were pretty much left alone, some were against the Muslims and were enemies). I understand it in that historical context with respect to Israel and not in the context of hating or killing Jews in general. I am not trying to mitigate anything, just to give some context. However, I also consider its use and the thinking and attitude behind it to be, if not odious, an extremely bad choice. It should always be clear in our minds and in our words and deeds that our argument is not with Jews or Judaism, but with Israel and Zionism. Moreover, the dispute is not and never has been a religious one, despite the efforts of some on both sides to transform it into one.

Having said that, and not at all by way of excusing what we hear in that video, this problem exists very much on both sides. Last week I attended a demonstration in front of the local Israeli consulate, and some of the signs and speech from the (surprisingly small number of) counterdemonstrators were quite horrible. For example, very large signs saying things like "Until Gaza is completely destroyed the job will not be finished," and "God is great, it's Islam that sucks."

I can say with confidence that anyone on our side who brought something similar would be asked to take it down or leave. Maybe it is because we have so many Jews with us in this area that we have this level of consciousness—I don't know. We have a few American anti-Semites who have been kicked out of so many demonstrations by now that they rarely bother to show up anymore. One of them used to come to all the Arab social events he could find out about. I suppose he expected to be welcomed as a "fellow Jew hater," but he was completely isolated and no one would talk to him, so he stopped showing up.

Beyond the Flotilla, the Crackdown Continues[10]

June 2, 2010

As I read the myriad of reactions to the Gaza Freedom Flotilla tragedy last Sunday, I'm struck by one recurring theme: the sense of astonishment that these activists responded to the Israeli Navy with violence.

In other words, they didn't act according to the script. They didn't behave like proper practitioners of civil disobedience. The implication: If they had responded like the nonviolent activists they purported to be, this whole tragedy could well have been avoided.

There's only one problem with this calculus: Nonviolent Palestinian protests[11] have actually been going on throughout the Occupied Territories for years—and the Israeli military has been responding to them with much the same kind of brutality that was used against the passengers of the *Mavi Marmara*.

A sampling of some incidents over the past year:

- In March 2009, Tristan Anderson, an American activist with the International Solidarity Movement (ISM), was shot in the head with a tear gas canister during a nonviolent protest, sustaining massive brain injuries.[12]
- Bassem Ibrahim Abu-Rahma, a popular nonviolent activist in Bil'in, was killed when he was hit in the chest by a tear-gas canister during a protest in April 2009.[13]
- In June 2009, 35-year-old Aqel Sadeq Dar Srour was shot in the chest and killed when he tried to assist Mohammad Misleh Mousa, a teenager who was shot by an Israeli soldier during a nonviolent demonstration in Ni'ilin. Mohammad was permanently paralyzed as a result of his injury.[14]
- This past April, Imad Rizka was critically injured when he was shot in the head with a tear-gas canister during a nonviolent protest in Bil'in.[15]
- Last Monday, Emily Henochowicz, a 21-year-old American ISM activist, lost her eye when she was shot in the face with a tear-gas canister during a peaceful protest of the flotilla incident at the Qalandiya checkpoint in the West Bank.[16]

These are not merely isolated incidents. Indeed, they are part of a concerted Israeli military policy to crush the grassroots nonviolent movements by means of lethal force, mass arrests, and detentions. As Israeli activist Jonathan Pollak observed this past December:

> Over the past six months, 31 Bil'in residents have been arrested, including almost all the members of the Popular Committee that organizes the

demonstrations. A similar tactic is being used against protesters in the neighboring village of Ni'ilin, which is losing over half of its land to Israel's wall and settlements. . . . Israeli lawyer Gaby Lasky . . . was informed by Israel's military prosecutors that the army had decided to end demonstrations against the Wall, and that it intends to use legal procedures to do so.

The Israeli army also recently resumed the use of 22-caliber sniper fire for dispersing demonstrations, though use of the weapon for crowd control purposes was specifically forbidden in 2001 by the Israeli army's legal arm. Following the killing of unarmed demonstrator Aqel Srour in Ni'ilin last June.[17]

Few are likely aware that nonviolent protest was happening within the Gaza Strip itself long before the flotilla set sail. American journalist Ashley Bates, who blogs from Gaza, has written extensively about Gaza's "Local Initiative against the Buffer Zone"—a nonviolent campaign organized by Gazan Saber Al-Zaaneen:

In July of 2008, Apache helicopters dropped fliers warning Palestinians that they were not permitted to go within 300 meters of the border. Mr. Zaaneen knew that Israeli soldiers had shot at people and destroyed farms and houses within one kilometer of the border. Feeling that Israel would continue encroaching unless Palestinians resisted, he began organizing nonviolent direct actions in the buffer zones, such as accompanying farmers as they tended their fields and searching for bodies of Palestinians killed by Israeli troops and left to rot. . . .

Every demonstrator must not bring weapons and must commit to nonviolence. "I don't resist because I want to die," he said. "I resist because I want freedom, land, education, opportunities, no occupation. This is the message of our movement. We want the whole world to know why the Palestinian people resist."[18]

Last April, Ms. Bates reported that Hind al-Akra, a 22-year-old female protester, was seriously injured when she was shot in the abdomen and seriously injured during a Buffer Zone protest. At the time, Ms. Bates wrote that "it seems only a matter of time before one of the protesters gets killed."[19]

Just five days later, her prediction came true: A protester named Ahmad Salem Deeb was shot by Israeli troops and died of blood loss shortly afterward.[20]

Immediately following the flotilla tragedy, Ms. Bates cited this telling observation by an ISM worker in Gaza:

I'm surprised that Israel would go this far with internationals. . . . The reality is that they are doing this sort of thing every day with Palestinians—farmers and fishermen are killed every day.[21]

We will likely be debating what exactly occurred aboard the *Mavi Marmara* for some time to come. In the meantime, similar tragedies are occurring throughout the Occupied Territories on a virtually daily basis. They are no less worthy of our attention.

Discussion

Miriam
I'm so glad you posted this. It is true that Palestinians in the occupied West Bank have been practicing nonviolence, and it is even truer that most of these nonviolent peaceful demonstrations do not make it into the mainstream news media. It's as though the media wants our impression of Palestinians to be violent, brutal, and savage. And because of the checkpoints scattered within the West Bank, Israel has made it even harder for Palestinians to mobilize their nonviolent efforts. Just because we might not hear about it doesn't mean it's not happening. Thank you, Brant, again, for your courage to speak out and to model Jewish values.

Shirin
Arundhati Roy said that to be effective, nonviolent action requires an audience. By its control over the media and the message, Israel denies it an audience and thereby renders it ineffective.

As I am sure you know, the Palestinians have a strong, if virtually completely unrecognized, history of nonviolent resistance going back to the twenties and thirties that continues to this day. I would not be the first person to suggest that Israel fears this far more than it fears terrorism.

Y. Ben-David
Giving all due credit to the peaceful Palestinian protesters, do you think that it is possible that thousands of Israelis killed or wounded in the big suicide bomber campaign that was supported by Palestinian public opinion, in addition to the thousands of rockets fired at Israel from Gaza, might have something to do with the image of the Palestinians being violent?

Miriam
Of course it is a tragedy when any person decides to go [down] the path of violence, be they any person of any faith. But I also think it is important to recognize that our media are very quick to report when

there are such violent tragedies, and not the nonviolent movement that has emerged among many Palestinians. I'm also not sure that we can assume that such violent acts are supported by "Palestinian public opinion." This seems like a huge generalization. When such things are said, I always wonder how many Palestinians one has met, how many real conversations have taken place, and why Jews, who are a complex people, look at others with one-dimensional thinking.

Gaza Witness: A Conversation with Ashley Bates[22]

June 18, 2010

Yesterday Ta'anit Tzedek hosted an incredibly powerful conference call with journalist/blogger Ashley Bates, who spoke to us from Gaza City. Ashley's personal testimony provided an extremely important antidote to the misinformation about Gaza that we've heard bandied about, particularly since the flotilla crisis.

At the opening of our conversation, I asked Ashley to address the claims of the Israeli government that "there is no humanitarian crisis in Gaza" and that no one is starving as result of Israel's blockade. I also asked her to address press reports that cite the upscale Roots Restaurant and well-stocked market stalls in Gaza City as proof that things are not nearly as dire as critics are claiming.

Ashley validated the reports that these kinds of goods are indeed available in the more affluent areas of Gaza. She added, however, that the only ones who can afford them are internationals such as herself or a relatively small number of affluent Gazans. She pointed out that the Gazan economy has completely collapsed as a result of the blockade, causing widespread unemployment and poverty for an overwhelming number of citizens. Ashley herself can afford to live a relatively comfortable life in a rented Gaza City apartment. Unlike most Gazans, she could afford to purchase her own electric generator—so she is unaffected by the daily eight-hour blackouts that are a familiar part of life in Gaza.

Ashley said that she saw no signs of starvation, but it was clear to her that the nutritional needs of Gazans are not being met. Eight out of 10 Gazans are on some form of international aid. In the refugee camps, Gazans are essentially living on diets devoid of fruits and vegetables. As a result, anemia and malnutrition are sharply on the rise, particularly among children.

She also witnessed considerable numbers of homeless Gazan families whose homes were destroyed during Israel's military assault in December 2008. Most have moved in with relatives or friends and live in very cramped quarters. Others rent apartments they cannot afford, relying upon the largess of landlords. Still others are forced to live in unstable, partially destroyed residences or in tents next to the rubble of their former homes.

Ashley said she was not qualified to comment as to whether this all constitutes a "humanitarian crisis." She did, however, call it "a crisis of human dignity"—and it is clear to her that these circumstances are a direct result of the blockade.

Gaza: Humanitarian Crisis or Collective Punishment?[23]

July 2, 2010

More than one Israeli politician has commented that there is "no humanitarian crisis in Gaza."[24] Fair enough. During Ta'anit Tzedek's monthly conference calls with Gazans, we have heard over and over that Gazan citizens do not want this crisis to be viewed as a humanitarian issue.

For instance, journalist Sami Abdel-Shafi told us in March that he believed casting Gaza as a humanitarian case is ultimately harmful to Gazans (80 percent of whom are dependent on foreign aid to survive). That is to say, the longer Gazans are kept dependent on humanitarian aid, the longer they will successfully be kept isolated from the international community:

> As long as the so-called "humanitarian" classification continues, I'm afraid we can stay like this for years. But the key is, why leave a population of more than 1.5 million people almost completely deprived of being educated and being developed and of the opportunity to be effective contributors to the regional economy, in addition to the economy of the world?[25]

The answer (as I'm sure Abdel-Shafi well knows) is that this is precisely the point. The blockade of Gaza has never been about Israel's security. From the very beginning, its aim has always been to isolate Hamas through the collective punishment of Gazans.

Of course Israel has long tried to make the case that its blockade is meant to keep weapons out of Gaza, but this justification has grown increasingly hollow over the years. (The surreal revelation that coriander was on the "forbidden list" is perhaps the most infamous example.[26])

I've noticed that even Israel has become less and less inclined to defend the blockade on security grounds. This past week, it was reported that Israel's defense establishment is urging the government not to cave in to growing international pressure and to permit Palestinians to export goods from the Gaza Strip.[27] As one defense official put it, "If this happens, we will lose all of our leverage over Hamas." When I read this, I couldn't help but think about Abdel-Shafi's comments. What possible security benefit could Israel gain from this kind of economic warfare?[28]

On a more heartening note, I just read in the Israeli press that "reliable sources" report that President Obama will insist on a full lifting of the blockade when Prime Minister Netanyahu visits Washington in two weeks.[29] According to the report, the president considers the continuing travel ban on Gazans to be (you guessed it) "collective punishment."

Here's hoping. . . .

Discussion

Y. Ben-David

What is going to be the result of Israel capitulating regarding the lifting of restrictions on good shipped to Gaza? A big political victory for Hamas. Now they will be viewed as the "authentic" representatives of the Palestinians, if not the "official" representatives. What will be the consequences of this for those of you who believe in "the peace process"? If Abbas and the Palestinian Authority are conducting these negotiations with Israel, do you really think they are going to make the concessions necessary for such an agreement against the wishes of Hamas? If there ever was a chance for an agreement (and I don't believe there ever was), this will kill it. So I don't understand why the "progressives" who claimed to support the "peace process" were so keen on giving extremist Hamas this triumph.

Shirin

They *are* the authentic representatives of the Palestinians. They were duly elected as such in an election that was determined to have been as free and fair as any election can be that is held under foreign military occupation. Israel and the US could have saved themselves, not to mention the Palestinians, an enormous amount of grief by accepting the results of the election *they* insisted upon.

You are also misinformed as to Hamas's positions regarding peace with Israel. You ought to update your information.

Richard

Would you be willing to update us on Hamas's positions regarding peace with Israel?

Shirin

Richard, there have been a number of statements from various Hamas officials, including no less than Khaled Meshal, that they are prepared to accept a Palestinian state that includes the West Bank and Gaza with East Jerusalem as its capital. This, of course, implies strongly that they will also accept Israel within the pre–June 1967 boundaries, but you do not need to depend upon this implicit acceptance, because Meshal himself and others have stated explicitly that if it is the will of the Palestinian people, they will accept Israel within the pre–June 1967 boundaries.

The real question has always been, of course, whether Israel will accept Israel within the pre–June 1967 boundaries, and the answer has always been no. Even in the time of Ben Gurion, the answer was no, as evidenced by numerous of his statements.

Kate

As always, thank for a cogent posting, Brant. It is difficult to find similar wisdom *anywhere*. In the last month I have heard several *divrei torah*—from Conservative rabbis who belong to the minyan I attend in West Rogers Park—advising us all to batten down the hatches, circle the wagons, refrain from criticism of the Netanyahu government, because Israel has done nothing wrong and those who criticize Israel want to destroy Israel, etc., etc. I feel like I am in a time warp: Is it the 1970s, and are we talking about Vietnam?

Sari Bashi on Gaza:
Control without Responsibility[30]

July 15, 2010

Today Ta'anit Tzedek sponsored an incredibly informative and thought-provoking conference call with Sari Bashi, executive director of Gisha Legal Center for Freedom of Movement. We were also joined by Reut Katz of Physicians for Human Rights—Israel, who shared information about the medical infrastructure in Gaza and the difficulties faced by Gazans needing medical treatment.

Toward the end of the call, I asked Sari why the crisis in Gaza always seemed to be so central to the Palestinian-Israeli conflict. Her incisive response:

> I think Gaza is a bit like the canary in the coal mine. What is being done now in Gaza is being done to a lesser extent in the West Bank, and we will see some of the terrible effects in the West Bank as well if we continue on the path we are on. The concern about Israel's behavior in Gaza is that it is exercising control without taking responsibility. It is controlling people's lives by controlling movement and access, but it is not taking responsibility for the effects of that control on a million and a half civilians who need to be able to access all of the things we've been discussing.
>
> In the West Bank, that process is also underway. Israel is dividing up the West Bank between Jewish areas, where the settlements are, and Palestinian areas—and it is slowly disengaging from responsibility for what happens in the Palestinian areas without giving up on control of those borders and of movement and access. And it can't be both ways: Either Israel continues to control movement and access but takes responsibility for that control, or if it wants to disengage from responsibility, it must let go of control—and that also means letting go of checking for security reasons what leaves and enters Gaza and the West Bank.[31]

Chapter 9

The Peace Process Is Dead

August–November 2010

By fall of 2010, I finally came clean on an issue I'd been dancing around for some time and stated publicly that I believed the peace process was dead. In truth this was a position I had long since accepted, but it was enormously painful for me to say it out loud. As the peace process was—and remains—the central political focus for liberal Zionism, I was well aware that by saying these words, I was politically flying "without a net," as it were. The final words of my first post say it all:

"Yes, there will need to be a political solution to this conflict. But until a present justice is consciously attached to a future peace, I believe in my heart that the peace process will remain as good as dead."

The Peace Process Is Dead[1]

August 22, 2010

Israelis and Palestinians are going back to the table, but no one really seems to be all that happy about it. Indeed, I can't remember a time when renewed peace talks were greeted with such widespread cynicism. And that's when you can even read about it at all—as I scour my usual media outlets for news and commentary on the peace process, I'm getting the distinct impression that this kind of thing is simply not considered to be news any more.

The only significant piece I've read recently is Ethan Bronner's front-page article in Saturday's *New York Times*. The first few paragraphs pretty much tell you everything you need to know:

> The American invitation on Friday to the Israelis and Palestinians to start direct peace talks in two weeks in Washington was immediately accepted by both governments. But just below the surface there was an almost audible shrug. There is little confidence—close to none—on either side that the Obama administration's goal of reaching a comprehensive deal in one year can be met.[2]

I used to believe that where there's talk, there's hope. (In fact, I think I've even written those very words on this blog once or twice before.) I don't think I really believe this anymore—not, at least, when it comes to the Israeli-Palestinian peace process. For almost two decades, the US and the international community have been brokering talks between both sides, and now it's come to this: Beyond the pro forma diplomatic statements, everyone seems to agree that it's really just a road to nowhere. And a half-hearted attempt to bring the "crippled and the helpless" to the bargaining table simply doesn't inspire hope. Quite the opposite.

I'm not even tempted anymore to engage in an analytical discussion of how, why, or where talks have failed. There are still more than enough pundits out there ready to parse the political maneuvering. To my mind, it's all fairly moot at this point. So many of us have been working overtime for years to advocate for the peace process. But while so many of us have held forth the two-state solution as a kind of Holy Grail, the prospect of a viable Palestinian state has grown increasingly remote.

Again, from Ethan Bronner:

> Most Palestinians—and many on the Israeli left—argue that there are now too many Israeli settlements in the West Bank for a viable, contiguous Palestinian state to arise there. . . . Support for many of the settlements remains relatively strong in Israel. In other words, if this view holds, the Israelis have closed out any serious option of a two-state solution. So the talks are useless.[3]

As someone who has fervently supported peace talks from the beginning, I write these words with great sorrow: It is time to face the facts and declare that the peace process is dead. I respect those who honestly disagree with such a position, but for myself at least, I cannot in good conscience advocate for a peace process that is so fatally flawed in so many ways. For me, the much more critical and pressing question at this point is not "how can we get both parties to the table?" but "how can we find a way to extend civil rights, human rights, equity, and equality for all inhabitants of Israel/ Palestine?"

That's really the crux of the issue for me: Peace without justice is no peace at all. Whether or not there is eventually a 1-state, 2-state, or 15-state solution, it will need to be a just solution. And at the moment, justice seems to be precisely what is missing from the peace process.

At the end of the day, Israel simply cannot claim to take the concept of Palestinian statehood seriously while it establishes Jewish settlements throughout the Palestinian territories with impunity. Israel cannot say it accepts the concept of a Palestinian capital in Jerusalem yet at the same time evict Palestinians from their homes in East Jerusalem with a clear intention of Judaizing these neighborhoods. And perhaps most critically, Israel cannot claim to meet the Palestinians across the peace table in good faith while it oppresses Palestinians on a daily basis.

My friend and colleague Cantor Michael Davis once said to me that the real problem with the peace process is that "we are focusing exclusively on the future at the expense of the present." I agree. For far too long we have been using the peace process as a shield to keep us from honestly facing the very real and troubling human-rights abuse Israel is committing on the ground right now. Yes, there will need to be a political solution to this conflict. But until a present justice is consciously attached to a future peace, I believe in my heart that the peace process will remain as good as dead.

Discussion

Steve
Netanyahu said yesterday that a future Palestinian state would have to be demilitarized and recognize Israel as the homeland of the Jewish people. But of course a demilitarized state is not a state at all—it doesn't have full sovereignty and cannot defend itself. What he wants is a Palestinian colony or protectorate.

And this is what all Israeli governments have wanted. The idea of a Palestinian state, an actual state, has been anathema to Israel since the beginning. The so-called "peace talks" have never been anything more than a charade, a convenient holding action. And it allows the US to make another pious pretense of being a broker for peace and justice.

rbarenblat
What a depressing post. And yet I can't argue with your points or your conclusion. Where do we go from here?

Rabbi Brant Rosen

Thanks for your important question. Here's my preliminary list:

We bear witness to what is occurring in Israel/Palestine.

We speak out publicly as Jews who are passionately concerned about the futures of all inhabitants of Israel/Palestine.

We demand that Israel be held accountable for its oppressive actions against Palestinians.

We call upon our government to make all future aid to Israel conditional on compliance with American policy on Israeli settlement activity.

We refuse to patronize companies or invest in funds that directly profit from the occupation.

And perhaps most important: We ignore the accusations of self-hatred and Israel-bashing and encourage other like-minded American Jews to join our call.

Shloime

I completely agree with you . . . that any discussion about an overall peace settlement must not exclude a constant focus on social justice within all the microaspects of society in Israel. I would be interested in knowing what suggestions you have along these lines for Jews outside Israel who would like to contribute to Israeli/Palestinian reconciliation. How can we discuss these issues within shuls while not coming across as anti-Israel (an old problem, by now)? . . .

. . . We should emphasize that all the communities within government rule should be treated with dignity, respect, and politeness, not with violence, displacement, and force. I am thinking of Sheikh Jarrah in East Jerusalem, the destruction of Bedouin villages, and the attacks on the olive trees and the Palestinian farmers who take care of them. I am wondering whether the question "What would I do?" can . . . move us beyond polemics and can form the basis of a human-rights Shabbat. I'll just add to this the idea that human rights should also [encompass] rights for the Earth: that there can be no justice without respecting the Earth and the living world as a whole.

I think we need to emphasize the question "What would I do if I were there?" as a way of moving beyond polemics and toward personal responsibility. Whichever author or authors of the Torah came up with the idea of being given the choice between life and death—therefore choosing life—was on to a wonderful, even revolutionary idea.

Eric

It's not just that we're given the choice between life and death. Both are set before us in the Torah, *by* the Torah—which is to say, we can draw on material from our deepest traditions to support either choice, either impulse, the best and the worst of us. "Everything is in it," as the Talmud says; we can't just follow but have to choose, ourselves, day after day after day.

Lisa

I don't actually know why I am bothering to ask but, can you tell me exactly what the Palestinian "leadership" would have to do before you would write that they have some responsibility in the failure of the peace process?? Apparently, denying Israel's right to exist, misappropriating humanitarian aid, hiding behind women and children, and murdering innocent people is not enough for you.

Rabbi Brant Rosen

The Palestinian leadership participating in the peace process is the PA, not Hamas (as you seem to be insinuating). If one was to ask whether or not the PA was holding up its own responsibilities in the peace process—which means largely guaranteeing and maintaining security in the West Bank—I'd say the answer is absolutely yes.

In fact, security in PA-administered territories has improved so much that the PA has now been coordinating security arrangements with the Shin Bet and the IDF.[4] (It seems to me that it is a genuine sign of the PA's willingness to adhere to the terms of the peace process that it is willing to be potentially viewed as "collaborationist" in the eyes of many Palestinians.)

In my opinion, the US and Israel have utterly hung the PA and the moderate Palestinian factions out to dry over the course of the peace process. If, following Oslo, Israel had shown good faith by not radically increasing its settlement of the territories, then the PA would have rightly been able to claim that its willingness to participate in the peace process was making a real difference on the ground and in the lives of Palestinians.

Instead, Israel's behavior during this period has only neutered the PA in the eyes of its constituents—while strengthening the hand of such groups as Hamas.

Richard

I didn't know that the PA recognized Israel's right to exist as a Jewish state. PA-sponsored materials consistently deny not only Israel's right to exist but also the Holocaust! I think it would be a step in the right direction for the PA to stop disseminating materials that advocate the evacuation of the Jews from Palestine, and I'm not talking about the West Bank.

Rabbi Brant Rosen

The PA has recognized Israel's right to exist since 1993. The addition of recognizing Israel as a "Jewish" state is another hoop that Israeli administrations have more recently inserted into the negotiating mix.

For more on this subject, here's what the very astute Mideast analyst Mitchell Plitnick had to say about this particular demand:

> [The] idea of Palestine recognizing not only Israeli sovereignty and its right to exist, but recognizing it as a Jewish state is a deal-breaker. . . a willful wrench that has been thrown into negotiations.
>
> . . . Recognizing Israel as the Jewish State demands that Palestinians . . . acknowledge that the dispossession they have endured for the past 62 years was justified. Whether one believes that Palestinian dispossession was inevitable, criminal, justified by war or a case of ethnic cleansing, surely everyone can agree that asking Palestinians to make such an admission is simply unreasonable.[5]

Re "PA-sponsored materials": You didn't provide any sources for this claim. If it is true, I would only say that every regime has its odious elements. For its part, the current Israeli administration includes a foreign minister who supports ethnic cleansing, advocating the transfer of Israeli Arab citizens out of Israel.[6]

What are you trying to say about the PA? That it is too odious a partner for peace talks? Are you serious here? If so, maybe you should get on the phone to Obama and Bibi (as well as the Shin Bet and the IDF) and explain to them that they are all engaging with a rejectionist, Holocaust-denying, genocidal regime.

Peace with Justice? A Dialogue[7]

August 27, 2010

Since my recent post on the current round of the Israeli-Palestinian peace process, I've received many responses. Here's one of the most thoughtful and challenging, sent to me by a good friend who asked not to be named. My response follows:

Dear Brant,

As the Midrash (Leviticus Rabbah 9) teaches, "Great is peace, since even in a time of war, one should begin with peace."

Even now, when the prospect of achieving peace seems so remote and some in the Netanyahu government seem so hostile, we as Jews are commanded to pursue peace. This doesn't mean that we should be Pollyanna-ish about the possibilities of success in the upcoming talks, but neither should we give up before they've started. There is always the possibility, however remote, that Netanyahu will decide to take the bull by the horns and do a Nixon-to-China-like move. Those of us who care deeply must encourage the best possible outcome. After all, if these talks fail and the Palestinian Authority disintegrates, where will this leave us in terms of security in the West Bank and international credibility? Where will it leave President Obama, who has hinged so much of his foreign policy on resolving the conflict? These are serious and weighty matters for Israel and the US.

I know that the political maneuvering around peace talks can be very discouraging for those like you who are trying to improve the situation on the ground. Politicians make all sorts of moves that are hard to swallow. Hillary Clinton, for example, started out very strongly on human-rights issues, leading the way for international financial assistance to Gaza following the war and strongly denouncing settlement building in East Jerusalem. To get to these talks, she has become much more restrained in response to both the failure of the settlement freeze policy and to fear of attacks from the right wing (both Jewish and Christian) in characterizing Obama as anti-Israel. There is a place for politics in moving things forward, but it operates in a very different manner than truth-telling. Mobilizing support from people with a broad range of perspectives involves compromises that can be very hard to swallow, but until we find a way to win over broader grassroots support, this is the price we will pay.

I admire your decision as a prominent rabbi to telling the truth about the on-the-ground situation in Israel and Palestine. This is extremely difficult to look at for many of us, and yet you have decided to unflinchingly dive in headfirst. However, I believe that your framing the political process in opposition to justice on the ground is quite problematic and ultimately more harmful to your dreams than helpful.

I cannot praise your glorification of hopelessness and the messianic idea that we cannot pursue peace until there is justice. We cannot stop seeking peace, and we cannot stop seeking justice, and we must use all the tools at our disposal, including politics and including truth-telling.

Most importantly, if you really want to "extend civil rights, human rights, equity, and equality for all inhabitants of Israel/Palestine" then you will need every possible ally. Please don't make yourself the leader of an exclusive club that turns away your natural allies for lack of moral purity. It's so much easier to stand on supposed high moral ground and criticize those who imperfectly seek to bring about change than to do the dirty work of making it happen. In the end, we all need each other if we're going to move this forward . . . .

Dear _____,

Thank you for your very thoughtful response. After receiving a great deal of feedback—and rereading my post—I realize now that my words conveyed no small amount of righteous anger and despair. That was partly by design, of course, but it was certainly not my intention to "glorify hopelessness." Knowing me as you do, you must know that I am not a hopeless person by nature and that I've long believed that hopelessness and cynicism are luxuries we simply cannot afford in this day and age.

Although I will plead guilty to occasional bouts of self-righteousness, I ultimately consider myself to be a realist like you. I also believe that in order to achieve peace, we must engage in "the dirty work of making it happen"— this was in fact the spirit in which I wrote my post. I was not interested in claiming a "moral high ground," but in simply facing facts: I do not believe any more that the peace process as it currently is defined offers a realistic hope for a true and lasting peace between Israelis and Palestinians.

To say that those who advocate for justice as part of the peace process are more interested in claiming an ivory tower "moral high ground" than actual results is exceedingly unfair. I do believe advocating for justice to be as much a part of the nitty-gritty as anything else in this process. To be clear: It is not my position, as you put it, that "we cannot pursue peace until there is justice." Rather, I'm suggesting that as long as we ignore an inherently unjust status quo in Israel/Palestine, any peace process will ultimately be built upon sand.

In my opinion, it is time to stop pretending that we have any kind of level playing field upon which successful negotiations might be built. Think of it this way: When we think of a US-brokered peace process, we invariably compare it to past efforts, such as the treaties between Israel and other Arab states. But when it comes to brokering a peace between Israel and Palestine, we face an entirely different situation. When two sovereign states come to the negotiating table, there is a relatively balanced power dynamic. When it comes to Israel/Palestine, however, that is simply not the case.

In truth, the Palestinians are the overwhelmingly disempowered party in this particular equation. Whether we are comfortable admitting it or not, Israel's founding entailed significant injustice toward the Palestinian people. This historical injustice is experienced and reexperienced daily through Israel's oppressive occupation. Whether we are comfortable saying it out loud or not, Israel is the party that wields overwhelming power over its ostensible peace partner in this equation.

Moreover, Israel also enjoys a "special relationship" with the US, the party that purports to be the "honest broker" in this process. Israel continues to receive billions of dollars in annual military aid from the US, with which it obtains the state-of-the-art weaponry, equipment, and security apparatus it uses to maintain its occupation over the Palestinians, their ostensible partner in negotiations. In short, there is a radically imbalanced power dynamic at play here. And it is not unrealistic to suggest that this injustice is an ongoing impediment to the success of the peace process.

Rather than looking to past Arab-Israeli peace treaties, I would suggest looking to the South African experience as a more helpful model. Indeed, this was a negotiation between two unequal parties that consciously pursued peace with justice. There was nothing "'messianic" about this process—the successful peace brokered between whites and blacks in South Africa involved the very real, difficult work of restorative justice. In this process, peace negotiations were pursued in the context of the South African regime's acceptance of responsibility for its oppressive behavior toward South African blacks.

I realize how immensely difficult it is for Israelis and many Jews to countenance such a comparison. I fully understand the psychology of vulnerability experienced by Israelis and many Jews vis-à-vis their relationship to Palestinians and the international community. But those of us who advocate a realistic peace in Israel/Palestine simply cannot afford to look the other way on these issues for fear of alienating our potential "allies."

I remember that you once told me that "shaming" Israelis is not the way to bring them to the table. But somehow, some way, Israelis will have to find a way to reckon with the inherent injustice that has become a part of the fabric of their society. As for American Jews, although it pains me to say so, those of us who care deeply about Israel will have to find a way to look this oppression in the face and call it out for what it really and truly is. Then we will have to have an honest conversation about how far we, as Americans and Jews, will be willing to go to end our complicity in this oppression.

Unless or until that happens, I believe that the latest version of the peace process is destined to go the way of previous incarnations: simply formalizing inequity. This is not the way to a real and lasting peace for Israelis and Palestinians.

You opened with one of my favorite Jewish texts. I'll close with another:

Rabban Shimon Ben Gamliel says: "The world stands on three things: On truth, on justice, and on peace, as it is written: 'render truth and peace—and justice in your gates.'" (Zechariah 8:16)

—Pirke Avot 1:18

Thank you for your challenging words. Please know that I take them very seriously. I hope that our dialogue will help in some small way to clarify these difficult and very painful issues for all who share our hopes and dreams for Israel/Palestine.

Discussion

Shloime Perel

It's worth remembering that for some years, the discussion on a peace treaty has focused exclusively on the possibility of a final agreement at the "top," so to speak. We should remember that a number of years ago, there was at least one widely publicized Israel/Palestine people-to-people peace agreement. And needless to say, there have been many contacts between peace-seeking Palestinians and Israeli Jews over the years. It would be wonderful if all these contacts and friendships could contribute to a formal peace agreement. Can all these people somehow mobilize themselves toward that end? Can we make peace a fashionable, trendy thing?

Martin Indyk on the Peace Process: Hoping against Hope[8]

August 29, 2010

A commenter on my last post asked me what I thought of Martin Indyk's recent *New York Times* op-ed, in which he expresses powerful optimism about the upcoming Israel/Palestine peace talks in Washington.[9]

Indyk's article represents a picture-perfect example of the inherent inequity of the peace process as it is currently defined.

Indyk lists four factors that he believes distinguish this round of direct talk from previous attempts. First, he claims that "violence is down considerably in the region."[10] Thanks to the PA's security measures in the West

Bank and Hamas's in Gaza, Indyk explains, Palestinian violence against Israelis has decreased considerably.

His analysis, however, completely leaves out the other side of the equation: Israel's violence against Palestinians, which remains as brutal and oppressive as ever. The examples are legion: Israel's military assault in Gaza in 2008–09 that left 1,400 dead, and the structural violence of its ongoing blockade of Gaza, which is having a devastating effect on Gaza's economy, health care system, infrastructure, and Gazans' freedom of movement. In the West Bank, the IDF continues its armed crackdown on weekly nonviolent protests and has increased its arrests and incarceration of nonviolent Palestinian leaders. Home evictions and demolitions continue throughout the territories, East Jerusalem, and even in Israel proper.

Indyk's myopia on this front is fascinating. Indeed, it offers an important window into a fundamental injustice that currently pervades the peace process—a process where only Palestinian violence against Israelis is considered germane to negotiations. It might reasonably be asked: Is this process about delineating the terms of an equitable peace treaty or dictating the terms of a Palestinian surrender?

Indyk's second factor: Israel's "settlement activity has slowed down considerably." To demonstrate his claim, he quotes from the Israeli Central Bureau of Statistics, which reports that

[No] new housing starts in the West Bank were reported . . . in the first quarter of this year. What's more, there have been hardly any new housing projects in East Jerusalem since the brouhaha in March, when Vice President Joe Biden, during a visit to Israel, condemned the announcement of 1,600 additional residential units. The demolition of Palestinian houses there is also down compared with recent years.[11]

It is a clear sign of Indyk's abiding prejudice that he turns to the Israeli government for an accurate report of facts on the ground. I'd suggest a more trustworthy source: Peace Now, which has been indefatigably tracking Israel's settlement activity in the West Bank. According to its most recent report, "there is almost no freeze or even a visible slowdown, despite the fact that legal construction starts have been frozen for 8 months [and] that the Government of Israel is not enforcing the moratorium."[12]

The report's main findings:

- At least 600 housing units have started to be built during the freeze, in more than 60 different settlements.
- At least 492 of those housing units are in direct violation of the law of the freeze.

- During an average year [when there is no freeze] approximately 1,130 housing units start to be built in eight months in the settlements. The new construction starts during the moratorium constitute approximately half the normal construction pace in the settlements.
- Some 2,000 housing units are currently under construction in the settlements, most of them started before the freeze was announced in November 2009.[13]

This means that on the ground, there is almost no freeze or even a visible slowdown, despite the fact that legal construction starts have been frozen for eight months. It also means that the Government of Israel is not enforcing the moratorium.

In short? Indyk's claim is misleading and spurious. Palestinians have been reasonably concerned about entering into direct talks while Israel's settlement activity continues. As things currently stand, the "freeze" is slated to be lifted next month—precisely the same time talks in Washington are scheduled to commence.

For factors three and four, Indyk points out that a majority of the public on both sides supports a two-state solution—and that there really isn't that much left to negotiate anyway. He blames Arafat exclusively for the breakdown of Camp David in 2000, a failure that left "Palestinians and Israelis mired in conflict."[14] This is, of course, the conventional Israeli narrative regarding the failure of Camp David: The Israelis made a generous offer, the Palestinians spurned it, and the Second Intifada ensued.

This is a simplistic, one-sided narrative that has long been challenged by compelling accounts of the actual negotiations. Most famously, this narrative asserts that Israel was prepared to offer 96 percent of the Occupied Territories to the Palestinians. It has since been pointed out that this number more accurately represented the percentage of the land over which Israel was prepared to negotiate. It did not include, among other things, East Jerusalem, the huge belt of Jewish settlements around the city, or a 10-mile-wide military buffer zone around the Palestinian territories. In fact, after factoring in an obligation to lease back settlements to Israel for 25 years, the total Palestinian land from which Israel was prepared to withdraw actually came closer to 46 percent.[15]

Regardless of which narrative we choose to believe, it is clear that 10 years after Camp David, many difficult issues remain unaddressed. In the meantime, Israel has continued to expand its settlement regime across Palestinian territories, which likely means that the amount of land from which it is prepared to withdraw has shrunk all the more. Under these circumstances, Indyk has little cause to treat the current round of negotiations as pro forma.

For the past 20 years the peace process has been defined by the same basic—and one-sided—parameters. Each time the process has been rebooted, we've heard the same kinds of hopeful tropes that Indyk expresses here. Each time we've been told that we have an unprecedented opportunity for peace. Each time we've been told that those who criticize the process are the "enemies of hope." But each time, this flawed political process has brought us no further along toward a viable two-state solution.

Perhaps it is time to envision a different process: one that takes values of justice and equity as seriously as it does peace. One in which the United States acts as a truly honest broker, in which Israel is held to account for its violence against Palestinians, its oppressive policies, and its ongoing settlement of the Occupied Territories. Then and only then will there truly be, as Indyk puts it, "hope in the Middle East."

Discussion

Bob
As long as the Palestinians insist on the "right" of return, there can never be peace. I've said that to a lot of Palestinian supporters; none have been able to refute it. I get a lot of blather about how it is their right (it isn't) or that international law requires it (it doesn't), but not one of them could come up with a realistic scenario for peace in which the Palestinians didn't give up the right of return. Their best was that the Israelis would let them return, and the Palestinians, after taking over Israel, would act toward the Israelis with fairness and equality. A manner completely at odds with how the Palestinians act toward each other and how all Muslim countries act to their minorities.

Eric
Bob, the tone of your comment—smug, triumphant, glib—brings something into focus for me this Elul.

Setting aside issues of international law for a moment, the Palestinian "right of return" is about a whole lot of people who wanted to go home, mostly to homes that don't exist anymore. Now it's also about their children and grandchildren, who are also people.

And you're making fun of them.

In the Judaism I know firsthand, here in the US, a new commandment, never explicitly articulated, has made its way into our hearts. Right there beside "love the stranger, because you were strangers in Egypt" I've been taught—in Hebrew school, in youth group, in summer camp, in "Israel advocacy" training—something else as well.

Put into words, it sounds like this: "Mock the Palestinians, because you were driven out of Spain, Europe, Egypt, Iraq, etc., and you never whined about a 'right of return,' now, did you?"

Mock their arguments, mock their supporters, mock their stories. They're nothing but "blather," and deserve a sneer.

Look, I don't like kids being murdered on buses and pizza stands, or old folks blown up at seder. I despise the glorification of armed struggle. I remember the old demands that every Jew not born in mandatory Palestine should leave, and I've read all too many poems and speeches that say the Zionist invader has no real connection (historical or emotional) to the land.

But this self-congratulatory obligation to make light of other people's suffering doesn't do much for me, either—especially as a core "religious" belief, as central as the v'ahavta. It's sour, small-minded, and cruel. Why on earth would I want to that to teach my children or bring them up in a community that espouses it?

Thanks for clarifying all this for me. Useful comment.

mmayer

The right to return, which is afforded to all, is covered under international law as follows:

To gain UN membership, Israel formally agreed to the UN GA Resolution 194 in regard to refugees and to the Partition Plan, Resolution 181. They also signed the Lausanne Protocol in 1949, thereby reaffirming their acceptance of 184 and 181. Their whole membership in the UN is contingent upon upholding Resolution 181 and 194.

The Partition Plan, 181, "provides that the Arab inhabitants of the Jewish state shall be protected in their rights and property." Further, their own Declaration of Independence provides that "the state of Israel will be ready to cooperate with the organs and representatives of the United Nations in the implementation of the resolution of the Assembly of November 29, 1947 [the Partition Plan], and will take steps to bring about the economic union over the whole of Palestine."

Resolution 194 (again, which Israel recognized in order to gain UN membership) states that "refugees wishing to return to their homes and live at peace with their neighbors should be permitted to do so at the earliest practicable date, and that compensation should be paid for the property of those choosing not to return and for loss of or damage to property which, under principles of international law or in equity, should be made good by the Governments or authorities responsible."

Chapter 42 of the Magna Carta: "It shall be lawful in the future for anyone . . . to leave our kingdom and to return, safe and secure by land and water."

Universal Declaration of Human Rights, Article 13, (2): "Everyone has the right to leave any country, including his own, and to return to his country."

Under the Fourth Geneva Convention (August 12, 1949), Article 49 states: "Individual or mass forcible transfers, as well as deportations of protected persons from occupied territory to the territory of the Occupying Power or to that of any other country, occupied or not, are prohibited, regardless of their motive"; Israel ratified the 1948 Geneva conventions in 1951.

The Settlement Freeze: Painted into a Corner?[16]

September 27, 2010

The deadline on Israel's "settlement freeze" has come and gone. On the West Bank, construction crews are gearing back up, and the settler celebrations have begun. Abbas is mulling over his options with the Arab League. Once again, the peace process seems to be hanging by a thread.

For their part, many analysts are now using the metaphor "painted into a corner" to dissect the impact of the settlement freeze. Israeli analyst Nahum Barnea, for instance, recently opined:

Three politicians—Barack Obama, Benjamin Netanyahu, and Mahmoud Abbas—painted themselves into a corner and didn't know how to get out of it.[17]

And none other than King Abdullah of Jordan said this on the *Daily Show* last week:

We all got painted into a corner on the issue of settlements, unfortunately, and where we should have concentrated was on territories and the borders of a future Israeli-Palestinian two-state solution.[18]

It's bewildering to me that the issue of settlements can somehow considered to be a pesky distraction to the peace process. How can talks on "territories and borders" proceed with anything resembling good faith if one side settles these disputed areas with impunity and the "honest broker" to the proceedings refuses to rein it in? How can we be expected to take such a process seriously?

We already know that one of the main reasons for Oslo's failure was its inability to deal with the settlement issue directly. Israel took the opportunity to significantly expand its settlement regime during the course of the "peace process." This has brought us to where we are today: In the wake of Oslo, more than half a million settlers now live throughout the West Bank in settlements and small cities, with special Israeli-only highways that effectively cut Palestinian territories into individual cantons separated by military checkpoints.

Have we learned nothing from past experience? Here's lesson number one: The settlements are not a side issue. Israel's settlement of the West Bank and East Jerusalem are—and have always been—a central obstacle to the peace process. Until Israel is made to cease and desist, I can't see how the latest round of talks can be considered anything but a charade.

Discussion

Cotton

What is difficult to understand is how most official pronouncements and editorials in this country continue to "encourage" Mr. Netanyahu to extend the freeze but at the same encourage Mr. Abbas not to leave the talks, ignoring the inherent inequity in the situation. While the Palestinians talked for 17 years, the settlements doubled in size. The US should back up its encouragement of Mr. Netanyahu with significant consequences if the freeze is not reinstated. How would we like to negotiate with someone for a sip of water from a glass, now half empty, from which the other continues to drink?

Steve

Israel and Netanyahu are not backed into a corner. There is no advantage for Israel to extending the deadline. Obama, Abbas, and even Jordan's Abdullah could be considered backed into a corner. This is called negotiations. Israel is thankfully not desperate for the so-called peace process. Maybe the other side is more desperate. Instead of placing pressure on Israel, why don't we wait and see what the other side is willing to do for the so-called peace? This includes the Gulf States as well.

Miriam

All this is rather simple: How can those who claim to want peace continue to build on others' (future) land? Additionally, Israel acts as though the settlement building must continue immediately, as though there is no room within Israel. This is a myth—there is plenty of room (ironically in the very "forests" that Israel built over destroyed Arab villages) for many people to build and return.

Rabbi Brian

Once again, thanks for your cogent analysis of the peace process. I am at the World Council of Churches meeting in Geneva, where I heard Afif Safieh, former Palestinian representative to the U.S., Holy See, UK. I first met Afif when he spoke in Beth Israel, a small Reconstructionist congregation in Delaware County, Pennsylvania. He still holds a position in the Palestinian Authority, so he must support the peace process, but talking with him confirmed for me that your analysis is accurate. He still believes in a two-state solution but doesn't know how it is possible given all that has happened, especially the vast Jewish settlement. This was the goal of the settlers and of all the Israeli governments that supported the enterprise, left and right. They have met their goal. A two-state solution is politically impossible now. I can't see how Palestinians will get a viable state. I think the plan even by Bibi and the right wing is to establish a state that will be a little, but not much, better than Gaza.

   A bantustan. I lived with such "independent states" in my younger years in South Africa.

On Zionism and Growing Pains[19]

October 22, 2010

As cochair of the newly created Jewish Voice for Peace Rabbinical Council, I've naturally been interested in the fallout from the Anti-Defamation League's naming JVP one of its "Top Ten Anti-Israel Groups in America." According to the ADL and its supporters, JVP is guilty of any number of Jewish communal sins. The most cardinal among them, apparently, is JVP's refusal to call itself a pro-Zionist organization, thus making it *treyf* in the eyes of the mainstream Jewish organizational community.

From the *New York Jewish Week*:

> The JVP website depicts a group that clearly puts most of the onus for the ongoing conflict on Israel and conspicuously refrains from calling itself "Zionist" even as it claims its positions are based on Jewish values.
>
> "We do not take a position on Zionism," said JVP's [Executive Director Rebecca] Vilkomerson, who is married to an Israeli and has lived in the Jewish state. "That's not a useful conversation; we have Zionists, anti-Zionists and post-Zionists."[20]

Zionism is, of course, the litmus test of communal loyalty in the old Jewish establishment. I've often been struck by the fact that although political Jewish nationalism is a relatively recent phenomenon in Jewish history, it has quickly become the sacred cow of the American Jewish community.

Indeed, in the organized Jewish community today, nothing will earn you a scarlet letter quicker than terming oneself an "anti-," "non-," or "post-Zionist." So when the JVP politely declines to display its Zionist credentials at the door, it's inevitable that the Jewish communal gatekeepers will be poised to pounce. *Jewish Week* quotes Ethan Felson of the Jewish Council for Public Affairs (JCPA) as saying that JVP

> plays a role in inoculating anti-Zionists and often anti-Jewish organizations and activists by offering a convenient Jewish voice that agrees with what they're saying—as if that voice is not coming from a radical fringe.[21]

This is nothing new. Jews have been accusing other Jews of being part of the "radical fringe" from time immemorial. This is how communal authority is typically wielded: Leaders determine the reach of their power by marking the boundaries of what they consider "normative" and by attempting to marginalize what they deem "beyond the norm."

Of course, boundaries tend to be moving targets. Invariably, yesterday's radicals become today's establishment. The outsiders eventually move inside. And little by little, the new authorities are compelled to redraw the boundaries of the norm yet again.

The Zionist movement was regarded as a small and insignificant Jewish fringe when it was founded in 19th-century Europe. Although it feels like ancient history today, even in the years prior to the establishment of the State of Israel in 1948, there were many respectable anti-Zionist institutions in the American Jewish community (the Reform movement being the most obvious example).

And in truth, even following the founding of the state, devotion to Israel was still not considered to be the *sine qua non* of American Jewish identity. It was only after the Six-Day War in 1967—a mere 40 years ago—that Zionism came to be considered an incontrovertible component of the American Jewish communal consciousness. In this regard, I found this line in the *Jewish Week* article to be particularly noteworthy:

> In another departure from the pro-Israel canon, JVP does not specifically endorse a two-state solution.[22]

Wow. It's an innocuous claim, but when you stop to think about it, it's pretty astounding to consider that the two-state solution is now considered to be a mainstream element of the "pro-Israel canon." I well remember when the mere suggestion of a Palestinian state was tantamount to heresy in the Jewish community.

A history lesson:

In 1973, a group of young rabbis and Jewish activists founded Breira, an "alternative" Jewish organization that sought to put progressive values on the agenda of the American Jewish community. When it was created, Breira was a national membership organization of more than 100 young Reform and Conservative rabbis (including Arnold Jacob Wolf and Everett Gendler) and many important American Jewish writers (including Arthur Waskow and Steven M. Cohen). In its first and by far most controversial public statement, Breira called for negotiations with the PLO and advocated for a two-state solution to the Israel-Palestinian conflict.

To make a long story short, in four short years, Breira—a vital organization of 1,500 members and prominent young Jewish leaders—was dead and gone, successfully blackballed by the organized Jewish community.

Today, when I hear Jewish organizations, such as the ADL and the JCPA, trying to marginalize JVP, I can't help but think about Breira: about the arc of Jewish communal history, and how it inevitably bends from the outside in. And I can't help but wonder at an old-school Jewish establishment trying desperately to hold on to communal paradigms that are slowly but surely slipping from their grasp.

Bottom line? Jewish Voice for Peace is an example of a new Jewish organization that speaks to a young, postnational generation of Jews who simply cannot relate to Zionism the way previous generations did. Indeed, increasing numbers of Jewish young people are interested in breaking down walls between peoples and nations—and in Israel they see a nation that often appears determined to build higher and higher walls between itself and the outside world. (It's a poignant irony indeed: While Zionism was ostensibly founded to normalize the status of Jewish people in the world, the Jewish state it spawned seems to view itself as all alone, increasingly victimized by the international community.)

Whether the old Jewish establishment likes it or not, there is a steadily growing demographic in the American Jewish community: proud, committed Jews who just don't adhere to the old narratives anymore, who are deeply troubled when Israel acts oppressively, and who are galled at being labeled traitors when they choose to speak out.

Felson calls the JVP "a particularly invidious group." Witness the introduction to its mission statement:

> Jewish Voice for Peace members are inspired by Jewish tradition to work together for peace, social justice, equality, human rights, respect for international law, and a US foreign policy based on these ideals.
>
> JVP opposes anti-Jewish, anti-Muslim, and anti-Arab bigotry and oppression. JVP seeks an end to the Israeli occupation of the West Bank, Gaza Strip, and East Jerusalem; security and self-determination for Israelis and Palestinians; a just solution for Palestinian refugees based on principles established in international law; an end to violence against civilians; and peace and justice for all peoples of the Middle East.[23]

Is it any wonder why JVP is growing steadily—and why this growth strikes fear in the hearts of the Jewish establishment?

No, I'm not surprised when I hear the invective of the Abe Foxmans and Ethan Felsons of the Jewish world. Painful as they are, I have to remind myself that their words are ultimately a sign of our Jewish communal health and vigor.

Yes, I suppose growing pains are brutal—but in the end, we shouldn't have it any other way.

Discussion

Ross

I believe that the change to Zionism that many organizations made after 1948 or 1967 was just a surface change, because the opposition to Zionism of these organizations before 1948 or 1967 was not opposition to hitching Judaism to nationalism or opposition to the belief in salvation by military force. These organizations were as devoted to nationalism and militarism before embracing Zionism as after. They just added devotion to Israeli nationalism and militarism to their devotion to US nationalism and militarism, which is a very small change. For an example in a logo of the pre-Zionist position of these groups, see the website of the American Council for Judaism,[24] the one holdover from pre-Zionist Reform Judaism. Note the red, white, and blue menorah.

Ironically, Judah Magnes, appalled by Reform Judaism's support of militarism during WWI, saw in Zionism a way for American Judaism to detach itself from American militarism by creating alternative, non-violent Jewish institutions in Palestine. He might not want to identify himself with the label "Zionist" today, since its meaning has been replaced with the very things he opposed.

Y. Ben-David

It is important to keep several things in mind:

1. Almost half of world Jewry lives in Israel today.
2. I believe that Israel is the *only* country in the world where the Jewish population is growing.
3. Israel today is *the* major center of Torah and Jewish studies in the world, which makes it the spiritual center of world Jewry.
4. Israel's legitimacy and its very physical existence are under ongoing threat.

Yes, it is true that Zionism was only supported by a minority of the Jews in the world before the rise of Nazism in 1933. The pros and cons of having a Jewish state were subject to debate for a long period of time. *But history has decided the issue.* The state is a fact. The vast majority of Jews in Israel accept the Zionist creed for defining the state's values, and this includes, in practice, the Haredim (ultra-Orthodox) community. The majority of Jews around the world support Israel's Zionist identity as well.

Certainly Jews today can say they don't support Zionism. But, as I said, the issue has been decided, just in the way the dispute in what became the United States was decided between the Patriots (pro-independence) and Tory (pro-British loyalists) in the 1770s and 1780s. Same with the dispute between the secessionists and Unionists before and during the US Civil War. The loyalist and secessionist philosophies are not considered legitimate political positions any more (and variations on the secessionist philosophy lasted until the desegregation of the 1960s), regardless of how one may feel in his heart about these issues today. It is not legitimate to argue for the breakup of the United States today.

Same with Israel. Much blood and treasure have been expended in setting up and preserving the state. Certainly it is legitimate to argue about the exact nature of the state, the relationship to the non-Jewish minorities in the state, and what the exact borders of the state may be in the future. But an Israeli who sees Jews, particularly outside Israel, demanding that Israeli military officers be put on trial for "war crimes" by international tribunals, or Jews demanding that the UN condemn Israel, or Jews organizing boycotts of Israel has every right to feel that these Jews are *directly* working against his interests, whatever their intentions may be.

There is one large group of Haredim who are militantly anti-Zionist. They oppose religious Jews cooperating with the state of Israel and its institutions (although, in practice, many do anyway). However, their philosophy is considered on the fringes by the larger Haredim community and has little influence. And yet it is important to note that they restrict their opposition to Zionism to being an *internal* argument within the Jewish people. They do *not* participate in campaigns against Israel on the international stage, because they are acutely aware of the anti-Semitic groups that often attach themselves to these movements and they don't want anything to do with them.

Thus, Jews outside Israel who actively work against Israel's Zionist core beliefs and its welfare on a day-to-day basis, even with the best of intentions, are condemning themselves to irrelevancy in the larger Jewish community and in the very historical progress of the Jewish people.

Thomas Z

If you mean by "Zionism" the existence of Israel, then everyone in JVP agrees with you. If you mean by "Zionism" the territorial expansion of Israel through settlements in the occupied areas, then many supporters of the existence of Israel disagree with you. Those are just two extremes of meaning. "Zionism" can mean very different things to different people and in different historical periods. It's impossible to interpret your note properly without knowing which of the many "Zionisms" you mean. It's possible that you haven't thought it out yourself.

Why opposition to repression by the Israeli government should be suppressed in the name of anti-Semitism, especially when internal opposition is completely without effect anyway, is not clear to me. It would be like the Catholic Church's suppressing opposition to priestly pedophilia in the name of protecting the Church. The evil goes on, unchecked, while the facade appears fine—for a while.

What Would You Call It?[25]

October 31, 2010

I'm fairly sure that if I used the word "apartheid" to describe the socio-political reality in Israel/Palestine, I'd be tarred and feathered six ways to Sunday by the American Jewish establishment.

Meanwhile, some truth-tellers in the Israeli press are openly using the "A-word" because—well, because it's just becoming impossible to ignore what's really going on in their country.

An article in *Ha'aretz* titled "Segregation of Jews and Arabs in 2010 Israel Is Almost Absolute" argued that

> under the guise of the deceptively mundane name "Amendment to the Cooperative Associations Bill," the Knesset's Constitution, Law and Justice Committee this week finalized a bill intended to bypass previous rulings of the High Court of Justice. If indeed this legislation is approved by the Knesset plenum, it will not be possible to describe it as anything other than an apartheid law.[26]

And from today's *Ha'aretz*, a piece titled "South Africa Is Already Here":

> Israel's apartheid movement is coming out of the woodwork and is taking on a formal, legal shape. It is moving from voluntary apartheid, which hides its ugliness through justifications of "cultural differences" and "historic neglect" which only requires a little funding and a couple of more sewage pipes to make everything right—to a purposeful, open, obligatory apartheid, which no longer requires any justification.[27]

Don't like the A-word? What would you call it?

Discussion

Richard
Can you define apartheid? I'm not really sure what it means independent of South Africa.

Rabbi Brant Rosen
From Article II, International Convention on the Suppression and Punishment of the Crime of Apartheid, UN General Assembly Resolution 3068, November 30, 1973:

For the purpose of the present Convention, the term "the crime
of apartheid," which shall include similar policies and practices
of racial segregation and discrimination as practiced in southern
Africa, shall apply to the following inhuman acts committed for
the purpose of establishing and maintaining domination by one
group of persons over any other racial group of persons and systematically oppressing them.[28]

Among the "inhuman acts" specified in the Convention, I'd highlight
these definitions apropos of Israeli policy:

- Denial to a member or members of a racial group or groups of the
  right to life and liberty of a person . . . by the infliction upon the
  members of a racial group or groups of serious bodily or mental
  harm, by the infringement of their freedom or dignity, or by sub-
  jecting them to torture or cruel, inhuman or degrading treatment or
  punishment.
- Any legislative measures and other measures calculated to prevent
  a racial group or groups from participation in the political, social,
  economic and cultural life of the country . . . [including] the right
  to leave and to return to that country, the right to a nationality,
  the right to freedom of movement and residence.
- Any measures including legislative measures designed to divide the
  population along racial lines by the creation of separate reserves
  and ghettos for the members of a racial group or groups . . . the
  expropriation of landed property belonging to a racial group.[29]

Richard
Do you think a Jewish state is apartheid by definition?

Rabbi Brant Rosen
I think it depends upon what definition of "Jewish state" you use.
Which is part of the problem: No one can seem to agree on what that
definition means in practice.

Indeed, this issue was never fully resolved by the state's founders.
Although Israel's Declaration of Independence states that the Jewish
state shall "ensure complete equality of social and political rights to all
its inhabitants irrespective of religion, race or sex," Israel never developed a Constitution that would guarantee this equality under rule of law.

Which brings us to where we are today. In 2001, Adalah issued a
report that explicitly identified more than 20 Israeli laws that actively
privilege Jews over non-Jews. The most important immigration laws,
the Law of Return (1950) and the Citizenship Law (1952), allow Jews

to freely immigrate to Israel and gain citizenship, but exclude Arabs who were forced to flee their homes in 1947 and 1967.

Israeli law also confers special quasi-governmental standing on the World Zionist Organization, the Jewish Agency, the Jewish National Fund, and other Zionist bodies, which by their own charters serve Jewish citizens only.

Various other laws, such as the Chief Rabbinate of Israel Law (1980), the Flag and Emblem Law (1949), and the State Education Law (1953) and its 2000 amendment, give recognition to Jewish educational, religious, and cultural practices and institutions and define their aims and objectives strictly in Jewish terms.

Is the very concept of a Jewish state ipso facto apartheid? That's really just an academic question. In the end, the facts on the ground represent the bottom line. And by whatever term you choose to term it, I believe we should be profoundly concerned over the institutional inequity that has been established—and continues to grow—in Israeli society.

Richard

What definition of a Jewish state would not qualify as apartheid? I can't imagine a Jewish state that does not in some way serve the worldwide Jewish community, which you would then call apartheid. You can bring as many racist laws as you want, but they don't mean anything if you think that the mere concept of a Jewish state is apartheid.

Eric

Richard—it sounds like you're saying it's better to have a Jewish state with racist laws than a state without such laws that isn't Jewish. But are you also saying that a Jewish state is inevitably an apartheid state? That there's no way that such a state could exist without meeting the UN definition of apartheid? That strikes me as somewhat more extreme than what Brant is saying here.

Y. Ben-David

I presume "progressive Jews" are asking these questions about whether we should consider Israel an "apartheid state" in order to get Jews and other Americans, particularly the American government, to be prepared to consider [stopping their support for] Israel, because the implication is that Israel, by supposedly having these "apartheid" laws, has lost its moral right to exist.

Fine. But why is the question not applied to all the other countries that have such laws? For instance, the Palestinians, Egyptians, and

Pakistan all have laws giving preference to Islam. The US gives generous amounts of aid and other support to all these countries. Pakistan was set up *specifically* as an ethnocentric Muslim state, and millions of Hindus and Sikhs were expelled from the country in order to make it "religiously" pure. Religious minorities are suffering massive violence there by the majority Sunni population. Yet these "progressive" Jews, as American citizens whose tax dollars support this state, have never asked any question about whether the government should stop support for them. Only Israel is subject to this scrutiny.

In Kashmir, India has used massive force to suppress an uprising by the Muslims there, who are the majority. They want independence. As a result of this violence, tens of thousands of Kashmiris have been killed in the last 20 years: far, far more than the number of Palestinians killed in the same period. Yet the "progressive Jews" have never questioned American support for India, nor have they demanded at least the possibility of applying BDS to India. Only Israel gets such scrutiny.

We may hear, "Well, as Jews, we have to be primarily concerned with cleaning up Israel's problems." That is merely ethnocentrism. "Progressive Jews" are proud of their commitment to all of humanity. Time to hear about all these other problem areas in the world and not just Israel at these "progressive" Jewish discussion groups.

Rabbi Brant Rosen

No, progressive Jews are asking these questions, because no one else in the Jewish community is asking them. There is no "implication that Israel has lost its moral right to exist." There is only the implication that Israel, which is overwhelmingly the largest beneficiary of unconditional US military aid, the state that we consistently refer to as "the only democracy in the Middle East," and the state that purports to represent Jews and Jewish values, should be expected to respect values such as human rights, justice, equity, and equality.

Yes, we progressive Jews are proud of our commitment to all humanity. That is why we are represented significantly in the leadership and membership of such organizations as Amnesty International and Human Rights Watch (institutions that focus scrutiny on a myriad of nations besides Israel).

As far as BDS is concerned, that is not a call for Jews to make. BDS is a call that is coming from the overwhelming majority of Palestinian civil society. If some progressive Jews support BDS against Israel, it is only because they choose to respond to that call. (If there was a call from Kashmiris in India for BDS, I suspect many progressive Jews would respond to that call as well.)

There are many human-rights abusers around the world, and they all receive their share of scrutiny in the public eye. But Israel is the only place, it seems to me, where these abuses are actively denied or explained away by a vociferous movement of advocates and supporters. If it feels as if my attention is unduly weighted toward Israel, it is largely because as a member of the Jewish community, I seek to right that balance.

I can't help but notice that you have chosen not to respond to the substance of my post. The thrust of your argument seems to be: "Well, Israel isn't the only human-rights abuser in the world." For a country that seeks to be considered to be part of the Western family of democracies, that feels like damning with faint praise.

Parsing the Latest Peace Process "Breakthrough"[30]

November 14, 2010

From today's *New York Times*:

> Prime Minister Benjamin Netanyahu of Israel has agreed to push his cabinet to freeze most construction on settlements in the West Bank for 90 days to break an impasse in peace negotiations with the Palestinians, an official briefed on talks between the United States and Israel said Saturday evening.
>
> In return, the Obama administration has offered Israel a package of security incentives and fighter jets worth $3 billion that would be contingent on the signing of a peace agreement, the official said. The United States would also block any moves in the United Nations Security Council that would try to shape a final peace agreement.[31]

Let's parse this now:

According to Peace Now's most recent research, in 6 short weeks, Israel has all but made up for the construction it lost during the 10-month freeze.[32] So that means we're back to square one. And because the new 90-day freeze is "nonrenewable," this latest breakthrough is essentially meaningless (except perhaps as a face-saving maneuver for the Obama administration).

We're also told that the new freeze would not include East Jerusalem, which was likewise never a part of the last freeze—when home demolitions, evictions of Palestinians, and plans for new Jewish construction continued apace.

I personally find American Jewry's deafening silence over what is going on in East Jerusalem to be beyond egregious. Can't find it in your heart to address the humanitarian implications? Fine. But if you are at all a proponent of the two-state solution, you should at least be concerned that Israel's actions have now made a shared capital in Jerusalem all but impossible.

This latest diplomatic "breakthrough" is nothing but a fig leaf. Does anyone really believe that anything substantive will be accomplished during a 90-day settlement (non-) freeze? When will our community find the courage to name these dangerously empty gestures for what they really and truly are?

Discussion

Ken B

I certainly agree that not enough Jewish organizations have spoken out on the issue of Jerusalem. However, "deafening silence" is not true, because there are organizations like Ameinu who regularly speak out on Jerusalem. In addition, Ameinu has actually raised much-needed funds for Sheikh Jarrah solidarity. It would be great if you used your blog and network to help these activists on the ground.

Secondly, I would suggest a little more of a "wait-and-see" attitude. The past suggests that all of your pessimism and cynicism is warranted, but *if* (and it is a big if) the next three months are used to establish future borders, that would be a huge breakthrough on the road to a two-state solution. Instead of immediately attacking the Obama administration and the Israeli government, I would urge all of us to focus on the importance of these next three months, if indeed negotiations resume.

Mike

I personally find it amazing that anyone could call this a breakthrough or view it as a step forward. It is almost like celebrating when a thief has finished robbing one neighborhood and then moves on to another—do we [rejoice] and celebrate that he won't be back to the first neighborhood for a few months?

I cannot read the minds of President Obama and Secretary Clinton, but could they really believe this *nareshkeit*? How can they sleep at night?

Richard

Do you want peace talks to happen? If so, why do you feel it necessary to convince people that Netanyahu's offer isn't sufficient to make them happen? It really bothers me that someone associated with Jewish Voice for Peace, Peace Now, "a pro-Israel, pro-peace lobby," is not really for peace. If you want peace now, you should want Abbas to sit down with no preconditions. Talking is better than not talking.

Also, you are very conveniently ignoring the political situation in Israel. Bibi is not in the best place, especially after his first 10-month settlement freeze was ignored by Abbas until the last day. In order to convince his ministers to approve another one, these conditions may be necessary.

Bibi doesn't view East Jerusalem as a settlement. (Only the most radical leftists refer to Ramot residents as settlers. And many leftists live in Ramot, or Gilo, or Har Homa, or any of the neighborhoods that the BBC refers to as "settlements.") You think that not agreeing to give up Jerusalem renders peace talks useless. I think that not agreeing to give up the Palestinian right of return renders peace talks useless. But talking is better than not talking. Peace now.

Did you ever stop to consider that "our community" isn't cowardly, but that they just disagree with you?

Rabbi Brant Rosen

Talking is not always better than not talking. The most obvious proof of that is the fact that peace talks have been occurring since 1991, and things have only gotten worse during that time. Israel's settlement regime in the West Bank has more than doubled, Palestinian lands have been expropriated and carved up into cantons, 1.5 million Palestinians in Gaza are living under siege, and the prospects for a viable, contiguous Palestinian state are now more remote than ever.

Talking is only of use if it occurs under fair and equitable circumstances—and this has never been the case during the so-called "peace process." What we have here is an occupier "talking" to the occupied, while the party ostensibly charged with brokering these talks forges a "special relationship" with the occupier.

Central to this relationship is the US's willingness to offer massive amounts of unconditional aid to Israel—and to look the other way when Israel behaves in ways which our government believes are counter to the cause of peace (i.e., its unchecked settlement of the territories that are ostensibly supposed to be part of negotiations).

When peace talks of this sort are allowed to go on, they are worse than merely ineffectual—they actually run counter to the cause of peace, because they create the illusion of progress while facts on the ground are allowed to deteriorate with impunity.

To conduct talks, as you say, "without preconditions" only compounds the problem. This kind of approach assumes talks between two relatively equal parties. But when the power dynamic is so radically unbalanced as it is here, there will need to be some effort to level the playing field for the talks to succeed.

The most obvious example of this, of course, is a total settlement freeze of all disputed territory in the West Bank and East Jerusalem. And yes, this includes places such as Ramot, Gilo, and Har Homa. This is how to negotiate seriously and in good faith. The political persuasion of those who live in these neighborhoods is not germane to the issue.

I'm struck that you speak of these "neighborhoods" so blithely, as if they are already ipso facto part of Israel. But let's take Har Homa, for instance. Before the peace talks commenced, Har Homa was nothing but empty land. No Israelis lived there, and it was entirely contiguous with Palestinian areas. Anybody drawing a logical border would have placed this area on the Palestinian side.

Today of course, Har Homa is considered part of Greater Jerusalem and part of an area that "everybody knows" will be part of the Jewish state in a final settlement. This has been Israel's consistent approach during the peace process: Keep "talking" while continuing to create facts in disputed territories. Again, this does not constitute good faith negotiations.

The more insidious aspect of Israel's policies in East Jerusalem involves the evictions and home demolitions it carries out in Palestinian neighborhoods. Here it uses legal loopholes to literally drive residents from their own homes (or destroy the homes entirely) for no other reason than they are not Jewish.

I believe these actions represent serious, egregious violations of human rights, and yes, I do grieve that more in our community are not speaking out against them. I realize that there are those who might "disagree" with me—but I've yet to hear any defense of these actions other than "these people don't have permits" (the Jerusalem municipality makes it virtually impossible for Arab residents to get permits) or "Jerusalem is the undivided capital of the Jewish state."

If anyone in our community has no problem with what Israel is doing in the Palestinian neighborhoods of East Jerusalem, I'm eager to hear your reasoning.

Mark
Another interesting piece of this, as long as we are parsing, is that the $3 billion in arms sales for these weapons of death we are selling Israel will come back to the US—this is a sale, remember. So we continue to feather the nest of our military contractors (aka the folks the US Congress works for) as part of this abominable charade of a "peace process." It's a war process. It's complicity with the continuing construction of apartheid in our time. Way to go, Hillary. Kudos, Barack. So much for the executive branch running foreign policy. It's the Masters of War, same as it ever was.

Seth
I fully agree with Brant that this is no breakthrough. Rather than repeat what he has said so well, [what] I want to point out is that all Bibi agreed to was to "push his cabinet," a cabinet with a foreign minister who says that peace is 10 years away and who supports loyalty oaths and other discriminatory programs. Then there is the Israeli version of the Religious Right who only care about enriching themselves and protecting their version of a theocracy.

If Bibi was truly serious about negotiations he would dissolve his current government and form a national unity government with Tzipi Livni as foreign minister.

Y. Ben-David
Why on earth do you think things would be different if Tzipi were foreign minister, or even if she were prime minister? If you would just recall a little while back, there was a left-wing government under Kadima and Labor. Olmert offered the Palestinians the Western Wall, the Jewish Quarter of the Old City, and all the other Jewish holy places over the pre-'67 lines, but Abbas *turned the offer down*. Why do you assume a left-wing government today would be any more able to make "peace" than the current "right-wing" government that instituted a unilateral settlement freeze, something no "peace government" had ever done before? Oh, I forgot, the previous leftist "peace government" did bring about two bloody wars, though.

Seth
Frankly, I am not sure that things will be different with a unity government, but I am not convinced that Netanyahu and Lieberman are sincere in their actions. Let's not forget that Netanyahu has still not dismantled the "outposts," has ignored frequent violations of the

so-called freeze, and still persists in serious limitations on essential items for Gaza.

Sure, we can all look back, trying to demonize the Palestinians or the Israelis. From my perspective neither has done enough for peace.

Budrus and the Wall:
Palestinian Nonviolent Resistance[33]

November 24, 2010

Just saw the independent film *Budrus* last night. I think it's a brilliant film in so many ways. I simultaneously experienced it as a compelling "how-to textbook" on grassroots organizing, an honest portrait of real nonviolent resistance in action, an up-close document of the human impact of the occupation, and a compassionate profile of life in one West Bank village.

It is also a masterfully constructed film that often transcends the documentary genre itself. Filmmakers Julia Bacha, Ronit Avni, and Rula Salameh present us with a true story that has a genuine dramatic arc.

The story in short: In 2003, Ayed Morrar, a remarkable Palestinian community leader, organized a nonviolent resistance movement to save his village, Budrus, from being destroyed by Israel's Separation Barrier. He brought together an impressive coalition of local Fatah and Hamas members, along with Israeli and international solidarity activists, to resist the wall's construction.

After some initial success, Budrus was put under military curfew and its resistance effort threatened to come apart. In the end, however, after 10 months of steadfast resistance, the Israeli government relented and redrew the route of the fence, saving the village.

There is no question that *Budrus* is a profound and authentic document of what well-organized nonviolent resistance can truly achieve. It's the kind of story that would move you even if it weren't actually true. And I won't deny that the story of these villagers' courage left me deeply inspired.

And yet . . .

I must also confess to having a nagging feeling that there was one critical puzzle piece left out of the story. The film is essentially the document of one village, and it more or less takes place within the bubble of this village's exclusive universe. But I was somewhat disappointed that *Budrus* failed to explore the overall context of institutional oppression in which this one village's story took place.

The film does indeed explain how the barrier cut significantly into Palestinian lands rather than simply following the route of the Green Line. The filmmakers, however, never address the reasons why Israel chose to do this. There are many references to Israel's security needs, but notably, no one ever asks the critical question: Why, if security was the only reason for the barrier, didn't Israel build it along the internationally recognized border between the West Bank and Israel proper?

The answer, of course, is that this wall is not just about security. It is also very much about the settlements and about Israel's desire to create its own unilateral border in advance of a final negotiated settlement. To wit: It is ultimately about taking land away from Palestinians.

If the film had included but one talking head to address this reality, viewers would understand the true stakes of Budrus's struggle. But by leaving this context unexamined, the filmmakers essentially document one village's travail without really explaining how it fits into a much larger injustice.

In truth, it must also be admitted that Budrus's victory was, and continues to be, notably exceptional. While the film mentions briefly at the end that this kind of nonviolent resistance is ongoing in other West Bank villages, none of these villages has experienced anything near the level of Budrus's success.

In fact, the exact opposite is happening. The Israeli military is brutally cracking down on the leaders of the popular committees that organize nonviolent campaigns. And although this repression is not regularly reported in the mainstream media, it is in fact unfolding on an almost-daily basis.

Last Monday, for instance, it was reported that Abdallah Abu Rahmah, a leader in the Bil'in campaign, was denied release from prison, even though he has completed his 12-month sentence in full. Just yesterday we learned that the 16-year-old son of another jailed Bil'in activist leader, Adeeb Abu Rahmah, was arrested by a "a group of masked soldiers [who] forcefully entered the house without showing a warrant."[34]

Adeeb, by the way, was sentenced to one year but remains in jail beyond his release date as the military prosecutors appeal his sentence. He will stay imprisoned "indefinitely"—which likely means for a long, long time.

These kinds of actions, tragically, are taking a huge toll on local nonviolent resistance campaigns. With many of their leaders in jail or targeted for imprisonment, local committees (with the notable exception of Sheikh Jarrah) are reporting lower numbers at their demonstrations. Those of us who are justifiably inspired by Budrus's story should find these developments deeply, deeply troubling.

Bottom line? Please see *Budrus* and encourage your friends to do the same. Buy copies when it comes out on DVD and give them to anyone you know who needs to know that despite media portrayals to the contrary, there is a significant and important nonviolent resistance movement in the Palestinian community.

But after you see it, please don't leave the film with the impression that this movement is experiencing the kind of success you've just witnessed. Israel is quite rightly threatened by Palestinian nonviolent resistance and is currently doing its level best to crush this movement under its military heel. Alas, it is too often succeeding.

To learn more about these campaigns, you should regularly visit the blog of activist Joseph Dana (josephdana.com), who has been indefatigably reporting from the ground in the West Bank and East Jerusalem. (He's probably uploaded enough video onto his site to make hundreds of documentary films on the subject.)

And if the film inspires you to make a difference yourself, please visit the website of Taayush Arab-Jewish Partnership (taayush.org) and send a much-needed donation.

Discussion

gitel sura

I very much agree with Rabbi Brant's analysis of the documentary *Budrus*, which points out both the positive and disappointing aspects of the documentary. One thing to add is that the Wall affecting Budrus was built quite close to the Green Line, and its intrusion into Budrus agricultural land was more from indifference than for the purpose of land theft. Nothing much was at stake for Israel to reroute the Budrus Wall.

In contrast, the Wall built near Bi'lin and other villages lies deep within Palestinian land and is used to scoop up the village land for huge Jewish settlements and the infrastructure that supports them. It is there that the villagers' struggle to regain their agricultural land has gone on for years in the face of brutal repression, including relentless military raids into the villages, lethal force against those demonstrating for their rights, and imprisonment of the human-rights activists.

This is not in any way to say that the struggle by the people of Budrus was not entirely courageous and inspiring. It is to say that the film, which is has been widely released and relatively well-received both in Israel and the US, tells the truth, but not the whole truth.

Clif

I saw *Budrus* today and concur with your review. I asked a friend who is completely blind to the real situation in both Israel and the Occupied Territories to accompany me to the showing of *Budrus*. As I expected, he did not take me up on it, although I offered a ride and the price of admission.

Chapter 10

Toward a New Model of Interfaith Relations

January 2010–June 2014

For the past several decades, liberal Jewish-Christian dialogue has assiduously avoided the issue of Israel/Palestine—a phenomenon Jewish theologian Marc Ellis has termed "the ecumenical deal."[1] Slowly but surely, however, mainline Christian denominations have been willing to stare down the (often withering) backlash of the Jewish communal establishment by advocating divestment from companies that profit from Israel's occupation. In turn, Jewish Voice for Peace and other Jews of conscience are increasingly standing with their Christian colleagues at their national conferences.

I do believe we are currently witnessing a new model of interfaith relations—one based in a willingness to act on our common prophetic values. The posts below offer a glimpse into this important new interfaith movement.

Jews/Christians and Israel/Palestine: Rediscovering the Prophetic[2]

January 16, 2012

Delivered January 15, 2012, at St. James Episcopal Cathedral in Chicago.

I am so pleased to be here with you this morning—and so very honored to have been invited to preach to you today. I'm touched and grateful to St. James for your gracious reception.

I'd like to start with a selection from the Hebrew Bible: 1 Samuel, chapter 3.

In an earlier chapter, we've already read that Samuel was born under somewhat remarkable circumstances. Before his birth, his mother Hannah had promised to dedicate him to divine service if only God would only bless her with a child. In chapter 3, the young Samuel is now serving under Eli the priest at the temple in Shiloh. We're told that in those days, "the word of the Lord was rare; prophecy was not widespread"—clearly a literary clue that this was all about to change.

Samuel is sleeping in the temple, next to the Ark of God. In the middle of the night, God calls out to Samuel, and Samuel, who thinks he hears Eli calling him, runs to the priest, and says "*Hineini*—Here I am." Eli replies, "I didn't call you—go back to sleep!" This happens again, and Eli, presumably with even greater exasperation in his voice now, sends Samuel back to bed.

When it happens a third time, Eli finally realizes what is going on. So he instructs Samuel, "If it happens again, say, 'Speak Lord, for Your servant is listening.'" When Samuel is called yet again, he follows Eli's instructions. God then reveals to Samuel that Eli's priestly house is about to be punished due to the corruption of his sons and his unwillingness to rein them in.

The next morning, Eli asks Samuel what God said, adding, "Please do not hold anything back." And so the young Samuel tells Eli everything: the good, the bad, and the ugly, if you will. Painful though it must have been, Eli accepts God's word as delivered by Samuel.

At the close of the chapter, we learn that Samuel grew up and "the Lord was with him." As the text puts it, God "did not leave any of Samuel's predictions unfulfilled." Thus, Samuel quickly gained a reputation through Israel as a trustworthy prophet. He would go on, of course, to be one of the greatest prophets in Israelite history.

Now, on the surface of this story, there is sort of an endearing slapstick quality to the young Samuel's discovery of his prophetic abilities. Because of this, I think it's too easy to misunderstand the real source of Samuel's greatness. What made Samuel a great prophet? Was it because he was promised to God by his mother? Was it because he had the ability to hear God talking to him when no one else could—not even Eli the priest himself?

No, I believe the key to his prophetic greatness lay in what came next. Samuel learned a harsh and painful truth about a very powerful man—a man who also happened to be his spiritual mentor—and he was willing to speak that unvarnished truth to him. He did not shrink from his prophetic responsibility, although the chances were probably strong that Eli could cast him out for delivering such a message.

This is, after all, the essence of being a prophet. A prophet isn't someone who can tell the future—and a prophet is certainly not special for being chosen to deliver God's divine message. No, the essence of being a prophet lies in one's readiness to speak painful, difficult, often public truths to power.

We will soon learn a great deal about the wages of power in the book of Samuel. The Israelites will eventually come to Samuel and tell him they want a king of their own, that they want to be "governed like all the other nations."

Samuel is grieved by this request—like all prophets, he takes it very personally. But God tells him, "Don't fret. It's not you they are rejecting, Samuel, it's me. They've just never understood where the real source of power in the world lies, despite my attempts to demonstrate this to them over and over again. If they think that putting their faith in military and political power will save them, fine. But they will soon find out where that path will lead them."

Of course, as they come to discover, kingship in ancient Israel doesn't go so well. The new nation becomes focused on militarism, becomes incorrigibly corrupt, splits in two, and eventually gets overrun from within and without. During this period, it is only the prophets who continue to speak the hard truth to power, who rail against the toxic ambitions of Israelite empire, who warn that this path will eventually be their downfall. And so it becomes.

I will say that, personally speaking, prophetic religion is my primary spiritual inspiration as a rabbi, as a Jew, and as a human being. I am driven by religion that speaks hard truth to power. By faith that holds unmitigated human power to account. I fervently believe that when religion advocates the cause of the powerless, when it stands with those who are victimized by the powerful, when religion proclaims that God stands with the oppressed and seeks their liberation—this is historically when religion has been at its very best. Conversely, when religion is used to promote empire, when it is used by the powerful to justify their rule, when it is wedded to militarism, nationalism, and political power—this is, tragically, when we witness religion at its worst.

I cannot help but read Jewish tradition with prophetic eyes. As a Jew, I've always been enormously proud of the classic rabbinical response to empire. I believe that the Jewish people have been able to survive even under such large and mighty powers because we've clung to a singular sacred vision. That there is a power even greater than Pharaoh, greater than Babylon, even greater than the Roman empire that exiled us and dispersed our people throughout the diaspora. It is a quintessentially Jewish vision best summed up by the prophetic line from the book of Zechariah: *Lo b'chayil v'lo b'koach*—"Not by might and not by power, but by my spirit, says the Lord of Hosts."

As a twenty-first-century American Jew, I cannot help but view the world through prophetic eyes as well. Painful though it is, if I am to be true to my understanding of my spiritual tradition, I cannot simply look away when I see my own country going down the road to empire, when I see our nation enmeshed in a state of permanent war around the world, with economic disparity growing ever larger here at home.

To be sure, these are not issues of concern for the American Jewish community alone. In my own interfaith activism, I have been deeply inspired by my clergy colleagues and other people of faith who share this prophetic vision. For me, this is the most critical aspect of interfaith relations—the movements that are created when faith traditions come together to hold power to account in a time of unacceptably growing gaps between the wealthy and poor, the privileged and the exploited, the powerful and powerless.

However, in order for this coalition to truly thrive—more specifically, in order for Jews and Christians to truly work together—we are going to have to find new ways to *talk* to each other. We must not park our prophetic values at the door whenever our conversations grow difficult. And one of the most difficult conversations has to do with the issue of Israel and Palestine.

In my opinion, the issue of Israel/Palestine is the one area in which true interfaith cooperation tends to break down. However, if we are to use the prophetic model as a guide for Jewish-Christian relations, then our communities cannot shirk sharing hard truths with one another.

Just as the Jewish community does not hesitate to hold the Christian church to task for its anti-Semitic oppression of Jews and Jewish communities throughout the centuries, I do not expect the Christian community to shrink from fully speaking its mind on the contemporary issue of Israel/Palestine. We cannot and should not dance around this issue. To my mind, there is simply too much at stake.

This is, needless to say, a painful issue for Jews to talk about among ourselves, let alone with others. But I would like to emphasize that there is by no means a uniformity of opinion on this issue in our community. While I have strong feelings about this subject, I do not pretend to speak for my congregation or the Jewish community at large—nor should any Jewish leader.

But at the same time, prophetic witness means not shying away from speaking your truth because you're worried about hurting feelings. You can't dwell on the prospect of being labeled any number of names, and you shouldn't allow yourself to be bullied or cowed into silence. On the contrary, acting prophetically means speaking your truth knowing full well that there will be strong opposition, but with the faith that there will also be those on the other side who are ready to hear your message and ready to work alongside you in your struggle.

So I'd like to suggest carving out a new place for interfaith relations between our respective communities. Not one that seeks dialogue for dialogue's sake, nor one that engages in political bartering, but one that finds common cause in prophetic witness.

Indeed, I hold on to this hope for my own community as well—and here I'd like to return to our lectionary chapter once more. If we read this story carefully, we may well discover that Samuel is not the only hero here. There is also Eli the priest—who is able to hear powerful rebuke, along with a prophecy of terrible consequences for his family.

What does he do? He has the wisdom, the humility, and the strong sense of self to ask Samuel for the whole truth—and when he hears it he is able to accept it. He is able to hear this difficult, harsh prophecy and not react with anger or defensiveness—for he knows it comes from a place of truth and righteousness.

I believe that Eli's response to Samuel's prophecy provides a powerful model for my own community. While I fervently hope that we find the strength to offer prophetic witness, I also pray that we find the courage to accept it as well—to overcome the fears that keep us from finding true partners in the struggle for liberation in our world.

So let us come together by facing down the glorification of corrupt power. Let us work together to affirm loudly that it is not by might and not by power but by God's spirit alone that we will create God's kingdom here on earth. And let us find a common worship in the God that stands with the oppressed, the marginalized, and the vulnerable.

I look forward to working together with you in this sacred work and, once again, I thank you so very much for inviting me to join you in worship this morning.

Discussion

Sarah

Dear Rabbi Rosen,

I read your article, and I'm concerned that you seem to leave God out of the Samuel story. As brave as it was for Samuel to face down Eli, it was God who gave Samuel the message (and probably the bravery to deliver it). I think if one wants to consider oneself a prophet, one has to be willing to wait for God to give one a message. The point isn't to take down power just because it is power, but rather to deliver God's truth to those in power. In addition, I come from a faith tradition that teaches that God appoints individuals [the] power to carry out His purposes that may or may not be clear to us humans. Because of this, those in power deserve some respect (if not as a moral person, for their position). I believe that as a citizen in a representative democracy, it is my duty to hold my elected officials to account for their actions through the re-election process. I, and the rest of the electorate in this country, hold ultimate power (again, in this country).

I am concerned that the viewpoint expressed in this article is overly simplistic in equating power with evil and powerlessness with good. Everyone is powerful in some way and powerless in others. The point of life is to use one's power to live a moral life. Just some thoughts to ponder.

Rabbi Brant Rosen

Sarah,

Thank you for your thoughtful reply to my sermon. While I respect your point of view, I think we have some fairly fundamental disagreements about the role of religion.

According to my understanding of Jewish tradition, prophecy is not about "waiting for God to deliver you a message." The rabbis of the Talmud made it clear that this form of prophecy "departed from Israel" after the death of Malachi, who they considered to be the final classical/Biblical prophet (see BT Sotah 48b and/or Yoma 9b for the original citation).

For my part, I would have grave suspicions about trusting the word of someone who claimed that God had "delivered" him/her a message. And I certainly don't follow religion that preaches people in power are put there by God to follow "His purposes." As I wrote in my sermon, I believe that when religion or God are used by mortal power to justify that power, tragedy will inevitably result.

So where does this leave the concept of prophecy today? I believe its spirit remains in the original prophets' fierce stand against corrupt human power and their willingness to call it out. I don't claim to know God's word, but I am certain of one thing: I do believe that God stands with the oppressed, the powerless, and the exploited, and that whenever we do what we can to stand with them, we are necessarily doing "God's work."

I don't disagree with you when you say that power is not inherently bad and that we are all "powerful and powerless" in some fashion. But I would only add that the veneration of human power is sacrilege—and that it is all too easy for the privileged and the powerful to claim the mantle of "powerless victim" while they commit (or assent to) oppression against others.

Sarah

Dear Rabbi Rosen,

Thank you for your response, it was certainly thought provoking for me. I agree that venerating human power is a bad thing and that it necessarily leads to evil being done in the world. What we venerate is what we pursue regardless of the methods of pursuit. That said, when I said that everyone is powerful and powerless in some fashion, I was defining power as the ability to choose our actions. Our choices are always limited by various factors (hence we are all powerless), yet I believe that we all have the ability to fundamentally choose our actions (we are powerful). I believe that there are very few cases of "true victims" in our world.

One case that comes to mind is that of the Sudanese and Somalis, whose countries are and have been torn apart by civil war on one hand and drought on the other. Yet even there, some Somalis exercise their power of choice to victimize others by becoming pirates. I feel that once a "victim" exercises his or her choice to victimize others, he or she can no longer be classified as a victim.

This applies to the Israel/Palestinian conflict as well. I know there are many Palestinians trying their best to live peaceful lives, to raise their children, and to eke out a living. My heart is with them. But it is hard when I see other Palestinians using their power of choice to choose to launch rockets at Israel or to blow themselves and others up in Israel. At that point, in my mind, those Palestinians change categories from victim to "victimizer."

Here's to hoping that we all use what power we do have to choose good.

Rabbi Brant Rosen

Sarah,

I find it hard to accept, as you put it, that there are few cases of "true victims" in our world. I think this flies in the face of the myriad of examples of structural oppression that have existed throughout history and continue to exist in our world today. If we use the case of Jim Crow in our own country, I suppose you could say that many individual African-Americans were able to "empower" themselves in any number of ways—not least of which was their refusal to adopt "victim mentalities"—but we must not ignore the fact that they ultimately lived within a larger context of injustice and oppression. And that true, lasting justice did not take place until this structure of oppression was finally dismantled.

To be sure, every historical situation is different and complex, but when it comes right down to it, oppression is really quite straightforward. I think we all know it when we see it. And I think it is just all too easy for people of privilege and power to evade responsibility by claiming "complexity" and by saying things like "there are no true victims in the world."

In the same way, while I do not condone the use of violence to achieve one's ends, I believe there is an important difference between violence wielded by the powerful (i.e., the state) and violence initiated by the oppressed against their oppressors. Like most Palestinians, I do not support rocket launching and suicide bombing, but I certainly understand the context of oppression within which it is occurring. Quite simply, these are acts of resistance against a brutal and unjust occupation.

I Support the Presbyterian (USA) Divestment Resolution[3]

February 22, 2012

As a Jew, a rabbi, and a person of conscience, I am voicing my support of the divestment resolution[4] being brought to the General Assembly of the Presbyterian Church (USA) this June.

This resolution, which has been a point of divisive contention between the PC (USA) and some American Jewish organizations for many years, recommends that the Church divest its funds from Caterpillar, Motorola, and Hewlett-Packard. It was put forth by the church's committee on Mission Responsibility Through Investment—an appointed body that recommended church divestment from companies engaged in "non-peaceful pursuits in Israel/Palestine."

I am deeply dismayed that along every step of this process, Jewish community organizations (among them the Anti-Defamation League, the Simon Wiesenthal Center, and the Jewish Council on Public Affairs) that purport to speak for the consensus of a diverse constituency have been intimidating and emotionally blackmailing the Presbyterian Church as it attempts to forge its ethical investment strategy in good faith.

It is extremely important to be clear about what is at stake here. First of all, this is *not* a resolution that seeks to boycott or single out Israel. Divestment does not target countries—it targets *companies*. In this regard, the PC (USA)'s ethical investment process seeks to divest from specific "military-related companies" it deems are engaged in "non-peaceful" pursuits.

We'd be hard pressed indeed to make the case that the Israeli government is not engaged in "non-peaceful pursuits" in the Occupied Territories and East Jerusalem. I won't go into detail here because I've been writing about this tragic issue for many years: the increasing of illegal Jewish settlements with impunity, the forced evictions and home demolitions, the uprooting of Palestinian orchards, the separation wall that chokes off Palestinians from their lands, the arbitrary administrative detentions, the brutal crushing of non-violent protest, etc.

All Americans—Jews and non-Jews alike—have cause for deep moral concern over these issues. Moreover, we have cause for dismay that our own government tacitly supports these actions. At the very least, we certainly have the right to make sure that our own investments do not support companies that profit from what we believe to be immoral acts committed in furtherance of Israel's occupation.

As the co-chair of the Jewish Voice for Peace Rabbinical Council, I am proud that JVP has initiated its own divestment campaign which targets the TIAA-CREF pension fund, urging it to divest from companies that profit from Israel's occupation. Among these are two of the three companies currently under consideration by PC (USA): Motorola and Caterpillar.

Why the concern over these specific companies? Because they are indisputably aiding and profiting from the oppression of Palestinians on the ground. Caterpillar profits from the destruction of Palestinian homes and the uprooting of Palestinian orchards by supplying the armor-plated, weaponized bulldozers used for such demolition work. Motorola profits from Israel's control of the Palestinian population by providing surveillance systems around Israeli settlements, checkpoints, and military camps in the West Bank, as well as communication systems to the Israeli army and West Bank settlers.

Why is Hewlett-Packard under consideration for divestment by the PC (USA)? HP owns Electronic Data Systems, which heads a consortium providing monitoring of checkpoints, including several built inside the West Bank in violation of international law. The Israeli Navy, which regularly attacks Gaza's fishermen within Gaza's own territorial waters and has often shelled civilian areas in the Gaza Strip, has chosen HP Israel to implement the outsourcing of its IT infrastructure. In addition, Hewlett Packard subsidiary HP Invent outsources IT services to a company called Matrix, which employs settlers in the illegal settlement of Modi'in Illit to do much of its work at low wages.

I repeat: By seeking to divest from these companies, the PC (USA) is not singling out Israel as a nation. The Presbyterian Church has every right to—and in fact does—divest its funds from any number of companies that enable non-peaceful pursuits around the world. In this case specifically, the PC (USA) has reasonably determined that these particular "pursuits" aid a highly militarized, brutal, and oppressive occupation—and it simply does not want to be complicit in supporting companies that enable it.

I am fully aware that several organizations in the Jewish community are already gearing up a full-court press to intimidate the PC (USA) from passing this resolution in June. JCPA president Rabbi Steve Gutow recently accused national Presbyterian leaders of "making the delegitimization of Israel a public witness of their church."[5] The Simon Wiesenthal Center has called the resolution "poisonous" and claims that by considering it the PC (USA) is "showing its moral bankruptcy."[6]

These sorts of statements do not speak for me, nor, I am sure, do they speak for the wide, diverse spectrum of opinion on the issue in the American Jewish community. There is no place for public bullying in interfaith relations—it is, needless to say, decidedly counter to principles of honest, good faith dialogue. To our Presbyterian friends: *Please* know there are many Jewish leaders who stand with you as you support the cause of peace and justice in Israel/Palestine.

In a recent open letter to the PC (USA), Rabbi Margaret Holub, my colleague on the JVP Rabbinical Council, expressed this sentiment eloquently with the following words:

> Your Church has long been active in pursuing justice and peace by non-violent means, including divestment, in many places around the world. As Christians, you have your own particular stake in the land to which both our traditions have long attachments of faith and history. We particularly acknowledge the oppression of Palestinian Christians under Israeli occupation and the justice of your efforts to relieve the oppression directed against your fellows.
>
> To advocate for an end to an unjust policy is not anti-Semitic. To criticize Israel is not anti-Semitic. To invest your own resources in corporations which pursue your vision of a just and peaceful world, and to withdraw your resources from those which contradict this vision, is not anti-Semitic. There is a terrible history of actual anti-Semitism perpetrated by Christians at different times throughout the millennia and conscientious Christians today do bear a burden of conscience on that account. We can understand that, with your commitment to paths of peace and justice, it must be terribly painful and inhibiting to be accused of anti-Semitism.
>
> In fact, many of us in the Jewish community recognize that the continuing occupation of Palestine itself presents a great danger to the safety of the Jewish people, not to mention oppressing our spirits and diminishing our honor in the world community. We appreciate the solidarity of people of conscience in

pursuing conscientious non-violent strategies, such as phased selective divestment, to end the occupation.[7]

I am proud that my name is under this letter, alongside those of many other members of our Rabbinical Council. If you stand with us, please join us in supporting the PC (USA) divestment resolution at their General Assembly in Pittsburgh this summer.

Discussion

Jordan G

On a practical, application-oriented level as an individual, have you personally divested from any mutual fund investments whose portfolios include the stocks or bonds of Caterpillar, Motorola Solutions and Hewlett-Packard, the companies you listed in your post? Have you presented this idea of personal divesting to your congregation? Have you accepted monies for yourself or the activist groups to which you belong, e.g., fees for speaking from congregants or others who work for these companies? Would you? Have you advised your congregation and its leadership against accepting monies for dues or other contributions from congregants or others who work for these companies? Would you?

Rabbi Brant Rosen

This campaign is not about "personal divestment," as you put it. Having said this, I do make an effort to engage in socially conscious investing, which includes, among other choices, avoiding companies that benefit from Israel's occupation. Yes, I do promote socially conscious investment to others as an ethical practice. (No, I have not advised my congregational leadership to reject dues from members who work at Motorola.)

Ken

I don't understand your "dismay" with the activities of the Jewish organizations. They have every right to use their power and influence to effect change where they believe a great wrong is being committed. It's the same right that you and the General Assembly of the Presbyterian Church are exercising. Many Jews and Christians do not agree with the interpretation of history and current events reflected in the General Assembly's resolution and your positions on these issues. Why is attempting to change and influence a decision-making process, or the way people think, only open to those who agree with your positions?

⟨⟨

American Christians Dare to Speak Their Conscience on Israel/Palestine[8]

October 23, 2012

Cross-posted with the Jewish Telegraphic Agency

There has long been an unwritten covenant between the Jewish establishment and Christian leaders when it comes to interfaith dialogue: "We can talk about any religious issues we like, but criticism of Israel's human rights violations is off limits."

Over the past few weeks, we've painfully witnessed what can happen when Christians break this covenant by speaking their religious conscience.

On October 5, fifteen prominent American Christian leaders released a letter that called on Congress to make military aid to Israel "contingent upon its government's compliance with applicable U.S. laws and policies."[9]

While most Americans wouldn't consider it unreasonable for our nation to insist that an aid recipient abide by U.S. laws, some Jewish organizations, including the Anti-Defamation League and the Jewish Council on Public Affairs, lashed out at their Christian colleagues, eventually walking out on a scheduled Jewish-Christian roundtable. They are now requesting that the Christian leaders come to a "summit meeting" to discuss the situation.

Considering the vehemence of such a response, one might assume that the Christian leaders' letter was filled with outrageous and incendiary anti-Israel rhetoric.

But, in fact, their letter is a sensitively worded and faithful call supporting "both Israelis and Palestinians in their desire to live in peace and well-being," as well as acknowledging "the pain and suffering of Israelis as a result of Palestinian actions," the "horror and loss of life from rocket attacks from Gaza and past suicide bombings," and "the broad impact that a sense of insecurity and fear has had on Israeli society."

Yes, the authors of the letter also expressed their concern over "widespread Israeli human rights violations committed against Palestinians, including killing of civilians, home demolitions and forced displacement, and restrictions on Palestinian movement, among others."

As painful as it might be for these Jewish groups to hear, however, these are not scurrilous or arguable "allegations." They have long been documented by international human rights groups, including the Israeli human rights organization B'tselem. The letter points out that a 2011

State Department Country Report on Human Rights Practices detailed widespread Israeli human rights violations committed against Palestinian civilians, many of which involve the misuse of U.S.-supplied weapons.

Why has the Jewish establishment reacted so violently to a relatively balanced and religiously based call? Because by speaking their conscience, these Christian leaders had the audacity to break the unwritten covenant: If you want to have a dialogue with us, leave Israel alone.

A recent Jewish Telegraphic Agency op-ed by Rabbi Noam E. Marans, who serves as director of interreligious and intergroup relations for the American Jewish Committee, provides an interesting window into the mechanics of this covenant. In his October 21 piece, "Christians' Letter Is an Unworthy Tactic," Marans says nothing about the substance of the letter itself, choosing instead to attack the Protestant leaders vehemently and reject the statement as nothing less than "the opening of a new anti-Israel front."

Marans went on to surmise that this reasonable, religiously based call for justice was the product of "certain leaders" who are frustrated with "their own failure to convince denominations to use divestment as a club to pressure Israel." Nowhere did he address the issue of Israeli human rights violations (except to refer to them as "allegations"). In the end, he suggested that this letter represents "the anti-Israel sentiment of some Christian leaders and their small but vocal, energetic, and well-funded following who are attempting to hijack the positive trajectory of Christian-Jewish relations."[10]

It is difficult to read such a statement without concluding that Marans's definition of "positive Christian-Jewish relations" means anything other than "no criticism of Israel allowed."

It is important to note that the letter to Congress was not written by a few angry church renegades; it was authored by fifteen prominent church leaders representing a wide spectrum of the Protestant faith community, including the Presbyterian Church (USA), the Evangelical Lutheran Church in America, the United Methodist Church, the National Council of Churches, the United Church of Christ, the Christian Church (Disciples of Christ), the American Friends Service Committee (a Quaker agency), and the Mennonite Central Committee.

While it is painful to read such accusations leveled at respected Christian leaders by a Jewish director of interreligious and intergroup relations, it is even more saddening that some Jewish organizations have chosen to walk away from a scheduled interfaith roundtable, then demand that the Christian leaders attend a "summit" on their own dictated terms.

It is not the role of Jewish organizations to dictate how their Christian partners can live out their conscience or their values, no matter how much they may disagree. Unpleasant realities cannot be discarded simply because these organizations regard such issues as off limits.

We can only hope that these Christian leaders will stand firm and that this sad episode will lead us to a new kind of interfaith covenant—one based on trust and respect, a willingness to face down our fear and suspicion of one another, and a readiness to discuss the painful, difficult issues that may divide us.

Will the American Jewish establishment be up to such a task?

Discussion

Dovid K

Since Jordan "invited" Israel into the disputed territories in 1967, life expectancy among the Arabs living there went from 48 years to 72 (compared with an average of 68 years for all the countries of the Middle East and North Africa), and Israeli medical programs reduced the infant-mortality rate of 60 per 1,000 live births in 1967 to 15 per 1,000 in 2000 (in Iraq the rate was 64; in Egypt, 40; in Jordan, 23; in Syria, 22). In addition, under Israel's systematic program of inoculation, childhood diseases like polio, whooping cough, tetanus, and measles were eradicated.

Isn't it obvious that you should be singing the praises of Israel's presence in the disputed territories?

Vicky

Firstly, I think you should note the difference between correlation and causation. The occupied territories [OPT] enjoyed a general economic boom post-'67 that aided quality of life. According to the World Bank's report on OPT economic development, this was partially attributable to a sharp increase in the number of educated Palestinians taking jobs in the Gulf states. Work in Israel—in primarily menial jobs—was also a contributory factor. The idea that anyone should be "singing the praises" of an occupying power because they improved the natives' lot by allowing them to clean the toilets is disturbingly paternalistic. That line of thinking went out of vogue with the British empire—or it should have done.

As for medical provision, it is impossible to talk about Israel's former role in the provision of healthcare in the OPT without mentioning the discrimination that existed. Neve Gordon flagged this up nearly twenty years ago, pointing out that government expenditure per capita on health care was $500 in Israel and between $18 and $20 in the OPT. The discrepancy is huge, and it clearly shows what kind of life the government values most. Quite aside from this, the occupation has also jeopardized Palestinian health and wellbeing in myriad ways—five minutes away from me in Bethlehem is a young woman who suffered a terrible bereavement as a child because it took the army over two hours to allow the ambulance to pass (and this after they shot her mother).

That young lady is just one of many. Then imagine what chronic water shortages mean for hospitals. What it's like to be a doctor who is barred from travelling to medical conferences, to be a mother giving birth at a checkpoint, to be a psychiatric team trying to treat trauma-related mental health conditions in an area where being traumatized is the norm and not the exception. The list goes on, and I wonder if you would feel able to bring up your line of argument ("But we run such a humane zoo—you'd be so much worse off without us . . .") in the presence of these people.

To my knowledge, the youngest child to have been arrested by the Israeli army to date is five years old. (Yahya al-Rishaq from Silwan.) The youngest attempted arrest involved a two-year-old in Kufr Qaddoum. Between five hundred and seven hundred children are arrested every single year (the preferred time being the middle of the night, as though to create maximum fear and disruption), usually on a charge of stone-throwing but often on no charge at all. In the face of this and all the other abuses that happen here, the church leaders' request that the US makes its military aid to Israel "contingent upon its government's compliance with applicable U.S. laws and policies" seems more than reasonable.

Sylvia

"Some Jewish organizations, including the Anti-Defamation League and the Jewish Council on Public Affairs, lashed out at their Christian colleagues, eventually walking out on a scheduled Jewish-Christian roundtable. They are now requesting that the Christian leaders come to a 'summit meeting' to discuss the situation."

Bad move, if anyone asks me.

What they should do is let Congress investigate the nature and purpose of that aid. I am confident that once they realize that two Iron Dome systems are insufficient to insure the protection of the Southern civilian population from rocket attacks from Gaza, they will increase that aid.

The two iron dome systems intercepted seven rockets out of eighty. This is 10% of what is needed.

And oh, they shouldn't forget while they're investigating, the cash given to the Palestinians this year which they have used to acquire bombs used against Jewish civilian refugees from Arab countries who live in the underdeveloped towns along the Gaza border.

I do not doubt for a moment that the moral conscience of the 15 churches will be just as moved by bombs on Jewish civilians as it is by anti-Palestinian graffiti.

Vicky

The US provides no military aid to fighters in the Gaza Strip. It does provide such aid to Israel, however, and therefore it should perhaps take more interest [in] how the Israeli military conducts itself. In the February of this year, sixteen-year-old Hanin Abu Jalala died from lung fibrosis, caused by white phosphorous. She spent the last three years of her short life in agonizing pain. She didn't die because of some defensive measure, because the Israeli army was trying to save you.

I could compare the Israeli and Palestinian civilian death tolls here or talk about the statistical likelihood of a resident of southern Israel being killed by a missile, but such comparisons make me uncomfortable. Human life is not something that should be quantified like that. It's enough to say here that there have been an awful lot of Hanins on the other side of that fence. I doubt you even know the name of one. Knowing them would be a better strategy for improving Israeli safety than hoping for the IDF to get some shiny new killing toys from the U.S. (you know as well as I do that Iron Dome is not the only thing the U.S. is funding—I doubt the churches would have such a problem if it were).

Your comment suggests that you are not thinking of people in Gaza as families and individuals who bear their own suffering, just as "Arabs"—the same amorphous crowd of people who are responsible for the situation of Mizrahi Jews in development towns. As though people in Gaza today are somehow responsible for the current Israeli government's urban budgetary allocations, the decision of a past government to house Mizrahi arrivals on the periphery, and what happened to Arab Jews in their former home countries. This is not about Arabs versus Jews. If you insist on conceptualizing like that, you cannot be surprised if people in the Abu Jalala family's position look at the rocket fire on the south and ask why they should care about that amorphous mass of people over there.

Recently a good friend of mine completed an MA in the U.K. It was the first time in her life that she left the Strip, thanks to a scholarship program for Gazan students. In the U.K. she "met" an Israeli for the first time. The girl sat down next to her at a fundraiser for the scholarship program, flipped open her phone, and began chatting in Hebrew. Sameeha froze. She spent several minutes wanting to talk to this girl and feverishly working out ways to open the conversation. In the end she decided that it was too difficult, and she left. Even "hello" was too hard.

This is the real serious problem here, not the fact that some churches want to cut down on the USA's flow of complimentary bombs and guns. When Rabbi Brant wrote the blog post series about the trip some of his congregation took to Rwanda, he quoted a victim of the Tutsi genocide: "If you knew me, you wouldn't kill me." Works both ways.

Some Final Thoughts on the United Methodist Divestment Vote[11]

May 7, 2012

After the United Methodist divestment resolution was voted down at the UM General Conference last week,[12] I've received my fair share of gloating responses from divestment opponents. (Award for the most colorful goes to "Tzahal," who sent in this attention-grabber: "BDS Fail, you f***ing KAPO.")

Actually, while many of us were disappointed by the final vote, I don't view this as a "fail." Not by a long shot.

First of all, as I reported from Tampa, I was deeply inspired to meet so many remarkable activists—Christians, Muslims, Palestinians, Israelis, and American Jews—who constitute a new community of conscience working for justice in Israel/Palestine.[13] This new interfaith/interethnic coalition is growing rapidly, and we are most certainly succeeding in raising conscience and awareness each time these kinds of resolutions are brought forth.

Beyond the final vote on this one specific resolution, we should consider it a success that these issues are increasingly discussed publicly by our religious communities. My fellow activists and I had numerous conversations with delegates in the convention hall and were heartened to engage so many people so honestly on this difficult issue. I was particularly gratified to speak with the numerous African delegates (who constituted 40 percent of the convention), who immediately understood the very real parallels to the legacy of colonialism in their own countries.

In addition, as my fellow activist Anna Baltzer recently pointed out,[14] while the divestment resolution did not ultimately pass, the UM General Conference did adopt a resolution that among other things urged the US government to "end all military aid to the region," called on all nations "to prohibit . . . any financial support by individuals or organizations for the construction and maintenance of settlements," and "to prohibit . . . the import of products made by companies in Israeli settlements on Palestinian land."[15]

I am coming away from this experience more convinced than ever that divestment is a critical tool in our quest for a just peace in Israel/Palestine. Over and over, I've heard that divestment is an unduly harsh and polarizing tactic—and that the emphasis should be on positive engagement and investment. This despite the fact that decades of political engagement by our government have failed miserably. This despite almost a decade's worth of failed attempts by church groups to engage companies such as Caterpillar, Motorola, and Hewlett/Packard—companies that literally profit from an oppressive, illegal occupation.

Add to this the testimonials of numerous Palestinian leaders who addressed the red herring of "positive investment" by explaining it wasn't charity they needed, but real, actual justice. In the words of Zahi Khouri, a prominent Palestinian Christian businessman and CEO of Coca-Cola Palestine:

> It may shock you, but whenever there is a viable project identified in Palestine, we can raise the funds. We don't need your financial help, your charity. What we need is to be able to operate freely. Divestment is the best, most immediate way that you can help us achieve that. We have been waiting for more than forty years; we need action now.[16]

Archbishop Desmond Tutu was so correct when he urged support of the divestment resolution by invoking Martin Luther King Jr.'s "Letter from a Birmingham Jail."[17] Then, as now, those who sought justice were counseled by religious leaders to "be patient" and to address the issue of oppression through engagement and non-confrontational tactics. Then, as now, there was an assumption that those who wielded corrupt power could somehow be "convinced" to give up their power voluntarily. Then, as now, this kind of patronizing counsel rings hollow and false in the ears of those who continue to suffer daily from ongoing injustice and persecution.

No, this was not a fail. There is a movement building, and this was only the beginning. Stay tuned. Similar resolutions will soon be considered in Pittsburgh at the General Assembly of the Presbyterian Church (USA) and the General Convention of the Episcopal Church in Indianapolis.

My new colleagues and I look forward to continuing this sacred work together.

⟨𝒮⟩

Zionism Unsettled—A Smart and Gutsy New Church Study Guide[18]

February 5, 2014

Just received my copy of *Zionism: Unsettled*[19]—an exciting new church study guide published by the Israel/Palestine Mission Network (IPMN) of the Presbyterian Church (USA). As someone who has been collaborating with Protestant church denominations on the issue of Israel/Palestine for a number of years now, I can say without hesitation that this is a much-needed resource: smart and gutsy and immensely important.

Zionism Unsettled is based on the upcoming anthology *Zionism and the Quest for Justice in the Holy Land*, to be published this summer by Wipf and Stock. While the anthology will be fairly academic in tone, *Zionism Unsettled* has digested its contents into a book and DVD for use by lay-people in congregational study settings. I'm thrilled that the IPMN has made this resource available to reach a much wider audience. (It was my honor to contribute an essay to that book, which has been adapted for a chapter in this study guide.)

Zionism Unsettled unsparingly examines Jewish and Christian forms of Zionism—with special attention to the way they have historically provided theological and ideological "cover" for the dispossession of the Palestinian people. It's a critical emphasis; indeed, while there are no lack of political analyses on this subject, far less attention has been paid to the ways in which religious ideology has shaped the political context in Israel/Palestine.

This guide fills that void powerfully with careful, impressively researched chapters on the history of political Zionism as well as examinations of evangelical and mainline Protestant Zionism. My own chapter, "A Jewish Theology of Liberation," proposes a Jewish alternative to land-based nationalism—namely, a Judaism based in values of universal values of justice and dignity for *all* who live in the land.

As a Jew, I'm especially appreciative that while *Zionism Unsettled* is strongly critical of Zionism, it doesn't flinch from extensive Christian self-criticism. The guide is particularly candid in its examination of the oppressive legacy of the post-Constantinian Church, replacement theology, and Christian anti-Semitism in general. In fact, throughout the guide there is a strong and palpable critique of exceptionalism of all stripes. In the end, the most basic criticism of *Zionism Unsettled* is leveled against the triumphalist claims of every empire that has conquered and colonized this land throughout the centuries:

> Exceptionalism is not unique to Zionism; rather it is present whenever exceptionalist religious ideology is fused with political power. Christian exceptionalist beliefs and actions contributed to the Nazi Holocaust, the genocide of Native Americans, and countless other instances of tragic brutality. Exceptionalist doctrines and behaviors within Islam have contributed to grievous human rights abuses such as the massacres during the closing days of the Ottoman Empire which crescendoed with the Armenian genocide in 1915.[20]

This is not to say I personally agree with everything in this guide. In particular, I'm not at all comfortable with the theological analysis of Dr. Gary Burge, who rightly criticizes Christian replacement theology (the belief that the Jewish covenant with God has been "replaced" by a new covenant in Christ), yet seems to reaffirm it when he suggests a concept of a "'suspended blessing' that will be restored at the end of history when 'all Israel will be saved.'"[21] It's not at all clear to me how this conception differs fundamentally from the "one covenant" theology he purports to disavow.

I was also disappointed by the chapter titled "A Palestinian Muslim Experience with Zionism," which does not at all apply to Islam the kind of critical pedagogy that characterizes the chapters on Christianity and Judaism. While this chapter rightly spotlights "the inclusive theology of the Qur'an," it fails to explore exceptionalist manifestations of Islam in the same unsparing manner that pervades the rest of the book. As a result, this chapter feels to me somewhat tacked on and represents a bit of a missed opportunity.

Despite my issues with *Zionism Unsettled*, however, I nonetheless find it to be a courageous work that has the potential to be a genuine game-changer in interfaith conversations over Israel/Palestine. While I have no doubt it will be enormously controversial in many liberal religious circles, I believe it is an essential resource that boldly reframes the terms of interfaith encounter in ways that are long overdue.

I deeply admire its bravery and look forward to the conversations it will most certainly inspire.

Discussion

Vicky
Interesting. Even though I am a Christian myself, Christian Zionism as a theological outlook (as opposed to a manifestation of post-Holocaust guilt) has always felt alien to me. Not being from the evangelical

Protestant circles where it's common, I haven't had much personal contact with it. But when I think about it, this Bible passage comes to mind: "Jesus also suffered outside the city gate to make the people holy through his own blood. Let us, then, go to him outside the camp, bearing the disgrace he bore. For here we do not have an enduring city, but we are looking for the city that is to come" (Hebrews 13:13–14).

As I read that passage, the exhortation to "go to him outside the camp" fits with Jesus's own teaching that we should look for him in prisoners, sick people, the desperately poor—people who are excluded and marginalized from society for whatever reason. ("Whatever you do to the least of these my brothers, you do also to me.") "For here we have no abiding city" is a reminder that there is no point in staying within the camp's boundaries anyway. What is the point of shoring up nationalist commitment when it won't last? Christian Zionism imbues a modern-day nationalist ideal with false spiritual significance at the expense of people who are condemned to remain outside the camp.

One day all countries and states will be gone, but those people will remain, and as Christians, how are we to stand before God and say, "Their homes were torn down in winter, but we glossed over it because we were more interested in the biblical symbolism of the state that did this to them," or, "Yes, the gospel says to visit the prisoners, but there were children in prison and we didn't even throw one glance their way because it was a lot more interesting to think about the state of Israel's significance to the end times"? It's idolatry. I am glad that this book is doing something to challenge it.

Reconsidering *Zionism Unsettled*: An Open Letter to Reverend Chris Leighton[22]

February 19. 2014

Dear Reverend Leighton,

I read with dismay your recent "Open Letter to the Presbyterian Church,"[23] in which you referred to the Israel Palestine Mission Network of the Presbyterian Church (USA) as "extremist" and called its newly published study guide, *Zionism Unsettled*, a "dishonest screed." As a rabbi who works actively alongside the IPMN—and whose words are quoted extensively in the guide—I am saddened by your words and feel compelled to respond.

As you might imagine, I take exception to your characterization of me as an accomplice to "sweeping denunciations of the Jewish people and their sacred traditions." Needless to say, if I felt for a moment that *Zionism Unsettled* represented an attack on Jews and Judaism, I obviously would never have agreed to be quoted in the guide.

Granted, *Zionism Unsettled* is not a perfect document—but while I might disagree with some of its characterizations and specific points of rhetoric, I do believe it shines a courageous and important light on the ideological roots of the political reality in Israel-Palestine. It certainly bears little resemblance to the "anti-Semitic," "ignorant" tome you so thoroughly excoriate in your letter.

I am tempted to respond point by point to your specific criticisms of the guide—and perhaps someday we will have the opportunity to debate them more thoroughly. For now, however, I'd like to address a paragraph in your letter that I found to be particularly troubling:

> Even a cursory study of history reveals the varied and complex forms that Zionism has taken over the centuries. The yearning for their national homeland has been woven into the Jewish community's daily life for millennia. The Torah (Deuteronomy) and the Tanakh (2 Chronicles) both end with images of yearning to return to the land; synagogues face Jerusalem; the Passover seder celebrated annually concludes with the prayer, "Next year in Jerusalem." To suggest that the Jewish yearning for their own homeland—a yearning that we Presbyterians have supported for numerous other nations—is somehow theologically and morally abhorrent is to deny Jews their own identity as a people. The word for that is "anti-Semitism," and that is, along with racism, sexism, homophobia, and all the other ills our Church condemns, a sin.

I believe your characterization of my sacred tradition is incorrect—and dangerously so. It is prejudicial in the extreme to equate Zionism with Judaism itself. Zionism—that is, the movement to create a Jewish nation-state in historic Palestine—is in fact a political movement that was born in nineteenth-century Europe. As such, it was a conscious and radical break with centuries of Jewish tradition that strongly cautioned against the establishment of an independent Jewish state in the land.

While it is certainly true, as you write, that the yearning for a "return to Zion" is suffused throughout Jewish tradition, it is important to note that this yearning was pointedly directed toward a far-off messianic future. The rabbinic sages repeatedly and forcefully forbade the "forcing of God's hand" through the creation of a humanly established, independent Jewish state in the land, which they believed would occasion disaster for the Jewish people. Throughout the centuries, the Jewish return to Zion functioned as a symbolic expression of hope—not as a political call to action.

Contrary to your assertion, *Zionism Unsettled never* makes the claim that the Jewish yearning for return "is somehow theologically and morally abhorrent." It simply makes the correct distinction between a centuries-old religious tradition that spiritualized the notion of return and the politicization of this idea by a modern nationalist movement.

In this regard, I find your use of the term "anti-Semitism" to slur those who oppose Zionism to be particularly pernicious. In fact, as I point out in the guide, before the establishment of the state of Israel, the political Zionist idea was hotly debated within the Jewish community itself. Many reputable Jewish figures, such as Rabbi Judah Magnes and Hannah Arendt, warned that the establishment of an exclusively Jewish state in a historically multi-religious and multi-ethnic land would inevitably result in conflict and a permanent state of war. It was certainly not "anti-Semitic" of them to suggest such a thing. On the contrary, they—and many others like them—were motivated by their concern for the security of the Jewish people as well as for the well-being of *all* peoples who lived in the land.

While it is true that Jewish anti-Zionism has become a dissident voice in our community since the establishment of the state of Israel, as a rabbi who works actively in the Jewish community, I can attest that there are growing numbers of Jews—particularly young Jews—who refuse to tie their Jewish identity so thoroughly to the highly militarized ethnic nation-state that Israel has become.

At the very least, there is a growing desire to allow non-Zionist voices to be part of the Jewish communal debate once more. One notable bell-wether of this phenomenon may be found in the Swarthmore Hillel student board's recent unanimous decision to defy the guidelines of Hillel International and declare itself an "Open Hillel." In a statement accompanying their resolution, these Jewish students noted:

> All are welcome to walk through our doors and speak with our name and under our roof, be they Zionist, anti-Zionist, post-Zionist, or non-Zionist. We are an institution that seeks to foster spirited debate, constructive dialogue, and a safe space for all, in keeping with the Jewish tradition.[24]

I trust you would never suggest that these Jewish students are driven by "anti-Semitism." On the contrary, they are clearly motivated by sacred Jewish values and a courageous refusal to reduce Jewish identity to one political ideology. It is particularly notable that a number of prominent liberal Zionist voices are publicly voicing their support for the students of

Swarthmore Hillel, indicating that our community may well be ready to return to a truly wide-tent debate on the role of Zionism in Jewish life.[25]

For all of this, however, *Zionism Unsettled* does not, as you suggest, attribute "the plight of the Palestinians to a single cause: Zionism." On the contrary, the study guide repeatedly points out that the political strife in Israel/Palestine is rooted in religious exceptionalist attitudes that are embedded within Judaism, Christianity, and American culture alike.

For many of us, *these* are the critical—and too often ignored—questions for interfaith dialogue: What will we do with those aspects of our religious traditions that value entitlement over humility? Do we believe that this land was promised by God to one particular group of people, or will we affirm a theology that promises the land to *all* who dwell upon it? Will we lift up the fusing of religion with state power and empire, or will we advocate a religious vision that preaches solidarity with the powerless, the disenfranchised, and the downtrodden?

There is much more I would like to say in response to your letter—and again, I hope that we might have the opportunity to debate the specifics more thoroughly. For now, I will only encourage you to reconsider your claim that *Zionism Unsettled* represents "a theological delegitimization of a central concern of the Jewish people."

As a Jew, I can only respond that it is not for you—or anyone—to blithely conflate the tenets of a modern nationalist movement with a venerable and centuries-old religious tradition. And it is certainly not "anti-Semitic" to say so.

Discussion

Michael Blum

I find it a *bit* ironic to have a Presbyterian minister quote my sacred texts to support his argument that I am an anti-Semite.

Bobby Greenberg

It is quite remarkable how a rabbi would so ardently jump aboard with a marginal Presbyterian group which tries to debase such a fundamental dream of his own Jewish people—and to further rationalize these canards with dubious rewritten history leaving out basic truths of the events that have occurred within the lifetimes of many still living.

Guest Post: Reverend Chris Leighton Responds to My Open Letter[26]

February 23, 2014

Reverend Chris Leighton has responded to my open letter of February 19, in which I addressed what I considered to be his troubling and unfounded attack on the newly released study guide Zionism Unsettled. *I have posted his words below. I genuinely appreciate his desire to enter into dialogue and will post my own response in several days.*

I appreciate the time and thought that you directed to my critique of *Zionism Unsettled.* I am not particularly interested in entering a debate that yields winners and losers and that drives combatants more deeply into their entrenched positions. I am interested in conversation that might enable people with deep disagreements to learn from one another, and I am acutely aware of how much more I have to learn in the ongoing struggle to understand and respond to the complexities of the Palestinian-Israeli impasse.

You make a number of observations that I want to ponder more deeply. You also indulge in some polemical excess that does not do justice to what needs to be said. At the end of the day, you believe that this congregational guide can prove a helpful resource. I think that it is so riddled with historical and theological flaws and so dismissive of the Jewish community that it will do much more harm than good. We disagree, and the most immediate question is whether our differences might prove worthy of some ongoing dialogue.

I wonder if we might begin more productively by examining some arguments that you make that I find puzzling. They may clarify our divergent readings of *Zionism Unsettled* and enable us to better understand when and where we speak past one another.

You make a strong case for the separation of Judaism from Zionism and, I think, rightly note the mistakes that arise when the two are collapsed. At the same time, to deny that Zionism and Judaism do not share deep historical and religious roots also strikes me as a serious error. You work with a very limited conception of Zionism as a nineteenth-century political movement that breaks from the Jewish tradition. I work with a much broader understanding of Zionism and see this movement as driven by a yearning for a Jewish homeland with deep biblical underpinnings. The blending of peoplehood, land, and Torah strikes me as integral to Jewish tradition. Even the more secular strains of Zionism that became predominant in the nineteenth century were suffused with biblical imagery, and so this movement was not as radical a rupture from the Jewish tradition as the more secular Zionists imagined.

So here is where I found your account confounding. Do you want to uncouple Zionism from Judaism altogether, or do you want to critique its more militant and "colonial" manifestations? Can all expressions and forms of Zionism be accurately placed into an ideological lump and legitimately condemned as a movement that leads "inexorably" to the displacement and mistreatment of Palestinians, as the IPMN guide indicates? Do you think that Jews do not belong to or have a legitimate claim to the land of Israel? Do you want to trace the problem to the UN's 1947 resolution to partition the land and to establish the State of Israel? Or do want to focus on the problems that emerged in the wake of the Six-Day War of 1967?

I have yet to see efforts to undo the establishment of the State of Israel produce constructive results. I have seen efforts to de-legitimize the State, to brand it as "an apartheid nation," and to punish Israel economically and politically polarize and fragment our communities. This is not to say that all anti-Zionists are anti-Semites. Yet it would be a terrible blunder not to acknowledge that many of them are. At another time we can circle back to clarify what constitutes "anti-Semitism" and its relationship to "anti-Judaism" before exploring who decides when it is fair and accurate to apply these categories. I do want to note that I did not throw around the term; indeed, I used it only once and quite specifically in my critique.

Back to the issue of a Jewish homeland. I believe that the quest for a home is deeply woven into the tissue of our humanity, and you would not deny that this yearning has occupied a prominent, if not central, role among Jews over the centuries. My impression is that you would not annul the longing to establish a Jewish homeland nor characterize this desire as intrinsically pernicious. Does the problem then take hold when Jews move from claims to a homeland to making their bid to establish a sovereign state? Homeland is okay. Sovereign state for Jews is not (unless divinely implemented).

When a Frenchman speaks of his homeland, or an Irishman, or American, or a Palestinian, or a Tibetan, are they designating an attachment to a specific land independent of the sovereignty on which the messy business of governments depends? Does not the search for a "homeland" aim at "sovereignty"? A national identity is difficult to construct and preserve without the power and freedom that is exercised by the state. One of the truly remarkable achievements of the Jewish people has been the ability to endure and even flourish over a remarkable span of history without the powers of a sovereign state. Yet to acknowledge the claims to homeland while denying Jews the opportunities and burdens of an independent state enshrines the status of Jews as "exceptional" and refuses them the rights and conditions that every other nation claims for itself. Your line of thinking seems to me to end up creating the very phenomenon that you and the guide condemn, albeit it is a different form of "exceptionalism."

Finally, I do not know of a nation, a religion, or even a family that does not hold to some kind of exceptionalism. Our national, religious, and familial identities are constructed on the basis of stories that distinguish us from others. Even when we insist that we are not superior to others (and hopefully we regard this task as a moral imperative), we support and sustain our nations, our religious communities, and our families with financial and psychological investments that give them priority. We live our lives treating our own with greater levels of time, energy, and resource— even as we strive to respond to the legitimate claims of those who need and demand our active engagement. Furthermore, I have yet to encounter a nation that does not fuse religion and politics—and overtly or implicitly make a claim to being exceptional. The challenge is how to identify and respond when the mixture turns toxic. I suspect that we agree that this is a vital responsibility of our religious leaders.

While keenly aware that your movement has for the most part rejected the notion of "chosenness," I do not think that this category invariably generates a sense of superiority. The rejection of "exceptionalism" strikes me as a thinly veiled rejection of a concept that remains prominent in much, if not most, of the Jewish world. The step from a condemnation of "exceptionalism" and "chosenness" to an indictment of Israel and the larger Jewish community as ethnocentrically racist is made without qualification.

The concept of "exceptionalism" (at least as it is defined and applied in this guide) strikes me as problematic. Are not the real problems to which you point a manifestation of "nationalism"? And if every country must be vigilant about the dangerous directions in which nationalism can move, why would the guide not acknowledge this challenge within Palestinian nationalism? It certainly would not be an arduous task to illustrate the problems by offering a brief overview from George Antonius to the Hamas Charter.

One example of dishonesty that I find troubling in the study guide is the unwillingness to offer a more comprehensive and balanced account. If the problem is that Jewish nationalism is different from other kinds of nationalism and deserving of condemnation, then the guide once again becomes guilty of the very error that it impugns. In other words, Zionism becomes an exceptional and inherently evil manifestation of nationalism. At best, I think that the analytic methods used in this guide are intellectually shoddy and the terminology reinforces the tendency to use confused and confusing generalizations—thereby reinforcing the polemical discourse that generates plenty of heat and a shortage of light.

These flaws point to a more serious issue, namely the unwillingness of the study guide to come clean on what it really believes is the necessary end game. Is the goal to help Israel achieve the democratic ideal embodied in its May 14, 1948, Declaration of the Establishment of the State of Israel, or to reject this national project, work to dismantle the current State of Israel, and create a new and different national entity? What do the authors really think necessary to overcome the plight of the Palestinians? It is essential to own up to the vision that animates this study guide, because the tools that are being deployed need to be appraised on the basis of the ends that they serve.

In my opinion, the vast majority of Presbyterians will not align themselves with a project that aims to disassemble the State of Israel. I think that the authors and editors of the guide know this and therefore have strategically decided to conceal the objectives for which they strive. Again, this strikes me as dishonest.

There is of course much more to be discussed. Perhaps these reflections will at the very least open up some points for further exploration.

Discussion

gwpj

This sentence in Rev. Leighton's reply to you is, I think, a very telling one in what it leaves out:

> I work with a much broader understanding of Zionism and see this movement as driven by a yearning for a Jewish homeland with deep biblical underpinnings. The blending of peoplehood, land and Torah strikes me as integral to Jewish tradition. Even the more secular strains of Zionism that became predominant in the nineteenth century were suffused with biblical imagery and so this movement was not as radical a rupture from the Jewish tradition as the more secular Zionists imagined.

What is missing is any mention of what happened to the Palestinian people when the Zionist project for a homeland began: the terrorism, the motivation to remove all traces of the Palestinian people, the denial of their existence ("a land without people for a people without a land"). I find this oversight astonishing and deeply saddening.

Vicky

That sentence leaves out other things. Firstly, "all" modern nationalism was midwifed in the nineteenth century. Along with the emergence of nation-states came a new way of fashioning history, with each state trying to give itself a long pedigree that was enshrined in school and college history curricula (the academic discipline of history as we understand it emerged hand-in-glove with the nation-state). The fact that nationalists of all stripes honestly saw their political movements as a blossoming of the ancient aspirations of a united people does not actually mean that this vision of the past is accurate. Conceptions of community do change over time and that is natural. This romanticized approach blots all that out.

He's also conflating separate issues. To begin with, civic nationalism (which he accepts unquestioningly as OK) is not the same as the ethnic nationalism on which Israel is built. Secondly, "peoplehood" and "ethnic nationalism" are not automatically the same thing. Feeling a commitment to the Jewish people does not necessarily translate as commitment to a Jewish nation-state. Spiritual respect for and closeness to the land isn't the same as demanding to own that land and administer it (at great cost to others, no less). There are religious Jews who live in the land but who don't support ethnic nationalism, and there are completely secular Jews who wouldn't dream of making aliyah from America yet who bang the drum for that nationalism.

Revisiting the early days of Zionism, Palestine was one of several places in consideration as a possible candidate for the Jewish state. It wasn't singled out as special then, whereas for religious Jews (who weren't nationalists) it meant everything. Zionism was hostile to religion from its inception and only after the Holocaust did it really become mainstream in religious Jewish communities. Its adoption was driven by terrible loss and trauma. The religious continuity he's arguing for just doesn't exist.

Historiographical problems apart, the real issue with his argument is ethics, as you say. It never fails to sadden me how Christian Zionist clergy are able to conveniently fit Palestinian suffering and oppression into a footnote, concentrating instead on some sweeping and highly sanitized epic drama of return and redemption that has more in common with Hollywood than it does with Jesus's teaching to stand with "the least of these."

During the First World War, there were clergy who set up patriotism as a religious duty and nationalism as a new gospel, with Christians who conscientiously objected to the fighting routinely being derided as cowards simply for having the courage to stand by the cross instead of by the flag. There is a problem when we introduce flags to churches. Any flag. It limits our ability to speak out when we need to. In the letter to the Hebrews, St. Paul tells us that we have no abiding city and that we must go to Jesus "outside the camp"—beyond borders, to a place that isn't us—in the same breath, which is why I am deeply disturbed that Rev. Leighton accepts nationalist exceptionalism so uncritically before going on to make out that ethnic nationalism is an intrinsic part of Jewish religion.

Since when did the state warrant the same kind of fidelity as God? Each justification I read for Christian Zionism feels more and more idolatrous. Millions of people are denied basic civil rights, including a say in the regime that rules over them, in order to preserve the Zionist dream—but the real cardinal sin is not their oppression, but the fact that giving them their rights would mean the "disassembly" of that dream, the apartheid state? Jesus did not say, "Whatever you do to the least of these my nation-states, you do also to me." We have a Christian responsibility to other people, not to uphold a structure of governance at any price, especially when we're not the ones paying it.

More Heat than Light: My Response to Reverend Chris Leighton[27]

February 26, 2014

Dear Reverend Leighton,

Thank you for your response to my open letter. While I'm also not particularly interested in turning our dialogue into a debate to be "won" or "lost," I do, however, take exception to much of what you wrote and feel compelled to respond in kind. I agree with you that our differences are worthy of ongoing dialogue. I can only hope that the airing of our disagreement might somehow be helpful to those who struggle with an issue that is of such critical importance to our respective faith communities.

I'd like to start with your observation:

> [To] deny . . . Zionism and Judaism do not share deep historical and religious roots . . . strikes me as a serious error. You work with a very limited conception of Zionism as a nineteenth-century political movement that breaks from Jewish tradition. I work with a much broader understanding of Zionism and see this movement as driven by yearnings for a Jewish homeland with deep biblical underpinnings. The blending of peoplehood, land and Torah strikes me as integral to Jewish tradition.

In writing this statement, you've chosen to sidestep my point that for thousands of years, the Jewish connection to the land was expressed as a spiritual yearning—*not* as a desire to create a sovereign Jewish nation. "Homeland" and "political nation" are two intrinsically different concepts and, as I've already written, Jewish tradition consistently regarded the notion of Jewish political nationhood to be anathema. Political Zionism was never "integral to Jewish tradition"; the concept was not even introduced into Jewish life until the nineteenth century.

By insisting on this point, your analysis of Jewish tradition and history betrays a characteristically Zionist bias that assumes the centrality of sovereign statehood. That is fine—you are certainly welcome to your biases. But you should at least be prepared to own them for what they are and not attempt to present them as normative.

The very concept of nation-statehood itself is a fundamentally modern notion. Like all modern forms of nationalism, Zionism arose to consciously create a sense of seamless continuity to the past through recourse to an ancient mythic history. But of course this is an artificial "continuity," one that owes more to modern political ideology than Jewish religious tradition.

It also has little to do with actual "history" as we know it today. As *Zionism Unsettled* notes, it is extremely problematic to use the Bible as a history book to lay claim to a particular piece of land. In the first place, the Bible is a profoundly ahistorical document, as we have long learned from literary scholars and archaeologists. Moreover, the Bible was certainly never intended to be "history" according to our current understanding of the term. The authors of the Bible did not purport to create a literal history of the events of their day—rather, it is a religiously inspired narrative that reflects ideas and values unique to the world of the ancient Near East.

This is more than just an academic point. As *Zionism Unsettled* points out, the use of the Bible as historical justification for a modern nationalist movement is not merely historically problematic—it has had tragic consequences for the inhabitants of historic Palestine, particularly when you consider Biblical passages that express entitlement to the land, a religious intolerance of the "foreign nations of Canaan," and commandments that require nothing short of their total dispossession—and, in some cases, even annihilation.

So, in one sense, we are in complete agreement when you write that "even the more secular strains of Zionism that became predominant in the nineteenth century were suffused with Biblical imagery." Perhaps we only disagree on the dark outcome of this phenomenon. We should not be unmindful of the ways early Zionist ideologues and the political founders of the state used the Biblical land traditions—and the ways they are currently wielded by Israeli politicians, settler leaders, and ultra-religious rabbis alike. This use of Biblical imagery must not be dismissed as mere religious rhetoric—these theological linkages have enormous power, particularly when we consider the expulsion of Palestinians from their homes in 1947–48 and the policies of displacement and transfer that continue to this very day.

You go on to ask:

> Do you want to uncouple Zionism from Judaism altogether, or do you want to critique its more militant and "colonial" manifestations? Can all expressions and forms of Zionism be accurately placed into an ideological lump and legitimately condemned as a movement that leads "inexorably" to the displacement and mistreatment of the Palestinians, as the IPMN guide indicates? Do you think that Jews do not belong to or have a legitimate claim to the land of Israel?

It is true that there are many different forms of Zionism—a fact that is extensively explored in *Zionism Unplugged* (see chapter 2). I would argue, however, that since the establishment of the state of Israel, the existence of these various "Zionisms" has largely become an academic point. In a very real way, the birth of Israel represents the ultimate victory of the values of political Zionism that were promoted by the founders of the state.

As someone who identified as a Zionist for most of his adult life, it is with no small measure of sadness that I acknowledge the ways political Zionism has "inexorably led to the displacement and mistreatment of the Palestinians." Perhaps most critically, I have come to reckon painfully with the ethnic nationalism at the core of political Zionism's *raison d'etre*—and its insistence upon the maintenance of a demographic Jewish majority in the land to safeguard the "Jewish character of the state." In the end, no matter how vociferously Israel might insist that it is, in fact, "Jewish and democratic," I do not believe it is ultimately possible to establish a demographically Jewish state without regarding the presence of non-Jews to be a problem.

In this regard, I do believe that *Zionism Unsettled* bravely shines a light on the tragic legacy of the Zionist idea, a concept that ultimately resulted in the forced depopulation of Palestinians from their homes (a phenomenon by now well attested to by Israeli historians) as well as the policies of dispossession that the Israeli government continues to enact even today. These events and policies do not exist in a vacuum—they are the logical end products of a very specific nationalist ideology that privileges the rights of one particular group over another.

You ask me if I believe Jews "do not belong to or have a legitimate claim to the land of Israel." Of course I believe that Jews have every right to live in the land. I'm not sure, however, what you mean by a "legitimate claim." If you mean "Can we Jews rightly maintain a religious connection to the land?" then my answer is certainly yes. If you mean "Do we have some kind of intrinsic right to exert our political sovereignty over this land and all who dwell in it?" then my answer is most certainly no. When it comes to nation-statism, it has historically been the case that "might makes right." The real question, it seems to me, is not "Who has the right to this land?" but rather "How can we extend full rights to *all* who live on this land?"

You write that you "have yet to see efforts to undo the establishment of the State of Israel produce constructive results." I'm struck that you equate an insistence upon equal rights for all to be tantamount to Israel's "undoing." But when it comes to a choice between a Jewish and a democratic state, as increasingly seems likely, what should be our choice? My community is fast approaching a reckoning: Which kind of state will ultimately be more "Jewish," one that unabashedly places Jewish rights above Palestinian rights or one that allows full and equal rights for all?

I also find your statement about "Israel's undoing" to be more than a little incendiary. By projecting nefarious designs onto an entire movement, this kind of rhetoric only exploits the deepest and darkest of Jewish fears. I will tell you that I have participated in the Palestinian solidarity movement for some years now and have yet to encounter the kind of anti-Semitic anti-Zionists you speak of. Are there anti-Semites in this movement? Undoubtedly. There are odious types on the margins of every political movement. But I can say without hesitation that the Palestinians and pro-Palestinian activists I have met and worked with have nothing but the deepest respect for Jews and Judaism at large and consistently endeavor, as I do, to draw a scrupulous differentiation between Zionism and Judaism.

I don't disagree with you that "the quest for home is deeply woven into the tissue of our humanity" and that this concept is deeply woven into the fabric of Jewish collective consciousness. But I must disagree with you strongly when you insist that "the search for homeland aim(s) at sovereignty." To me, this is an astonishingly narrow and reductionist reading of the notions of home and homeland.

You write that "a national identity is difficult to construct and preserve without the power and freedom that is exercised by the state." But, in fact, that is precisely what the Jewish people have done for centuries. Judaism as we know it was born in the wake of the destruction of the Second Temple as a profound and spiritually courageous response to the reality of dispersion and exile. As such, Jewish tradition is replete with teachings that respond to this trauma with a message of spiritual hope and renewal.

In one of my favorite rabbinic *midrashim*, for instance, Rabbi Akiba teaches, "Wherever the people of Israel were exiled, the Divine Presence was exiled with them." In other words, Judaism arose to assert that despite the experience of exile, the Jewish people would always be "home." God was no longer geographically specific to one particular land—spiritual meaning and fulfillment could be found throughout the diaspora, wherever the Jewish people might live. (The *midrash* ends, notably, on a messianic note: "And when they return in the future, the Divine Presence will return with them.")

In so doing, rabbinic Judaism transformed a land-based cultic practice to a global religion, enabling Jewish life to flourish and grow widely throughout the diaspora. This, I believe, represents the intrinsic beauty and genius of the Jewish conception of peoplehood: In a time of profound upheaval and crisis, we spiritualized the concept of "homeland" and redefined ourselves as a globally based, multi-ethnic, multi-cultural peoplehood that viewed the entire world as its "home." The concept of exile became, in a sense, a spiritual prism through which we viewed the world and our place in it. It might well be claimed that centuries of Jewish religious creativity resulted from this profound existential mindset.

As a Jew, I do not need you to tell me that this conception of Judaism is somehow "exceptionalist" because it "refuses the rights and conditions that every other nation claims for itself." With all due respect, it is not for you to take it upon yourself to define my Jewish rights and claims, particularly when this runs counter to centuries of Jewish tradition and experience. I understand that you have chosen to adopt the Zionist narrative of my history and that is certainly your right. But you do not have the right to preach to a Jew that his understanding of "homeland" must *ipso facto* be expressed through sovereign political statehood.

Moreover, there are numerous stateless peoples throughout the world. Would you go on to suggest that they too have the intrinsic right to "the opportunities and burdens of an independent state?" If so, where does this right come from and how might it possibly be implemented? If not, then why are you granting this unique right to the Jewish people? Quite frankly, I find your conflation of the concepts of "homeland" and "nation-state" to be hopelessly confused, creating myriads more problems than it purports to solve.

On the concept of exceptionalism, you write:

> I have yet to encounter a nation or religion that does not fuse religion and politics—and overtly or implicitly make a claim to being exceptional. The challenge is how to identify and respond when the mixture turns toxic.

Like the authors of *Zionism Unsettled*, I would go much farther than this. I believe that challenge is to identify and respond to those aspects of our respective religious traditions that assume our superiority over others—*and to thoroughly disavow them.*

It is all well and good to "support and sustain our nations, our religious communities, and our families with financial and psychological investments that give them priority." I'm even willing to admit that it is natural for a person or group to feel "chosen" in a way that doesn't automatically denote superiority. The problem occurs, as *Zionism Unsettled* rightly points out, when exceptionalism "exempts the chosen from the need to conform to normal rules, laws, or general principles that we use to hold other people accountable."[28]

As the study guide notes, religious exceptionalism has historically been at its most dangerous when it is wedded to state power. In illuminating this point, *Zionism Unsettled* actually devotes a significant amount of analysis to post-Constantinian Christianity and its legacy of anti-Semitism over the centuries. In so doing, it identifies the ultimate problem as the merging of religion and empire—not Zionism per se. You misrepresent the guide egregiously when you accuse it of treating Zionism as "an exceptional and inherently evil manifestation of nationalism." In fact, *Zionism Unsettled* repeatedly places political Zionism within the larger context of religious and national exceptionalism—a phenomenon that has historically proven to be, to paraphrase your words, a uniquely toxic mixture.

Finally, you bemoan the lack of a more "comprehensive and balanced account" in *Zionism Unsettled.* I would suggest that this lack of balance does not originate in the guide but rather the in Israel-Palestine conflict itself. To be sure, this conflict does not and has never constituted a level playing field. Rather, it has pitted one of the most militarized nations in the world—one that enjoys the near-unconditional support of the world's largest superpower—against a people it has dispossessed from its land, a people whose yearning for home now reflects, as you so eloquently put it, "a quest . . . that is woven into the very tissue of [its] humanity."

I do believe this is the most critical place where you and I part company. You express your religious faith through your work in the world of interfaith dialogue—an arena that assumes balance and equity on two equal "sides." I view my faith as refracted through my work as an activist who stands in solidarity with a people that is seeking its liberation. As such I do not view this conflict in any way as a balanced equation. On the contrary, I seek to re-right what I believe to be an inherently *unbalanced* situation.

I realize full well that, by saying such things, I leave myself open to further accusations of "polemical excess that does not do justice to what needs to be said." So be it. I would only ask you to consider that rhetoric has a fundamentally different function in the world of dialogue than in the arena of political transformation. I understand that in your world, words are typically wielded in the furtherance of creating "more light than heat." But when there is very real oppression occurring, as I truly believe is the case here, it is not at all inappropriate to turn up the heat, no matter how upsetting this may be for Israel and its advocates.

I do not know if you have ever visited Palestinians in the West Bank or Gaza and witnessed firsthand the deeply oppressive reality of their daily existence. If you haven't, I encourage you to do so. I encourage you to talk to Palestinians who live in villages whose livelihood has been choked off by a wall that separates them from their agricultural lands in order to make way for the growth of Jewish settlements. I encourage you to meet with Palestinians whose weekly non-violent demonstrations against the wall are met regularly with brutal force by the Israeli military. Speak to Palestinian mothers and fathers whose children have been abducted in the middle of the night by the IDF and subjected to interrogation in Israeli prisons. Get to know Palestinians who have had their residency rights revoked and/or their homes demolished so that Jewish "demographic facts" can be created on the ground. Talk with Palestinians in Gaza who are being collectively punished by a crushing blockade and subjected to life inside what has essentially become one of the largest open-air prisons in the world.

I believe that, if you take the time to do so, you will invariably come to find that these men and women represent spiritual teachers just as compelling as the American Jews and Christians with whom you regularly engage in dialogue. At the very least, I hope they might somehow challenge your views on "what needs to be said" about this conflict.

While you may well consider the above to be just another example of my "polemical excess," I would only say that my convictions come from a faithful place—and from a religious tradition that exhorts me to stand with the oppressed and call out the oppressor. I also believe these same religious convictions inform the very heart of *Zionism Unsettled* and, whatever its specific flaws, I find it to be an enormously important and courageous resource. You claim that the "vast majority of Presbyterians will not align themselves with a project that aims to disassemble the State of Israel." Of course, the guide does nothing of the kind. It does, however, call for disassembling an inequitable system that privileges one group over another and replacing it with one that guarantees full rights for all. For this it makes no apology, nor should it.

You certainly know the Presbyterian community better than I, but I will say that I have met and spoken with many Presbyterians—and members of other Protestant denominations—who have expressed gratitude for this new guide and are eager to use it in their churches. As with my own faith community, I do sense that we are currently in the midst of a paradigm shift on the issue of Zionism, and I am not anywhere near as certain as you that the "vast majority" of Christians or Jews are so ready to denounce such ideas as abject anti-Semitism.

Again, thank you for taking the time to respond to my open letter. I agree with you that there is much more to be discussed. Whether or not we engage in further exploration together, I hope and trust that our conversation might still be helpful to those who have read our exchange.

Discussion

Reverend Chris Leighton

It might be worth stepping back and examining the character of our exchange. While we have managed at a few points to articulate points of disagreement, my sense is that more often than not we have spoken past one another. I think that there has been a failure to frame questions and concerns that might help us and your blog readers learn very much—and the disputational character of our interplay is symptomatic of most "debates" about the Palestinian-Israeli conflict. It seems to me that a lot of folks have made up their minds about where the blame lies, and it is extremely difficult to get outside the foregone conclusions. I certainly discovered very quickly that I was not going to change your mind, and I must admit that you have not put forth any compelling thoughts that lead me to view *Zionism Unsettled* more positively.

This sense of futility took hold at two key points in your latest response. You asked me if I had ever visited the West Bank and/or Gaza. You wanted to know if I had looked the suffering of Palestinians in the face and confronted the horror. And your assumption was that if I had your experience and sensitivity, your moral perspicacity and powers of empathy, then I would reach the same conclusions as you. That anyone could engage the same dreadful facts and then reach different conclusions about the source of the problem and the appropriate response—well, this was simply beyond your imagining.

In addition to being needlessly patronizing, it may give your readers the false impression that I have sheltered myself (or been manipulated by others) and thereby avoided the disruptive encounter with the injustices suffered by Palestinians. Our organization makes certain that groups that we lead are exposed to the harsh realities on the ground and that we engage both Palestinians and Israelis, including Jews, Christians and Muslims who have divergent, often conflicting experiences. Is there more to see? Absolutely. Have we failed to grasp the enormity of the anguish experienced by Palestinians and Israelis? Of course. Yet the romanticized and one-dimensional narratives that insist that you cannot be pro-Palestinian without being anti-Israeli have long been shattered.

The second moment in your response that disclosed the barrenness of our exchange came into focus when you accused me of "preaching to a Jew" what his understanding of a homeland should be. What I presented as a description of the prevailing Jewish ethos, you regarded as a prescriptive and unwarranted demand. Who was this *chutzpadik* Christian to tell you what it means to be a good Jew? I am well aware that there are Jews who reject claims to "chosenness" and who regard "Zionism" as a betrayal of Jewish ethics. You are not alone. That said, it is still an accurate assessment to note that yours is a minority position, even if it is much more compatible with Protestants' sensibilities.

At the end of the day, I still do not know if you believe that a two-state solution is viable. I do not know if you regard the State of Israel (as established by the UN in 1947) as a failed project, given its deep grounding in a Zionist vision. My impression is that you dream of a bi-national state. This wish strikes me as a romantic vision (also with roots in the nineteenth century) that is unattainable in the foreseeable future—and the revolutionary zeal that clings to such a political transformation promises an entirely new level of bloodshed. I certainly find little ground for confidence that religious and ethnic pluralism is currently gaining a secure democratic footing in the region. And so I struggle to hold out for a two-state compromise that might over time evolve into a more creative and healthy political arrangement. It is a fragile possibility, but despair is a condition that I believe both of our traditions insist we can ill afford.

From the Presbyterian General Assembly: Jews and Christians in Support of Divestment[29]

June 17, 2014

I've just returned from two days in Detroit at the Presbyterian Church (USA) General Assembly (GA), where I joined together with Christian and Jewish friends and colleagues to help support overtures being brought to the plenum that further the cause of justice in our country and around the world—particularly in Israel/Palestine.

During my very full sojourn in downtown Detroit, I had the opportunity to testify in a committee meeting that was deliberating on an overture that presented new parameters for Interfaith Relations. I also attended the extensive committee discussions on the overture that is garnering a great deal of attention from around the world: divestment of the PC (USA)'s funds from three companies that profit from Israel's occupation: Caterpillar, Motorola Solutions, and Hewlett-Packard.

This overture has a ten-year history behind it. Although it has been brought to previous GAs, each convention brings brand-new commissioners, so while many attendees are all too familiar with this particular overture, many (if not most) of the ones who will actually be voting are relatively new to the issues involved. Even so, I had the pleasure of speaking with a number of commissioners who are considering it with an impressive level of thoughtfulness and seriousness.

Some of the most profound moments of my experience at the GA came from the realization that I am truly part of a large and growing interfaith movement for justice that has fast become an important spiritual home for me. I came to the GA with a large delegation from Jewish Voice for Peace, which has worked closely with PC (USA) members on this issue for nearly a decade.

These inspired Presbyterian activists have become our dear friends and true spiritual teachers. This past Monday night, it was my great honor to offer a keynote speech at a dinner sponsored by the Israel/Palestine Mission Network of the Presbyterian Church (USA). As I spoke, I was deeply moved to look out at the room and see so many old and new colleagues, all part of this very special community of conscience.

There is much more to unfold as the GA continues to deliberate this week. As of this writing, the committee discussing the divestment overture will soon be deciding whether to refer it to plenum. In the meantime, from Rabbi Margaret Holub, writing in the *Jewish Forward*:

> Our greatest hope is that the Jewish people would hear selective divestment from these corporations as what it is—a form of *tochechah*. It is a rebuke from our neighbors in the American religious landscape, calling us to task for a cruel policy that brings pain to their own brothers and sisters in the Palestinian Christian community and to all who live under Israeli occupation. Far from being hate speech, it is the speech of conscience.
>
> We believe in fact that the Presbyterian Church has many new friends to gain in the Jewish community and beyond it through its courageous witness. We may not share all of our beliefs or political commitments. Such is the beauty and difficulty of coalition work, or of any kind of spiritual companionship. We have much to learn from each other, and in long-term relationships our differences are as important as our points of convergence.[30]

⟨𝒟⟩

The Presbyterian Divestment Vote: Toward a New Model of Community Relations[31]

June 23, 2014

In the wake of the Presbyterian Church (USA)'s recent decision[32] to divest from three companies that profit from Israel's occupation, Jewish establishment leaders have been expressing their displeasure toward the PC (USA) in no uncertain terms.

Anti-Defamation League director Abe Foxman stated last week that church leaders have "fomented an atmosphere of open hostility to Israel."[33] Rabbi Noam Marans, director of interreligious relations at the American Jewish Committee, declared that "the PC (USA) decision is celebrated by those who believe they are one step closer to a Jew-free Middle East."[34] And Rabbi Steve Gutow, president of the Jewish Council for Public Affairs, publicly accused the PC (USA) of having a "deep animus" against "both the Jewish people and the State of Israel."[35]

Given such extreme rhetoric, it may come as a surprise to many that the same overture that called for the Presbyterian Foundation and Board of Pensions to divest from Caterpillar, Inc., Hewett-Packard, and Motorola Solutions also included resolutions to:

- Reaffirm Israel's right to exist as a sovereign nation within secure and internationally recognized borders in accordance with the United Nations resolutions;
- Declare its commitment to a two-state solution in which a secure and universally recognized State of Israel lives alongside a free, viable, and secure state for the Palestinian people;
- Reaffirm PC (USA)'s commitment to interfaith dialog and partnerships with the American Jewish, Muslim friends and Palestinian Christians and call for all presbyteries and congregations within the PC (USA) to include interfaith dialogue and relationship-building as part of their own engagement in working for a just peace;
- Urge all church institutions to give careful consideration to possible investments in Israel-Palestine that advance peace and improve the lives of Palestinians and Israelis.[36]

Do these sound like the words of a "hostile" church committed to a "Jew-free Middle East"?

In truth, these are the words of a religious community struggling in good faith to walk the path of justice while remaining sensitive to the concerns of their Jewish sisters and brothers.

Such a description certainly comports with my own personal experience. I attended the Presbyterian General Assembly last week as part of the Jewish Voice for Peace delegation and had lengthy conversations with numerous GA commissioners. When I asked them to share their feelings about the divestment overture, many responded with a similar refrain: In their hearts they wanted to vote in favor, but they hesitated because they were worried what it might do to their relationships with their Jewish family and friends and colleagues.

This theme occurred repeatedly during the committee and plenum debates as well. Commissioners who opposed the overture relied less on political arguments than upon their concern for their personal relationships with Jews and with the Jewish community at large. Many commissioners who spoke in favor of the overture expressed similar concerns even as they decided to cast their votes as a matter of deeply held conscience.

In the end, the process that led up to the final vote on divestment was one of genuine discernment and faithful witness. To be sure, the final wording of the overture is a nuanced statement by a church that clearly seeks to follow its sacred mission of justice in Israel/Palestine even as it cherishes its longstanding relationship with the Jewish community.

As a Jew, I was deeply saddened that so many Jewish establishment leaders saw fit to resort to what can only be called emotional blackmail in order to fight against a Presbyterian overture that they didn't like. But for all the undue pressure, I have no doubt that the heavy-handed nature of these tactics ultimately contributed in no small way to the success of the final divestment overture.

Notably, during the plenum discussion, one commissioner commented that he was "offended" to see some Jewish opponents to the overture wearing T-shirts that said "Love Us or Leave Us." Another asked if Reform movement president Rabbi Rick Jacob's offer to broker a meeting in Jerusalem between Presbyterian leaders and Benjamin Netanyahu *if* they voted down the overture was somehow a thinly veiled threat.

As a Jewish supporter of divestment, I will say without hesitation that this vote was first and foremost a victory for Palestinians, who continue to suffer under Israel's illegal and immoral occupation. On a secondary level, however, we might say that this was a victory for a religious community that refused to let its sacred convictions be stymied by cynical pressure.

As for us, the Jewish community is left with the very real question: Are we truly prepared to write off one of the largest American Christian denominations over this vote—a vote that was taken in good faith and with profound deliberation? On a deeper level, we might well ask ourselves honestly: Have the Jewish communal establishment's bullying tactics finally reached the end of their usefulness?

Indeed, when it comes to the issue of Israel/Palestine in interfaith relations, the unwritten rule of the Jewish establishment has always been "toe our line or feel our wrath." By voting for divestment, the PC (USA) declared itself ready to stand down this ultimatum.

There is now every reason to believe other denominations will now follow suit. Will our community continue to respond with cynical threats, or will we finally be ready to model an approach to community relations grounded in trust, understanding, and mutual respect?

Discussion

David R

Were the four resolutions mentioned in Brant Rosen's posting there from the beginning? If not, when and by whom were they inserted?

In addition to passing this resolution to divest from three American companies, has the Presbyterian Church (USA) passed any resolutions opposing incitement to terrorism by Palestinians, Jew-hatred by Palestinians, attacks on innocent Israeli citizens, or Hamas's charter stating that they will never accept a Jewish state in any borders and that their "obligation" is to kill all Jews everywhere?

Steven Lindsley

As a PCUSA pastor who followed the General Assembly proceedings closely, I can say that the four resolutions language was, in fact, in the overall resolution when it was brought to the floor. In other words, this was not inserted as an afterthought. I also believe this language serves to address and answer your other points. As a denomination we are very much for peace and against any ongoing acts of violence and terrorism.

Chapter 11

Tzedek Chicago

August–November 2014

In July 2014, Israel launched another brutal Israeli assault on Gaza, killing 2,104 Palestinians—including 1,462 civilians and 495 children.[1] I wrote the first two posts in this chapter while participating in the anti-war protests in Chicago that took place during that terrible, tragic summer.

It was also during this time that I decided to resign from my congregation. Several months after leaving Jewish Reconstructionist Congregation, I founded a new non-Zionist congregation, Tzedek Chicago.

For Tisha B'Av: A Lamentation for Gaza[2]

August 1, 2014

This Monday night begins the Jewish fast of Tisha B'Av: a day of mourning for the calamities that have befallen the Jewish people over the centuries. Among other things, the traditional Tisha B'Av liturgy includes chanting the Biblical book of Lamentations.

Given the profoundly tragic events currently unfolding in Gaza, I offer my reimagining of the first chapter of Lamentations. I share it with the hope that on this day of mourning we might also mourn the mounting dead in Gaza— along with what Israel has become.

A Lamentation for Gaza

Gaza weeps alone.
Bombs falling without end
her cheeks wet with tears.
A widow abandoned
imprisoned on all sides
with none willing to save her.

We who once knew oppression
have become the oppressors.
Those who have been pursued
are now the pursuers.
We have uprooted families
from their homes, we have
driven them deep into
this desolate place,
this narrow strip of exile.

All along the roads there is mourning.
The teeming marketplaces
have been bombed into emptiness.
The only sounds we hear
are cries of pain
sirens blaring
drones buzzing
bitterness echoing
into the black vacuum
of homes destroyed
and dreams denied.

We have become Gaza's master
leveling neighborhoods
with the mere touch of a button
for her transgression of resistance.
Her children are born into captivity.
They know us only as occupiers
enemies to be feared
and hated.

We have lost all
that once was precious to us.
This fatal attachment to our own might
has become our downfall.
This idolatrous veneration of the land
has sent us wandering into
a wilderness of our own making.

We have robbed Gaza of
her deepest dignity
plunged her into sorrow and darkness.

Her people crowd into refugee camps
held captive by fences and buffer zones
gunboats, mortar rounds
and Apache missiles.

We sing of Jerusalem,
to "a free people in their own land"
but our song has become a mockery.
How can we sing a song of freedom
imprisoned inside behind walls we have built
with our own fear and dread?

Here we sit clinging to our illusions
of comfort and security
while we unleash hell on earth
on the other side of the border.
We sit on hillsides and cheer
as our explosions light up the sky
while far below, whole neighborhoods
are reduced to rubble.

For these things I weep:
for the toxic fear we have unleashed
from the dark place of our hearts
for the endless grief
we are inflicting
on the people of Gaza.

Discussion

Dr. Sapir H

Mourning songs are a not a strategy.

The tragic situation is that the moderate majorities—those who wish to end the conflict by peaceful means—are desperate and radicals dictate conditions to everyone. There is an urgent necessity to create a broad peacemaking coalition of the majority on both sides against the extremes.

From Dr. Sapir Handelman—an Israeli who just went into the shelter because Hamas was firing missiles from a populated area . . .

David B0

Is it possible to feel sorry for the Palestinians that they have blown yet another chance to have a state of their own? That they have taken the goodwill of the world and turned it into terror tunnels and rockets aimed at innocent citizens?

We as Jews in Israel don't have to apologize for living.

I think you need to understand this. The Gazan residents have been taken captive by Hamas and if anything Israel is doing them a favor by trying to lift the siege of Gaza by Hamas.

It's a very sad situation but you need to keep it in perspective: the perspective of thousands of years, not just what endears you to fair weather friends.

rene

David,

Thanks for your rational response to this one-sided garbage.

Rabbi Rosen, whoever you are, please write a Lamentation for the 200,000 Syrians killed by their own government, the hundreds of thousands left homeless.

What is a people to do if rockets are constantly rained down on them? Do you prefer to see Jews with bowed shaven heads being marched meekly off to slaughter? Do you get it that this is what the Palestinians want, what they are taught? I am appalled by your website and the one-sided trash it reflects.

Irwin W D

How dare you, HOW DARE YOU! call yourself a Jew, let alone a Rabbi. Appeasing enemies to the Jewish people. You low class piece of excrement! You should be excommunicated.

Cynthia

I just read the news of your decision to quit JRC. Although I am not a member of the congregation, after reading some of your political ramblings here and elsewhere, I thank God for your departure. You are truly a sick and twisted individual devoid of any logical moral sense. If you cannot understand cause and effect and attribute them accurately, you cannot possibly equitably judge your fellow Jews in Israel, much less your fellow human beings. And your writings on the Middle East conflict clearly betray a deep and perhaps deliberate misunderstanding of cause and effect within the historical context of Israel's creation and its current existentially precarious position vis-a-vis the Arab world—including the Palestinian Arabs.

Somehow, despite terrible losses over the centuries, the Jews have survived all external and internal enemies. Although it sometimes takes what seems an interminable amount of time, the truth does will out. Your departure from the Jewish rabbinical community and from your congregation in Evanston will, in no small measure, contribute to a return of much needed integrity and sanity to the universe.

Andrew

With all due respect, Rabbi—your comments are shocking to me as a Jew and American. Please visit Sderot and see the terror that's been inflicted on those innocent people every day for the last eight years. I've been there and I've seen and felt it. A strong, safe, and free Israel is an insurance policy that the Jewish community possesses. We should cherish it and protect it—not try to destroy it.

Robin S

This is so beautiful and sad. Thank you for your posts and your commitment to speaking the truth.

David C

Brant, you are truly a Prince of the American Jewish Freak Show. You and your Christianized Jewish flock should be ashamed of yourselves. I really hope that that the Gazan Islamofascists called Hamas that our kids had to fight off, give their blood for, and which instead you write poems of lamentation for will soon come nipping at your ankles in Evanston in the form of ISIS. Or better, someday ISIS in the US will use your kids as protective shields as they carry out their terror acts on the American homeland as your media is now predicting. You spend your life convincing Jews, who are so ignorant of anything Jewish, that Israel was the aggressor.

Why don't you write poetry for the Sderot children who spent their childhood under constant missile attack from Gaza (thousands to be exact), the place that Israel gave up for peace to be the Singapore of the Middle East. Our only crime was having technology to knock down their missiles while their leaders sat in bunkers under Shifa Hospital. You have learned nothing about the tragedy of Tisha B'Av. SHAME ON YOU. You are not a rabbi. I want see if you have the guts to post this IN FULL, you sick freak.

With love from Haifa, Israel.

Seth

My lament is as much for the destruction of Gaza as for the loss of the Jewish soul.

Disruptions over Gaza: Notes from a Summer Protest[3]

November 10, 2014

I had planned to write this post several months ago, but when circumstances in my personal/professional life recently took a dramatic turn, I took an extended hiatus from blogging. I'm happy to say I'm finally coming up for air—and that readers of this blog can fully expect to see increasing posts in the near future. I'm leading with one that deals with an event from this past summer. Although it deals with news that is now a few months old, I believe it is a story that remains tragically relevant.

Back on August 21, I participated with a small group of activists from Jewish Voice for Peace–Chicago that disrupted a fundraiser sponsored by the Jewish United Fund (JUF) of Metropolitan Chicago. At the time, Israel's military onslaught on Gaza was in full swing and the JUF, like many Jewish federations across the country, was actively raising funds for the war effort.

It is important to note that Jewish federations are more than merely a network of social-service agencies; they seek to serve as the official face of the Jewish community. Given their prominence as community spokespeople, their unquestioning, knee-jerk support of Israel's policies and actions has been painfully problematic—particularly when it comes to a war as controversial as Israel's "Operation Protective Edge" this past summer.

It is safe to say that increasing numbers of us in the Jewish community were morally repulsed by Israel's actions during the months of July and August. We understood full well that this military onslaught was a war of choice,[4] not self-defense. We watched as the Israeli military killed 2,100 Palestinians in two months, the overwhelming majority of whom were civilians—including nearly 500 children.[5] We listened over and over as the Israeli government and its apologists justified its bloodshed by claiming that Hamas used its civilian population as "human shields"—a false claim that has been repeatedly disproved by human rights observers.[6]

While JUF chairman Bill Silverstein claimed at the fundraiser that "world Jewry is standing behind [Israel],"[7] there were, in fact, a myriad of public Jewish protests against Operation Protective Edge throughout the United States. In addition to Chicago, Jewish Voice for Peace (JVP) chapters organized protests in New York, Los Angeles, Washington, DC, Boston, San Francisco, Detroit, Raleigh/Durham, St. Louis, and San Diego, among others. In a protest against one prominent corporate enabler of Israel's war machine, the Seattle chapter of JVP staged a "die-in" at Boeing headquarters in Tukwila, WA, temporarily closing the entrance to the facility. Here in Chicago, JVP staged an act of non-violent civil disobedience inside Boeing's corporate office, resulting in the arrest of five activists.

In addition, IfNotNow (INN), a new grassroots initiative spearheaded by young Jews, held public prayer vigils at Jewish communal institutions across the country. INN's dramatic inaugural vigil in New York City was held on July 28 in front of the offices of the Conference of Presidents of Major Jewish Organizations. After a statement was read, memorial candles were lit and placed on the ground. Nine activists were arrested during this prayerful act of Jewish civil disobedience. It was my honor to participate in such a vigil here in Chicago, which took place on August 7 in front of the JUF offices downtown.

While all these actions differed in approach and tone, together they provide evidence of a growing movement of Jewish conscience against Israeli militarism and the devastating human toll it has exacted in Israel/Palestine. During Israel's similar military onslaught on Gaza in 2008 and 2009, this movement was barely in its nascent stages; by the summer of 2014, I think it is safe to say, it had found its voice in an immensely powerful way. It was particularly notable that many of them were organized by young Jews in their twenties, reinforcing the findings of an August Gallup poll that found a majority of Americans between the ages of eighteen and twenty-nine considered Israel's actions in Gaza to be "unjustified."[8]

It is also important to note that these protests have been deeply rooted in Jewish values, symbols, and liturgy. The JVP Chicago members who organized and carried out the disruption at the JUF fundraiser were most certainly motivated by the sacred Jewish imperatives that exhort us not to stand idly by, to pursue justice, and not to follow the multitude to do wrong. I was particularly proud that our group was multi-generational, ranging in age from twenties to sixties.

While I did not participate in the actual disruptions, I was present in the Hilton Towers ballroom to give my fellow protesters support, film the action taking place, and tweet pictures of the disruptions as they unfolded. There were a series of five disruptions during the course of the evening. The first occurred as Chicago mayor Rahm Emanuel spoke; two members of our group stood up, held up a banner that read "Shame on Israel," and repeatedly chanted, "We are Jews, shame on you. Stop killing children now!"

Security grabbed their banner away immediately, and they continued chanting as they were escorted from the room. Three other pairs of protesters and an Israeli-American also disrupted speakers at various points during the program. Each time, the response of the crowd grew angrier—

the final pair of activists were physically struck and had water thrown in their faces by attendees. (I myself was eventually asked to leave and was also escorted from the room by security. I can only assume someone from JUF recognized me and outed me to the program staff).

Speaking personally, I will say without hesitation that my participation in this action was a profound, even sacred experience. It took place during a terrible, tragic time in which I, as a Jew, was being implicated in crimes that were being committed by a state purporting to act on behalf of the Jewish people. In my hometown of Chicago, the organization that claimed to represent my community was openly urging on the war effort and publicly raising funds to support it.

It is difficult to describe the sense of anguish and alienation I felt as I sat in that room, listening to speaker after speaker urge on the war effort without expressing an iota of concern over the scores of innocents that Israel was killing daily. The only mention of the Gazan dead arose when speakers defensively and cynically wielded the canard of "human shields."

I was sitting directly behind the first pair of disrupters. They stood up just as Rahm Emanuel had announced that he and his wife were pledging five thousand dollars to the JUF's Israel Emergency Campaign. (Why exactly the mayor of Chicago was so publicly and dramatically taking sides in an international conflict is another troubling question for us to ponder.[9]) I must say that when I saw my friends stand up, point their fingers at Emanuel, and exclaim "Shame on you!" it truly felt like a redemptive moment. It was if my own soul as a Jew—indeed, as a human being of conscience—had finally been given back its voice.

Following the action, I heard criticisms that our disruption ran counter "to the values of dialogue." If we were looking to convince members of the Jewish community of the worthiness of our cause, we were told, this kind of jingoistic, disruptive sloganeering was just not the way to do it.

Of course, such a critique utterly misses the point of our protest. We were not seeking "dialogue" with members of our community; on the contrary, we were protesting war crimes being committed in our name. We certainly did not have any illusions that our action would convert anyone in that ballroom to our cause. Our target audience was not the attendees of the JUF fundraiser—rather, we sought to send a message to the world at large, to state loudly and openly that the entire Jewish community is not, in fact, marching lock-step in support of Israel's war effort.

We also heard the critique that our actions were just downright rude: rude to our civic leaders, rude to the speakers and guests, rude to decorum of this function, and rude to the JUF as a whole.

Yes, our action was disruptive—that was, in fact, its point. But if these disruptions felt rude and impolitic, the discomfort felt in that room was beyond miniscule in comparison to the horrors that were being inflicted at that very moment on the people of Gaza. Our protest was at its very core, an act of *tochechah* (reproof), hearkening back to the Biblical dictum: "You shall surely rebuke your neighbor and incur no sin because of that person" (Leviticus 19:17).

When I think of this kind of criticism, I can't help but think back to Dr. Martin Luther King Jr.'s "Letter from a Birmingham Jail," in which he addressed a very similar critique leveled at him by liberal clergy who urged him not to "cause tension" in their city through public acts of non-violent civil disobedience.

As King wrote to his Birmingham colleagues:

> Nonviolent direct action seeks to create such a crisis and foster such a tension that a community which has constantly refused to negotiate is forced to confront the issue. It seeks to so dramatize the issue that it can no longer be ignored. My citing the creation of tension as part of the work of the nonviolent-resister may sound rather shocking. But I must confess that I am not afraid of the word "tension." I have earnestly opposed violent tension, but there is a type of constructive, nonviolent tension which is necessary for growth. Just as Socrates felt that it was necessary to create a tension in the mind so that individuals could rise from the bondage of myths and half-truths to the unfettered realm of creative analysis and objective appraisal, we must see the need for nonviolent gadflies to create the kind of tension in society that will help men rise from the dark depths of prejudice and racism to the majestic heights of understanding and brotherhood.[10]

It is now three months since the cease-fire that ended the carnage of that terrible summer. We have already forgotten about Gaza: With the increasing shortness of our news cycles and attention spans, it has all but disappeared from our view.

But of course, the tragedy continues. The death and destruction inflicted on the people of that tiny strip of land still reverberates through the agony of the injured and the traumatized and through the grief of so many who lost parents, siblings, children, and friends. As a Gazan friend recently told me, no one—*no one*—in Gaza is untouched by the pain of grief.

As a Jew, I will never forget the tragedy of those two months, nor will I remain silent over the crimes that continue to be committed in my name. But I am heartened by those in my community who are increasingly finding the courage of their convictions. It is truly my honor to be counted with the disrupters, the "non-violent gadflies" who seek to "dramatize the issue so that it can no longer be ignored."

Discussion

abulnaalgodon

Brant, your voice in this medium is most welcome and I'm grateful you feel sufficiently restored to be writing here again, but I confess to continuing [to] regret your voice will no longer be identified as that of a congregational rabbi. I sincerely hope the congregation you faithfully served for so many years and which I deeply respect will not forget its voice in calling for justice even when it is "disruptive."

I am often reminded that the rabbi whom I attempt to follow was often considered rude and was certainly disruptive on several occasions. The "authorities" were frequently not pleased. I am reassured that when any of us summon the courage to follow faithfully we are drawing on the same deep moral core that lies at the heart of our respective traditions.

Vicky

I'm glad to see you posting again, Brant. I wondered where you were.

This summer a very close friend in Gaza was bereaved when a tank shell hit her aunt and uncle's home (next door to hers) and killed her two little cousins, aged four and seven. Her updates were chilling (and their absence was terrifying—electricity shortages meant that she couldn't be in touch all the time and I was often left wondering if her family were still alive). Then I would go to Hebrew class and have to listen to people who treated the mere sound of a siren in Jerusalem as though it were the Blitz but who were happy to dismiss two thousand dead Gazan bodies as not bad at all compared to Syria. The fact that some lives are far cheaper than others under this regime has never been clearer to me.

I am grateful for your continued activism on behalf of people like my friend Sameeha and her dead cousins, who aren't considered quite so deserving of life and dignity.

Tzedek Chicago: A New Jewish Congregation Puts Justice on the Agenda![11]

July 5, 2015

I'm honored and very, very excited to announce the creation of a new Jewish congregation: Tzedek Chicago. We recently held our launch program in our new home at Luther Memorial Church in the Lincoln Square neighborhood of Chicago, and I'm sure all who were present would agree there was a joyous excitement in the room as we shared our vision for our new congregation.

We'll continue to reach out to potential members during the summer and will officially kick off our religious programmatic calendar with High Holiday services this fall. I will be serving as the spiritual leader of Tzedek Chicago on a part-time basis while continuing in my full-time position as the Midwest regional director for the American Friends Service Committee. I feel blessed indeed to be returning to congregational life in addition to my important work at AFSC, which has itself become a meaningful professional, spiritual, and political home for me in so many ways.

How to describe our new congregation? Let me begin by sharing our core values with you.

We value . . .
. . . a Judaism beyond borders:
We celebrate with a Judaism that builds more bridges, not higher walls. Our community promotes a universalist Jewish identity—one that seeks a greater engagement in the world around us. Within our congregation, we view our diversity as our strength. Membership is not restricted to Jews or those who are partnered with Jews; our community welcomes all who share our values.

We advocate for a world beyond borders and reject the view that any one people, ethnic group, or nation is entitled to any part of our world more than any other. Guided by the values in Jewish tradition that bids us to care for the earth that we share with all peoples and all life, we promote personal behaviors and public policies that will ensure preservation of our planet's natural resources and its survival for future generations.

. . . a Judaism of solidarity:
We are inspired by prophetic Judaism: our tradition's sacred imperative to take a stand against the corrupt use of power. We also understand that the Jewish historical legacy as a persecuted people bequeaths to us a responsibility to reject the ways of oppression and stand with the most vulnerable members of our society. We emphasize the Torah's repeated teachings to stand with the oppressed and to call out the oppressor.

We actively pursue partnerships with local and national organizations and coalitions that combat institutional racism and pursue justice and equity for all. We promote a Judaism rooted in anti-racist values and understand that anti-Semitism is not separate from the systems that perpetuate prejudice and discrimination. As members of a Jewish community, we stand together with all peoples throughout the world who are targeted as "other."

. . . a Judaism of non-violence:

We honor those aspects of our tradition that promote peace and reject the pursuit of war as a solution to our conflicts. We openly disavow those aspects of our religion—and all religions—that promote violence, intolerance, and xenophobia.

Our activism is based upon a vision of shared security for the world; we support the practices of nonviolence, civil resistance, diplomacy, and human engagement. We take a stand against militarism and colonialism, particularly when it is waged in our name as Jews and Americans.

We oppose all forms of communal, family, and interpersonal violence and support organizations working to strengthen community health and peaceful, supportive coexistence. In all aspects of our communal life, we expect our members to treat each other with respect, engagement, and openness to the differences among us.

. . . a Judaism of spiritual freedom:

We promote spiritual exploration and encourage our members' diverse beliefs. Some of our members adhere to more traditional views of the divine while others view God as a human expression of our highest, most transcendent aspirations. Others do not define themselves as religious but identify with the humanist and cultural aspects of Jewish tradition.

We honor the inherent integrity of all faith traditions and reject all forms of religious exceptionalism. We actively partner with other faith communities in ways that celebrate our shared values and common humanity. In our activism, we actively work for religious freedom in our country and throughout the world.

. . . a Judaism of equity

In accordance with the Torah's imperative that there should be no needy among us, we work in solidarity with those who assert that poverty has no place in a civilized and moral society—and that all people have the right to safe food and water, safe living spaces, health care, and education.

We are committed to transparent and egalitarian governance and decision-making in our congregational life. We value the contributions of all members equally, regardless of age, gender, sexual orientation, wealth, or social standing.

. . . a Judaism beyond nationalism

While we appreciate the important role of the land of Israel in Jewish tradition, liturgy, and identity, we do not celebrate the fusing of Judaism with political nationalism. We are non-Zionist, openly acknowledging that the creation of an ethnic Jewish nation state in historic Palestine resulted in an injustice against its indigenous people—an injustice that continues to this day.

We reject any ideology that insists upon exclusive Jewish entitlement to the land, recognizing that it has historically been considered sacred by many faiths and home to a variety of peoples, ethnicities, and cultures. We oppose Israel's ongoing oppression of the Palestinian people and seek a future that includes full civil and human rights for all who live in the land—Jews and non-Jews alike.

I'm leading with this list because Tzedek Chicago is first and foremost *a values-based community*. What we do will be deeply informed by the values that drive us. By establishing this new congregation, we are very consciously attempting to create a Jewish spiritual home for the growing numbers of American Jews who cherish these values and seek a spiritual community in which to express them.

I've served as a congregational rabbi in liberal Jewish congregations for most of my adult life. While I have found this work professionally meaningful and spiritually nourishing in its own right, I am now eager to explore a fundamentally different approach to Jewish congregational life. In particular, I'm interested in building an intentional Jewish community that views the pursuit of social justice as its central driving force.

I realize, of course, that by espousing values such as these, our new congregation crosses any number of the contemporary Jewish community's red lines. I certainly have no illusions how a Jewish congregation that describes itself as "non-Zionist" and that openly protests "Israel's ongoing oppression of the Palestinian people" will be received by the Jewish establishment. Given centrality of Zionism and Israel advocacy in Jewish communal life, it would be fair to say that Tzedek Chicago is very much a dissident congregation in the Jewish world.

I do believe, however, that we *must* make room in our community for Jews whose values dissent from what the communal establishment deems "mainstream." It bears noting that dissent has historically occupied a venerable and even sacred place in Jewish life. Our congregation consciously and proudly seeks to lift up this dissident legacy—one which has long been indigenous to Jewish tradition itself in so many critical ways.

Indeed, the values I've listed above reflect a distinct liberatory narrative that runs through the heart of Judaism and Jewish history. It is a narrative rooted in the Exodus story that tells of a God who stands by the oppressed and demands that we do the same. It resonates through the words of Biblical prophets who spoke dangerous truths to power. It can be found in the courageous example of ancient rabbis who responded to the trauma of exile at the hands of the world's mightiest empire by creating a religion with a universal message of healing and hope.

Among other things, the founding of Tzedek Chicago is an attempt to reclaim this Jewish narrative of liberation. As such, it reflects our desire to stand down a decidedly different Jewish narrative that has taken hold of the Jewish community since the end of the Holocaust and the establishment of the state of Israel—one that teaches that traumas of the past will inevitably become our future unless the Jewish people embraces the ways of empire, nationalism, physical might, and militarism.

There is clearly much more to say about this phenomenon (and those who have followed this blog surely know that I've had a great deal to say about it over the years). For now, I'll only add this: There are increasing numbers who believe this new Jewish narrative represents a betrayal of our most sacred legacy—and who seek to place solidarity, liberation, and justice back on the agenda.

Finally, as I am filled with awe and gratitude to have reached this moment, I can only conclude with:

Source of all that lives and all that is:

We are so very grateful that you have given us life, sustained us, and brought us to this very sacred new beginning.

Glossary

Abbas, Mahmoud. (1935–) President of the Palestinian National Authority, 2005 to present. Also known as "Abu Mazen."

aliyah. To immigrate to Israel; Hebrew for "ascent."

Anti-Defamation League (ADL). An American Jewish organization founded in 1913 to combat anti-Semitism and discrimination; in recent decades has increasingly focused its efforts on Israel advocacy.

apartheid. "Separate but equal" system of institutionalized racism used by the South African government 1948–1994. Used more broadly to denote any system of enforced racial or ethnic segregation.

Arafat, Yasser. (1929–2004) First president of the Palestinian National Authority (1996–2004); leader of the Palestinian Liberation Organization (PLO) (1986–1996); founder of the Fatah political party; awarded Nobel Peace Prize along with Yitzhak Rabin and Shimon Peres for the Oslo Accords in 1994.

Ashkenazi. Term commonly used to describe Jews of Central and Eastern European ancestry.

B'tselem. An Israel-based human-rights group (btselem.org).

Barak, Ehud. (1942–) Israeli defense minister (2007–present); served as Israel's prime minister (1999–2001); affiliated with the Labor Party until 2011, now affiliated with the Independence Party. Participated in the failed Camp David peace talks with Yasser Arafat and Bill Clinton in 2000.

BDS. Acronym for Boycott/Divestment/Sanctions, a strategy of nonviolent resistance employed by anti-apartheid activists toward South Africa during the 1980s; advocated toward Israel by a Palestinian civil society call in 2005.

Bibi. *See* Netanyahu, Benjamin.

dayenu. A popular Passover song; in Hebrew: "it would have been enough."

Decalogue. The Ten Commandments.

Deir Yassin. A Palestinian village attacked by Jewish paramilitaries Irgun and Lehi (see separate entries) on April 9, 1948; 107 villagers were killed, including women and children. News of the massacre spread fear among Palestinians, precipitating their flight from towns and villages.

Dershowitz, Alan. (1938–) Prominent law professor, Israel advocate, and public intellectual.

dhimmitude. A neologism commonly understood to denote a state of submission or surrender to Islamic or Sharia law, specifically that of non-Muslim minorities in Muslim states.

diaspora. A people bound together by a national or ethnic identity who are no longer geographically concentrated in their place of origin. The Jewish diaspora refers to Jewish communities located outside the historic land of Israel.

Divrei Torah. Plural of D'var Torah; sermons or commentaries on the weekly Torah reading.

dunam. A unit of measurement equivalent to 1,000 square meters.

Etzel. See *Irgun.*

Fatah. A prominent Palestinian political party founded by Yasser Arafat; nationalist in orientation and affiliated with the PLO.

Foxman, Abraham. (1940–) National director of the Anti-Defamation League from 1987 to present.

Galut Jewry. *Galut* is Hebrew for "exile"; term used to describe Jews living in the diaspora.

goyishe kop. Yiddish term literally meaning "gentile brain"; usually used in a sarcastic way to mean "stupid."

Haftarah. Sections from the Biblical books of the Prophets. Chanted liturgically on the Sabbath and holidays.

Haganah. A Jewish paramilitary organization active before the founding of the state of Israel, 1920–1948; after Israeli independence, became the core of what would become the Israel Defense Forces.

halas. Arabic for "enough," "finish," or "stop."

Hamas. A Palestinian political party founded in 1987; Sunni Islamist in orientation; currently the elected government of the Gaza Strip.

Herzl, Theodor. (1860–1904) Viennese journalist who founded the modern Zionist movement; the central theorist of political Zionist thought.

Hezbollah. A prominent Lebanese political party founded in 1982; Shi'a Islamist in orientation; has a strong paramilitary wing as well as an electoral wing that holds seats in the Lebanese parliament and oversees a broad range of social services programs.

IDF. *See* Israel Defense Forces.

Intifada. Arabic word meaning "uprising" or "shaking off." The Palestinian uprising of 1987–1993 is referred to as the First Intifada; the Palestinian uprising of 2000–2005 (roughly) is considered the Second Intifada.

Irgun. A Jewish paramilitary organization active before the founding of Israel that split off from the Haganah; became part of the Israel Defense Forces after Israeli independence.

Irredentism. A movement active in Italy in the late 19th and early 20th centuries that sought to incorporate all "ethnically Italian" territories into a unified state of Italy; the term has come to signify any national group that seeks to annex lands it considers ethnically or traditionally its own.

Israel Defense Forces (IDF). The Israeli military. At Israel's founding, incorporated existing Jewish paramilitary groups; today all Jewish Israeli youth must serve in the IDF.

Jewish Defense League. An American political group, ultranationalist in origin and devoted to armed resistance to anti-Semitism; founded by Rabbi Meir Kahane in 1968.

JRC. Jewish Reconstructionist Congregation, the author's former congregation in Evanston, Illinois.

Kadima. A major Israeli political party founded in 2005 by Ariel Sharon; liberal to centrist in orientation.

Kahane, Meir. (1932–1990) New York rabbi and founder of the ultranationalist Jewish Defense League.

Kaplan, Mordecai. (1881–1983) American rabbi; founder of Reconstructionist Judaism and a prominent teacher, thinker, and theologian in the American Jewish community.

kavanna. Hebrew term meaning "direction of the heart"; having the proper mindset for prayer.

Knesset. The Israeli parliament.

Labor Party. A major Israeli political party founded in 1968; social democratic in orientation.

Lehi. A Jewish paramilitary organization active before the founding of Israel, 1940–1948; became part of the Israel Defense Forces after Israeli independence.

Levant. A geographic region encompassing the land at the eastern end of the Mediterranean Sea that has been a historical cultural crossroads; includes Israel/Palestine, Lebanon, Syria, and Jordan.

Lieberman, Avigdor. (1958–) Current deputy prime minister of Israel (2006–present), Knesset member, and minister of foreign affairs; founder and leader of the nationalist Yisrael Beiteinu party.

Likud Party. A major Israeli political party; center-right in orientation; since 2009, controls the Israeli government under the leadership of Prime Minister Benjamin Netanyahu.

Livni, Tzipi. (1958–) Leader of the Kadima political party and a member of the Knesset (2009–present).

Mechilta of Rabbi Ishmael. A classical rabbinic book of homiletical and interpretive commentary.

Meshal, Khaled. (1956–) Chairman of the Hamas Political Bureau (1996–present).

midrash. Classical rabbinic homiletical and exegetical literature.

minyan. A Jewish prayer quorum consisting of at least 10 people.

Mitchell, George. (1933–) United States Special Envoy for Middle East Peace appointed by President Obama (2009–2011); served in the US Senate, including as Democratic Senate majority leader.

Mizrahi Jews. Jews of Middle Eastern or North African origin.

Nakba. Arabic word meaning "catastrophe"; the Palestinian term for the physical dislocation of the Palestinian people that occurred during the months leading up to and following the founding of the state of Israel on May 14, 1948. *See also* Yom Ha'atzmaut.

nareshkeit. Yiddish word for "foolishness."

Netanyahu, Benjamin ("Bibi"). (1949–) Current prime minister of Israel (since 2009; also from 1996–1999) and Knesset member; member of the Likud party.

nonviolence. Strategies of resistance to oppression that reject using violence to achieve their ends; has many historical precedents; pioneered by the Mahatma Gandhi's *satyagraha* anticolonial movement in India and in the United States by the African American civil rights movement under the leadership of Dr. Martin Luther King Jr.

PA. *See* Palestinian National Authority.

Palestine. A name used since antiquity to refer to the southern part of the Levant, although boundaries have varied. Today "Palestine" may refer to the political entity administered by the Palestinian National Authority (recognized as a state by 122 countries, although not the United States, Israel, or the United Nations); to the Arab ethnic and cultural group with roots in that region; or to the entire area, by those who do not recognize the State of Israel.

Palestinian Liberation Organization (PLO). A Palestinian political and paramilitary organization; founded in 1964 at an Arab League summit for the purpose of the liberation of Palestine through armed struggle; in 1993, recognized the state of Israel and in return was recognized by the United Nations and Israel as the sole representative of the Palestinian people and granted permanent observer status at the UN.

Palestinian National Authority. The quasi-independent governing body of the Palestinian territories created according to the terms of the Oslo Accords.

Qassam. A type of rocket used by Hamas and other Palestinian groups to attack Israel from Gaza.

sabra. Hebrew name for the "prickly pear" cactus; slang for an Israeli-born Jew, meaning someone who is tough on the outside but sweet and tender on the inside.

Sderot. A town in Southern Israel, less than a mile from Gaza, which has been the target of near-constant rocket assault campaigns from inside Gaza; it has become a national symbol in Israel of the suffering of Jewish Israelis during the Gaza conflict.

separation barrier. A barrier built by Israel to separate Palestinian and Israeli land and settlements. Israel claims its purpose is security; critics point out that the route does not follow the internationally recognized boundary between Israel and the West Bank, that it incorporates additional Palestinian territory, and that it separates Palestinians' homes from their workplaces or farmlands. The barrier is a fence in some sections; in others, a concrete wall six to eight meters high. Although it is still under construction, the completed wall will be almost 450 miles long. Also known by critics as the "apartheid wall."

Shalit, Gilad. (1986–) An IDF soldier captured by Hamas during a conflict in 2006; he was held hostage until 2011, when he was released as part of a prisoner exchange between Hamas and Israel. Shalit's case became a *cause célèbre* among Israelis and the Jewish diaspora.

Sharon, Ariel. (1928–2014) Prime minister of Israel (Likud party) 2001– 2006; widely regarded in Israel as a war hero for his military leadership in the War of Independence, the Six-Day War, and the Yom Kippur War. Became a controversial figure due to his role as defense minister during Israel's 1982 war in Lebanon. In 2006, he suffered a stroke and lapsed into a permanent coma.

shiva. Jewish ritual of a seven-day mourning period observed for the dead. Observing shiva is also referred to as "sitting shiva."

shul. Yiddish word for "synagogue."

Talmud. A central Jewish legal text containing rabbinic debate and Scriptural commentary. Produced in various phases in a variety of rabbinical academies throughout Babylonia and Jerusalem during the second to fifth centuries.

Tanakh. The "Hebrew Bible"; consists of the Torah (the five books of Moses), the prophets, and the "writings," which include historical and poetic books.

tikkun olam. Hebrew term meaning "to repair the world"; in modern Judaism, signifies social justice and service to the community.

Tisha B'Av. A somber Jewish fast day that commemorates the destruction of the Second Temple in Jerusalem and the subsequent tragedies that have befallen the Jewish people throughout history.

Torah. The Five Books of Moses; in English, Genesis, Exodus, Leviticus, Numbers, and Deuteronomy.

Tzedek. Hebrew for "justice."

v'ahavta. A scriptural selection (Deuteronomy 6:4–9) recited as part of the daily Jewish liturgy; begins, "And you shall love the Lord your God with all your heart, with all your soul, and with all your might."

White Intifada. A term used to describe the current Palestinian nonviolent resistance movement; "white" because it is ongoing and not acute; it is not causing a major mobilization of the military but has the effect of building Palestinian resistance and growing international solidarity.

white phosphorus. A highly flammable chemical used in munitions to produce smoke and very hot fire; it is also poisonous if absorbed through the skin, and white phosphorus burns are often lethal. Used by Israel in Gaza and by the US in Iraq and Afghanistan. Its legality according to chemical weapons treaties is in dispute.

Yishuv. Hebrew word meaning "settlement"; usually used to describe the Jewish community in in Palestine before 1948.

Yisrael Beiteinu. A major Israeli political party; strongly nationalist and anti-Arab/Palestinian in orientation, with a base of mostly Soviet-born Israelis.

Yom Ha'atzmaut. Israel's Independence Day, celebrating the founding of Israel on May 14, 1948. *See also* Nakba.

Yom Kippur. The Day of Atonement, in which Jews fast and atone for their sins; the holiest day of the Jewish religious calendar.

Zionism. An ideology of Jewish nationalism. Refers primarily to the establishment and building up of a politically independent Jewish state in the historic land of Israel. The Zionist movement was founded by Theodor Herzl in 1897 largely in response to anti-Semitism in Europe. Other ideological schools of Zionism include cultural, labor-socialist, and religious Zionism; today the term is broadly used to denote support for the state of Israel and/or its actions.

Notes

Chapter 1

1. Post archived at http://bit.ly/Zh1M. Wherever titles have not been changed, links to blog posts have been shortened to save space.
2. This last sentence refers my participation in a citizen diplomacy delegation to Iran with Fellowship of Reconciliation during November–December 2008. I wrote extensively about my experiences on this trip (see http://rabbibrant.com/2008/12/09/home-from-iran-final-thoughts/).
3. W. Gunther Plaut, ed., *The Torah: A Modern Commentary* (New York: Union for Reform Judaism, 1981), 1645.
4. http://bit.ly/GOBdSK
5. Barack Obama, speech delivered in Sderot, Israel, on July 23, 2008. Video, http://bit.ly/5NWSJl; transcript, http://nyti.ms/GYyQ4Z.
6. http://bit.ly/2myYDt
7. Ruthie Blum, "It's the Demography, Stupid," interview with Arnon Soffer, *Jerusalem Post*, May 21, 2004. The interview, which has been removed from the *Jerusalem Post* website, is reproduced in full in the blog post, http://bit.ly/2myYDt.
8. Labor Beat, "Mass Chicago Rally for Gaza," YouTube video of demonstration in Chicago on January 2, 2009, at http://www.youtube.com/watch?v=tdf1l_aO4oc&feature=channel_page.
9. http://bit.ly/GYFt64
10. This was a reference to a YouTube video entitled "Thousands of Israelis Protest the War in Gaza." Produced by Israel Social TV, it includes numerous interviews with demonstrators, including veteran Israeli peace activist Uri Avnery. See http://www.youtube.com/watch?v=mc9DN2Oi0-w.
11. http://bit.ly/GM1Pcn
12. http://bit.ly/GNmmMT
13. Richard Silverstein, "Gaza Phase 3: IDF Marches into Hell (Gaza City)," *Tikun Olam*, January 15, 2009, at http://www.richardsilverstein.com/tikun_olam/2009/01/15/gaza-phase-3-idf-marches-into-hell-gaza-city/.
14. Originally published under the title "Gaza: The Arrow Cannot Be Taken Back," http://rabbibrant.com/2009/01/20/gaza-the-arrow-cannot-be-taken-back/.
15. Sabrina Tavernise and Taghreed El-Khodary, "Shocked and Grieving Gazans Find Bodies Under the Rubble of Homes," *New York Times*, January 19, 2009, at http://

www.nytimes.com/2009/01/19/world/middleeast/19gaza.html.

16. http://rabbibrant.com/2009/01/29/rabbis-and-the-third-rail/

17. Originally published under the title "Gaza: Soldiers Are Speaking Out," http://rabbibrant.com/2009/03/20/gaza-soldiers-are-speaking-out/.

18. Ethan Bronner, "Soldiers' Accounts of Gaza Killings Raise Furor in Israel," *New York Times*, March 20, 2009, at http://www.nytimes.com/2009/03/20/world/middleeast/20gaza.

19. Ibid.

20. Richard Silverstein, "IDF Testimony of Possible War Crimes," *Tikun Olam*, March 20, 2009, at http://www.richardsilverstein.com/tikun_olam/2009/03/20/idf-testimony-of-possible-war-crimes/.

21. BBC News, "Gaza Soldier Accounts 'Hearsay,'" *BBC News* Online, March 30, 2009, at http://news.bbc.co.uk/2/hi/7972490.stm.

22. B'Tselem, "Calls for Independent Investigation into Military's Conduct During 'Operation Cast Lead,'" *B'Tselem* website, March 30, 2009, at http://www.btselem.org/gaza_strip/20090330_jag_closes_file_of_soldier_testimonies.

Chapter 2

1. http://bit.ly/GQBxnm

2. Ethan Bronner, "A Hard-Liner Gains Ground in Israel," *New York Times*, February 8, 2009, at http://nyti.ms/J7rt7w (accessed March 20, 2012).

3. For the complete text of Israel's Declaration of Independence, see http://stateofisrael.com/declaration/.

4. Susan Nathan, *The Other Side of Israel* (New York: Doubleday, 2005).

5. http://bit.ly/1E5E8

6. Naomi Klein, "Israel: Boycott, Divest, Sanction," *Nation*, January 26, 2009, at http://www.naomiklein.org/articles/2009/01/israel-boycott-divest-sanction (accessed March 20, 2012).

7. Joel Bleifuss, "To Boycott Israel . . . or Not?," *In These Times*, March 30, 2009, at http://www.inthesetimes.com/article/4311/to_boycott_israelor_not/ (accessed March 20, 2012).

8. Thomas L. Friedman, "Campus Hypocrisy," *New York Times*, October 16, 2002, at http://nyti.ms/I36OnH (accessed March 20, 2012).

9. The article has since been removed.

10. http://bit.ly/zZhwc

11. Amaya Galili, "Nakba: Not a Dirty Word," *YNet*, April 29, 2009. Article is in Hebrew; this translation is by Mark Braverman. Original Hebrew article available at http://www.ynet.co.il/articles/0,7340,L-3706047,00.html (accessed March 20, 2012).

12. http://bit.ly/J7qg04

13. For coverage of the event, see Philip Weiss, "Led By a Rabbi, Jews and Palestinian-Americans Mark Nakba in Passover-Derived Ceremony," *Mondoweiss*, May 15, 2009, at http://mondoweiss.net/2009/05/led-by-a-rabbi-jews-and-palestinian

americans-mark-nakba-in-passoverderived-ceremony.html (accessed March 21, 2012).

14. Walid Khalidi, ed., *All That Remains: The Palestinian Villages Occupied and Depopulated by Israel in 1948* (Washington, DC: Institute for Palestine Studies, 1992).

15. Reuters, "Lieberman's Party Proposes Ban on Arab Nakba," *Ha'aretz*, May 14, 2009, at http://www.haaretz.com/news/lieberman-s-party-proposes-ban-on-arab -nakba-1.276035 (accessed March 20, 2012).

16. http://bit.ly/GZ2MeP

17. Hanan Greenberg, "Soldiers Stationed in Bilin: Gaza Is Easier," *YNet*, May 22, 2009, at http://www.ynetnews.com/articles/0,7340,L-3720056,00.html (accessed March 20, 2012).

18. Mary Elizabeth King, *A Quiet Revolution* (New York: Nation Books, 2007).

19. Rory McCarthy, "Non-Violent Protests against West Bank Barrier Turn Increasingly Dangerous," *Guardian* (UK), April 27, 2009, at http://www.guardian .co.uk/world/2009/apr/27/israel-security-barrier-protests (accessed March 20, 2012).

20. http://bit.ly/GOoAxN

21. Helene Cooper, "U.S. Weighs Tactics on Israeli Settlement," *New York Times*, May 31, 2009, at http://www.nytimes.com/2009/06/01/us/01prexy.html (accessed March 20, 2012).

22. Idith Zertal and Akiva Eldar, *Lords of the Land: The War over Israel's Settlements in the Occupied Territories, 1967–2007* (New York: Nation Books, 2009).

23. Yuval Azoulay, Nadav Shragai, and Natasha Mozgovaya, "U.S.: We Will Continue to Support Israel at UN," *Ha'aretz*, June 1, 2009, at http://www.haaretz.com /news/u-s-we-will-continue-to-support-israel-at-un-1.277069 (accessed March 20, 2012).

24. Marshal Breger, "Bush, George Herbert Walker," *Jewish Virtual Library*, undated, at http://www.jewishvirtuallibrary.org/jsource/judaica/ejud_0002_0004_0_03769 .html (accessed March 20, 2012).

25. http://bit.ly/IVHila

26. Benjamin Netanyahu, speech delivered at Tel Aviv's Bar Ilan University, June 14, 2009. Transcript and audio available at http://www.mfa.gov.il/MFA/Government/ Speeches+by+Israeli+leaders/2009/Address_PM_Netanyahu_Bar-Ilan_ University_14-Jun-2009.htm (accessed March 20, 2012).

27. Ibid.

28. Barack Obama, speech delivered in Cairo, Egypt, on June 4, 2009. White House transcript available at http://www.nytimes.com/2009/06/04/us/politics/04obama .text.html?pagewanted=1&_r=1 (accessed March 20, 2012).

29. Editorial, "Why Obama Is Wrong on Israel and the Shoah," *Jerusalem Post*, June 7, 2009, at http://www.jpost.com/Opinion/Editorials/Article.aspx?id=144737 (accessed March 20, 2012).

30. Benjamin Netanyahu, speech delivered June 14, 2009.

31. Adele Berlin, Marc Zvi Brettler, and Michael Fishbane, eds., *The Jewish Study Bible* (Oxford: Oxford University Press, 2004), 1990–2000.

32. http://bit.ly/H3avr7

33. Philip Rizk, *This Palestinian Life*, documentary film, 2009. See http://this palestinianlife.org/ (accessed March 21, 2012).

34. Ibid.

Chapter 3

1. http://bit.ly/2W6s4x

2. Human Rights Watch, "Israel/Egypt: Choking Gaza Harms Civilians," February 18, 2009, http://www.hrw.org/en/news/2009/02/18/israelegypt-choking-gaza -harms-civilians.

3. ANERA, "The Loss of Lives Is a Tragedy," undated, http://www.anera.org/gaza /Gaza_flotilla.php.

4. International Crisis Group, "Gaza's Unfinished Business: Executive Summary and Recommendations," Middle East Report No. 85, April 23, 2009, http://www .crisisgroup.org/en/regions/middle-east-north-africa/israel-palestine/85-gazas -unfinished-business.aspx.

5. http://rabbibrant.com/2009/07/14/jewish-fast-for-gaza-an-exchange/

6. http://rabbibrant.com/2009/07/24/flesh-of-our-flesh/

7. Francis Brown, S. R. Driver, Charles A. Briggs, *Brown-Driver-Briggs Hebrew and English Lexicon* (Peabody, MA: Hendrickson, 1996).

8. http://bit.ly/GNs3KL

9. http://www.jpost.com/LandedPages/PrintArticle.aspx?id=154130. Reprinted with permission.

10. David Forman, "Counterpoint: American Rabbis 'Fast for Gaza,'" *Jerusalem Post*, August 27, 2009, http://www.jpost.com/Opinion/Columnists/Article.aspx?id =153078.

11. Gisha Legal Center for Freedom of Movement, "Lift the Closure—Give Life a Chance," YouTube video, June 17, 2009, http://www.youtube.com/watch?v =LZ9FjcoOEpQ.

Chapter 4

1. A full audio file of this conference call can be found at: http://fastforgaza.net /audio/goldstone-10-18-2009.

2. Richard Goldstone, interview with Gal Beckerman, "Goldstone: 'If This Was a Court Of Law, There Would Have Been Nothing Proven,'" *Jewish Daily Forward*, October 7, 2009, http://forward.com/articles/116269/goldstone-if-this-was-a -court-of-law-there-wou/

3. Alan Baker, "Just What Did Goldstone Expect?," *Jerusalem Post*, October 18, 2009, http://www.jpost.com/Opinion/Article.aspx?id=157889.

4. The report's full text, executive summary, translations, and related press releases can be found at http://www2.ohchr.org/english/bodies/hrcouncil/specialsession/9 /FactFindingMission.htm.

5. United Nations, "UN Fact Finding Mission Finds Strong Evidence of War Crimes and Crimes against Humanity Committed during the Gaza Conflict; Calls for End to Impunity," press release, September 15, 2009, archived at http://www.unhchr .ch/huricane/huricane.nsf/view01/9B63490FFCBE44E5C1257632004EA67B?open document.

6. Ibid.

7. Ron Kampeas, "Israel, Jewish Groups Seek to Discredit New U.N. Report on Gaza War," *JTA*, September 15, 2009, archived at http://www.jta.org/news/article/2009 /09/15/1007893/israel-groups-target-the-source-in-countering-goldstone-report.

8. Ibid.

9. Ibid.

10. Ibid.

11. United Nations, "UN Fact Finding Mission Finds Strong Evidence."

12. http://bit.ly/GNs3KL

13. http://bit.ly/YNsjD

14. A full audio file of this call can be found at http://fastforgaza.net/node/88.

15. Richard Goldstone, "Statement on behalf of the Members of the United Nations Fact Finding Mission on the Gaza Conflict before the Human Rights Council," Human Rights Council 12th Session, September 29, 2009, p. 4. Archived online at https://www.umhltf.org/Goldstone_Report.html#Richard_Goldstone_Statement.

16. http://rabbibrant.com/2009/10/13/dirty-laundry/

17. http://bit.ly/leIE9

18. See the vote breakdown at http://clerk.house.gov/evs/2009/roll838.xml.

19. A summary is available at http://www.govtrack.us/congress/bills/111/hres867.

20. John J. Mearsheimer and Stephen M. Walt, *The Israel Lobby and U.S. Foreign Policy* (New York: Farrar, Straus and Giroux, 2007).

21. Fred Abrahams, "On Israel, Congress Tolerates Abuse," *Huffington Post*, November 4, 2009, archived at http://www.huffingtonpost.com/fred-abrahams /on-israel-congress-tolera_b_345056.html.

Chapter 5

1. Originally published as "On Jewish Hearts and Minds: A Response to Daniel Gordis," http://rabbibrant.com/2009/10/23/on-jewish-hearts-and-minds-a -response-to-daniel-gordis/.

2. Daniel Gordis, "The I's Have It," *Jerusalem Post*, October 18, 2009, http:// danielgordis.org/2009/10/18/the-is-have-it/#more-1360.

3. Ibid.

4. Ibid.

5. Charles S. Liebman and Steven M. Cohen, *Two Worlds of Judaism: The Israeli and American Experiences* (New Haven, CT: Yale University Press, 1988).

6. http://bit.ly/1rwlqr

7. Anshel Pfeffer, "IDF Chief Rabbi: Troops Who Show Mercy to Enemy Will Be 'Damned,'" *Ha'aretz*, November 15, 2009, http://www.haaretz.com/print-edition

/news/idf-chief-rabbi-troops-who-show-mercy-to-enemy-will-be-damned-1.4175.

8. Ben Lynfield, "Army Rabbi 'Gave Out Hate Leaflet to Troops,'" *Independent*, January 27, 2009, http://www.independent.co.uk/news/world/middle-east/army -rabbi-gave-out-hate-leaflet-to-troops-1516805.html.

9. See "Soldiers Speak Out" in chapter 1 of this volume.

10. Shamir Yeger and Gal Einav, "In the Name of God," *YNet*, February 2, 2009, http://www.ynetnews.com/articles/0,7340,L-3665302,00.html.

11. Katya Adler, "The rise of Israel's military rabbis," *BBC Newsnight*, September 7, 2009, http://news.bbc.co.uk/2/hi/programmes/newsnight/8232340.stm.

12. Zachary Goelman, "Secular Israeli Soldiers Burdened with Biblical Bric-a-brac," *Epichorus*, February 3, 2009, http://epichorus.blogspot.com/2009/02/secular-israeli -soldiers-burdoned-with.html.

13. See Kalonymos Kalmish Shapira, *Sacred Fire: Torah from the Years of Fury 1939- 1942* (Lanham, MD: Jason Aronson, 2002).

14. http://bit.ly/IeTVmX

15. Nir Hasson, "Israel Stripped Thousands of Jerusalem Arabs of Residency in 2008," *Ha'aretz*, December 2, 2009, http://www.haaretz.com/print-edition/news/israel -stripped-thousands-of-jerusalem-arabs-of-residency-in-2008-1.3006.

16. Liel Kyzer, "Clashes in Sheikh Jarrah as Jews Move In, Arabs Move Out," *Ha'aretz*, December 2, 2009, http://www.haaretz.com/print-edition/news/clashes-in-sheikh -jarrah-as-jews-move-in-arabs-move-out-1.3025.

17. Ir Amim, "Evictions and Settlement Planes in Sheikh Jarrah: The Case of Shimon HaTzadik," Ir Amim website, June 25, 2009, 1, http://www.ir-amim.org.il/eng/_ Uploads/dbsAttachedFiles/SheikhJarrahEngnew.pdf.

18. Rory McCarthy, "Families Evicted from their East Jerusalem Homes after 50 Years," *Guardian* (UK), August 24, 2009, http://www.guardian.co.uk/world/2009 /aug/24/west-bank-east-jerusalem-evictions.

19. Nir Hasson, "Israel Building Jewish Homes with One Hand, Destroying Arab Homes with the Other," *Ha'aretz*, November 19, 2009, http://www.haaretz.com /print-edition/news/israel-building-jewish-homes-with-one-hand-destroying -arab-homes-with-the-other-1.3896.

20. Marcy Newman, "Ethnic Cleansing in East Jerusalem," *Electronic Intifada*, March 10, 2009, http://electronicintifada.net/content/ethnic-cleansing-east-jerusalem /8123#.Tsku5E9VJZg.

21. Benny Morris, *The Birth of the Palestinian Refugee Problem Revisited* (Cambridge: Cambridge University Press, 2004), 127–28.

22. Yitzhak Rabin, *The Rabin Memoirs* (Berkeley: University of California Press, 1996).

23. Sandy Tolan, *The Lemon Tree: An Arab, a Jew, and the Heart of the Middle East* (London: Bloomsbury, 2007).

24. http://bit.ly/I5qwQe

25. See "In Search of Perspective in Bil'in" in chapter 2 of this volume.

26. Popular Struggle Coordination Committee, "Bil'in Leader Abdallah Abu Rahmah Arrested during Military Night Raid," Bil'in Village website, December 10, 2009,

http://www.bilin-village.org/english/articles/testimonies/Bilin-leader-Abdallah
-Abu-Rahmah-arrested-during-military-night-raid.

27. Quoted in Michael S. Kochin, *Five Chapters on Rhetoric: Character, Action, Things, Nothing, and Art* (State College: Pennsylvania State University Press, 2009).

28. Amira Hass, "Their Power of Endurance," *Ha'aretz*, August 9, 2006, http://www
.haaretz.com/print-edition/opinion/their-power-of-endurance-1.194706.

29. http://rabbibrant.com/2010/02/24/tel-aviv-stick-to-your-own-kind-stay-with
-your-own-kind/

30. Gideon Alon and Aluf Benn, "Netanyahu: Israel's Arabs Are the Real Demographic Threat," *Ha'aretz*, December 18, 2003, http://www.haaretz.com
/print-edition/news/netanyahu-israel-s-arabs-are-the-real-demographic
-threat-1.109045.

31. Dimi Reider, "Tel Aviv Presents: Municipal Program to Prevent Arab Boys from Dating Jewish Girls," *Coteret*, February 24, 2010, http://coteret.com/2010/02/24
/tel-aviv-presents-municipal-program-to-prevent-arab-boys-from-dating-jewish
-girls/.

Chapter 6

1. http://bit.ly/7TCCbK

2. Taghreed El-Khodary and Ethan Bronner, "Israelis Say Strikes Against Hamas Will Continue," *New York Times*, December 27, 2008, http://nyti.ms/I3jtqY.

3. http://bit.ly/9OEabT

4. World Council of Churches, "The Kairos Palestine Document," December 11, 2009, http://www.oikoumene.org/en/resources/documents/other-ecumenical
-bodies/kairos-palestine-document.html.

5. Ibid.

6. See "Is BDS Anti-Semitism?" in chapter 2 of this volume.

7. http://bit.ly/ayQ6gs

8. Gal Beckerman, "JCPA Taking Direct Aim at Anti-Israel Boycotters," *Jewish Daily Forward*, February 24, 2010, http://forward.com/articles/126327/.

9. Gal Beckerman, "Palestinian-Led Movement to Boycott Israel Is Gaining Support," *Jewish Daily Forward*, September 16, 2009, http://www.forward.com
/articles/114212/.

10. http://bit.ly/HmfN05. Published as the Jewish Voice for Peace 2010 Passover insert.

11. http://bit.ly/HvTV5u

12. Sara Benninga, "Sheikh Jarrah Speaker Breaks It Down Further," *Israel: The Only Democracy in the Middle East?*, March 20, 2010, http://theonlydemocracy
.org/2010/03/sheikh-jarrah-speaker-breaks-it-down-further/.

13. Isabel Kershner, "Israel Confirms New Building in East Jerusalem," *New York Times*, March 24, 2010, http://www.nytimes.com/2010/03/25/world/middle
east/25jerusalem.html.

14. Benjamin Netanyahu, speech to AIPAC, Washington, DC, March 22, 2010,

transcript and video at http://www.mfa.gov.il/MFA/Government/Speeches+by+
Israeli+leaders/2010/PM_Netanyahu_AIPAC_Conference_22-Mar-2010.htm.

15. Lara Friedman and Daniel Seidemann, "Jerusalem, Settlements, and the
'Everybody Knows' Fallacy," *Middle East Channel*, March 19, 2010, http://mideast
.foreignpolicy.com/posts/2010/03/19/jerusalem_settlements_and_the_everybody
_knows_fallacy.
16. Menachem Usshiskin, quoted in Nur Masalha, *Expulsion of the Palestinians: The
Concept of "Transfer" in Zionist Political Thought, 1882-1948* (Washington, DC:
Institute for Palestine Studies, 1992), 37.
17. http://bit.ly/cnZ2iT
18. UCSD Divest for Peace, "Resolution in Support of Peace and Neutrality
Through UC Divestment from U.S. Corporations Profiting from Occupation,"
undated, http://www.ucsddivestforpeace.org/divestment-resolution/.
19. On April 5, the ASUC voted 12-7, with one abstention, to uphold the President's
veto. At a final vote on April 29, the student senate voted 13 to 5 to uphold the
veto—one vote short of the total necessary for an override.
20. Editorial, "Troubling UC Berkeley Student Senate Bill on Israel," *J Street*, April 5,
2010, http://jstreet.org/blog/troubling-uc-berkeley-student-senate-bill-on-israel/.
21. Desmond Tutu, quoted in "Archbishop Desmond Tutu to UC Berkeley: Divesting
Is the Right Thing to Do," *Salem News*, April 11, 2010, http://www.salem-news
.com/articles/april112010/desmond-tutu-dt.php.
22. Naomi Klein, "Open Letter to Berkeley Students on their Historic Israeli
Divestment Bill," *Common Dreams*, March 31, 2010, http://www.commondreams
.org/view/2010/03/31-9.
23. See "Is BDS Anti-Semitism?" in chapter 2 of this volume.
24. Sydney Levy and Yaman Salahi, "Why Are American Jewish Groups So Intent
on Defending Illegal Israeli Settlements and Other Human Rights Violations?,"
undated, http://jewishvoiceforpeace.org/content/why-are-american-jewish
-groups-so-intent-defending-illegal-israeli-settlements-and-other-hum.
25. http://bit.ly/8ZOYS5
26. "The Pilots' Letter," English translation, *Courage to Refuse*, September 25, 2003,
http://www.seruv.org.il/english/article.asp?msgid=55&type=news.

Chapter 7

1. http://bit.ly/b3vlXV
2. See http://www.theparentscircle.org.
3. Originally published as "Pride and Prejudice: A Conversation With an Israeli-
American Friend," http://rabbibrant.com/2010/04/27/pride-and-prejudice-a-
conversation-with-an-israeli-american-friend/.
4. Originally published as "Pride and Prejudice #2: Our Conversation Continues,"
http://rabbibrant.com/2010/05/01/pride-and-prejudice-2-our-converation
-continues/.

5. Saul Singer, "Stop Palestinian Denial of Jewish Peoplehood," *Bitter Lemons*, April 26, 2010, http://www.bitterlemons.org/previous/bl260410ed9.html#isr2.

6. Originally published as "Pride and Prejudice #3: My Response to David," http://rabbibrant.com/2010/05/03/pride-and-prejudice-3-my-response-to-david/.

7. Originally published as "Pride and Prejudice #4: Our Dialogue Concludes," http://rabbibrant.com/2010/05/08/pride-and-prejudice-3-our-dialogue-concludes/.

8. Jamila al-Shanti, interview by Ashley Bates, *Dispatches from Gaza*, April 30, 2010, http://gazadispatches.blogspot.com/2010/04/im-against-sept-11th-but-i-support.html.

Chapter 8

1. http://bit.ly/bug36E

2. Isabel Kershner, "Deadly Israeli Raid Draws Condemnation," *New York Times*, May 31, 2010, http://www.nytimes.com/2010/06/01/world/middleeast/01flotilla.html.

3. Avi Trengo, "Predictable Israeli Fiasco," *YNet*, May 31, 2010, http://www.ynet news.com/articles/0,7340,L-3896841,00.html.

4. Zvi Bar'el, "Whatever Turkey Does, It Will Be Bad for Israel and Good for Hamas," *Ha'aretz*, May 31, 2010, http://www.haaretz.com/news/diplomacy-defense/analysis-whatever-turkey-does-it-will-be-bad-for-israel-and-good-for-hamas-1.293306.

5. Tovah Lazaroff and Yaakov Lappin, "Barak: Flotilla Organizers to Blame," *Jerusalem Post*, May 31, 2010, http://www.jpost.com/LandedPages/PrintArticle.aspx?id=176998.

6. Reut Institute, "The Delegitimization Challenge: Creating a Political Firewall," February 14, 2010, http://www.reut-institute.org/Publication.aspx?Publication Id=3769.

7. http://bit.ly/9hfCxl

8. http://fastforgaza.net/node/146

9. Clip from Al-Jazeera, May 29, 2010, "Gaza Flotilla Participants Invoked the Killing of Jews," YouTube video, posted by Palestinian Media Watch, May 31, 2010, http://www.youtube.com/watch?v=b3L7OV414Kk.

10. http://bit.ly/c1mREM. Cross-posted at *Huffington Post*, June 2, 2010.

11. Edith Garwood, "Palestinian Nonviolent Resistance Has Strong Roots," *Amnesty International Blog*, January 28, 2010, http://blog.amnestyusa.org/middle-east/palestinian-nonviolent-resistance-has-strong-roots/.

12. Rory McCarthy, "Parents of Critically Injured US Peace Activist Demand Justice from Israel," *Guardian* (UK), March 23, 2009, http://www.guardian.co.uk/world/2009/mar/23/tristan-anderson-israel-protest.

13. Ali Waked, "Relatives: Bilin Protestor Was Persistent in His Struggle," *YNet*, April 19, 2009, http://www.ynet.co.il/english/articles/0,7340,L-3702943,00.html.

14. Al-Haq press release, "The Wilful Killing of Aqel Srour Following a Ni'lin Demonstration against the Annexation Wall: A Deplorable Illustration of

Impunity's Slippery Slope," October 13, 2010, http://bit.ly/IKjq5i.

15. Bil'in Popular Committee, "Serious Head Injury in Bil'in Today," April 23, 2010, http://www.bilin-village.org/english/articles/testimonies/Serious-Head-Injury-in-Bilin-Today.

16. Nathan Guttman, "American Jewish Student Loses Eye During West Bank Protest of Israel," *Jewish Daily Forward*, June 9, 2010, http://www.forward.com/articles/128662/.

17. Jonathan Pollak, "The Ongoing Repression of Palestinian Protesters," *Huffington Post*, December 18, 2009, http://www.huffingtonpost.com/jonathan-pollak/the-ongoing-repression-of_b_397132.html.

18. Ashley Bates, "The Leader of Gaza's New Wave of Bil'in-Inspired Demonstrations," *Dispatches from Gaza,* April 6, 2010, http://gazadispatches.blogspot.com/2010/04/leader-of-gazas-new-wave-of-bilin.html.

19. Ashley Bates, "Unarmed Female Protester is Lucky to be Alive," *Dispatches from Gaza*, April 24, 2010, http://gazadispatches.blogspot.com/2010/04/unarmed-female-protester-nearly-killed.html.

20. Ashley Bates, "Growing Instability in Gaza," *Dispatches from Gaza*, April 29, 2010, http://gazadispatches.blogspot.com/2010/04/palpable-instability-in-gaza.html.

21. Ashley Bates, "Gazans Unite Against Flotilla 'Massacre,'" *Dispatches from Gaza*, May 31, 2010, http://gazadispatches.blogspot.com/2010/05/gazans-unite-against-israeli-massacre.html.

22. http://bit.ly/bLZL9S. Audio recording available at Jewish Fast for Gaza website, http://fastforgaza.net/node/153.

23. http://bit.ly/dbQoYe

24. Attila Somfalvi, "Lieberman: Gaza Flotilla 'Violent,'" *YNet*, May 28, 2010, http://www.ynetnews.com/articles/0,7340,L-3895506,00.html.

25. Audio recording available at Jewish Fast for Gaza website, http://fastforgaza.net/node/131.

26. Amira Hass, "Why Won't Israel Allow Gazans to Import Coriander?," *Ha'aretz*, May 7, 2010, http://www.haaretz.com/print-edition/news/why-won-t-israel-allow-gazans-to-import-coriander-1.288824.

27. Yaakov Katz, "Officials: Don't End Gaza Export Ban," *Jerusalem Post*, June 30, 2010, http://www.jpost.com/MiddleEast/Article.aspx?id=179953.

28. Sheera Frenkel, "Israeli Document: Gaza Blockade Isn't about Security," McClatchy-Tribune News Service, June 9, 2010, http://www.mcclatchydc.com/2010/06/09/95621/israeli-document-gaza-blockade.html.

29. Didi Remez, "Yediot: In Summit with Netanyahu, Obama Will Demand Full Lifting of Gaza Blockade," *Coteret*, June 27, 2010, http://coteret.com/2010/06/27/yediot-in-summit-with-netanyahu-obama-will-demand-full-lifting-of-gaza-blockade/.

30. http://bit.ly/94honK

31. Audio recording available at Jewish Fast for Gaza website, http://fastforgaza.net/node/157.

Chapter 9

1. http://bit.ly/cgE88J
2. Ethan Bronner, "In Mideast Talks, Scant Hopes from the Beginning," *New York Times*, August 20, 2010, http://www.nytimes.com/2010/08/21/world/middle east/21assess.html?_r=2.
3. Ibid.
4. Avi Issacharoff and Amos Harel, "Shin Bet Visits West Bank Cities to Boost Security Ties with PA," *Ha'aretz*, July 10, 2010, http://www.haaretz.com/blogs /2.244/mess-report-shin-bet-visits-west-bank-cities-to-boost-security-ties-with -pa-1.301345.
5. Mitchell Plitnick, "Webcasting Hasbara," *Realistic Peace in Israel-Palestine*, July 12, 2010, http://realisticpeace.wordpress.com/2010/07/12/webcasting-hasbara/.
6. J Street, "Who is Avigdor Lieberman?," undated, http://jstreet.org/who-avigdor -lieberman/.
7. Originally published as "Peace with Justice in Israel/Palestine: A Dialogue," http:// rabbibrant.com/2010/08/27/peace-with-justice-in-israelpalestine-a-dialogue/.
8. http://bit.ly/debSeC
9. Martin Indyk, "For Once, Hope in the Middle East," *New York Times*, August 27, 2010, http://www.nytimes.com/2010/08/27/opinion/27indyk.html.
10. Ibid.
11. Ibid.
12. Peace Now, "Eight Months into the Settlement Freeze," August 2, 2010, http:// www.peacenow.org.il/eng/node/99.
13. Ibid.
14. Indyk, "For Once, Hope in the Middle East."
15. Robert Malley and Hussein Agha, "Camp David: The Tragedy of Errors," *New York Review of Books*, August 9, 2001, http://www.nybooks.com/articles/archives /2001/aug/09/camp-david-the-tragedy-of-errors/?page=1.
16. http://bit.ly/99tat1
17. Nahum Barnea, "Painted into a Corner," *YNet*, September 26, 2010, http://www .ynetnews.com/articles/0,7340,L-3959986,00.html.
18. King Abdullah II, interview by Jon Stewart, *Daily Show*, September 23, 2010, video available at http://www.indecisionforever.com/2010/09/24/jon-stewarts-extended -interview-with-jordans-king-abdullah-ii/.
19. Originally published as "On JVP, Zionism and Jewish Community Growing Pains," http://rabbibrant.com/2010/10/22/on-jvp-zionism-and-jewish-community -growing-pains/.
20. James D. Besser, "ADL List Fuels Debate over What's Anti-Israel," *New York Jewish Week*, October 20, 2010, http://www.thejewishweek.com/news /international/adl_list_fuels_debate_over_whats_anti_israel.
21. Ibid.
22. Ibid.
23. Jewish Voice for Peace, "Mission Statement," http://jewishvoiceforpeace.org

/content/jvp-mission-statement.
24. American Council for Judaism, http://www.acjna.org/acjna/default.aspx.
25. Originally published as "Jews and Arabs in Israel: What Would You Call It?,"
http://rabbibrant.com/2010/10/31/jews-and-arabs-in-israel-what-would-you
-call-it/.
26. Amnon Be'eri-Sulitzeanu, "Segregation of Jews and Arabs in 2010 Israel Is Almost
Absolute," Ha'aretz, October 29, 2010, http://www.haaretz.com/print-edition
/opinion/segregation-of-jews-and-arabs-in-2010-israel-is-almost-absolute
-1.321728.
27. Zvi Bar'el, "South Africa Is Already Here," Ha'aretz, October 31, 2010, http://
www.haaretz.com/print-edition/opinion/south-africa-is-already-here-1.322052.
28. Article II, International Convention on the Suppression and Punishment of the
Crime of Apartheid, UN General Assembly Resolution 3068, November 30, 1973.
The full text of the resolution is available through the UN website at http://
daccess-dds-ny.un.org/doc/RESOLUTION/GEN/NR0/281/40/IMG/NR028140
.pdf?OpenElement.
29. Ibid.
30. http://bit.ly/aG6RVS
31. Mark Landler, "Netanyahu Agrees to Push for Freeze in Settlements," New York
Times, November 14, 2010, http://www.nytimes.com/2010/11/14/world/middle
east/14mideast.html?_r=1&hp.
32. Peace Now, "In 6 Weeks the Settlers Almost Made Up for the 10 Months Settlement
Freeze," November 13, 2010, http://www.peacenow.org.il/eng
/content/6-weeks-settlers-almost-made-10-months-settlement-freeze.
33. Originally published as "My 'Budrus' Review," http://rabbibrant.com/2010/11/24
/my-budrus-review/.
34. Popular Struggle Coordination Committee, "Israeli Soldiers Raid the Home of
Imprisoned Bil'in Activist Adeeb Abu Rahmah; Arrest His Son," Popular Struggle
blog, November 23, 2010, http://www.popularstruggle.org/node/434.

Chapter 10

1. Marc H. Ellis, "Exile and the Prophetic: The Interfaith Ecumenical Deal Is Dead,"
Mondoweiss, November 12, 2012, http://mondoweiss.net/2012/11/exile-and-the
-prophetic-the-interfaith-ecumenical-deal-is-dead.
2. https://rabbibrant.com/2012/01/16/jewschristians-and-israelpalestine
-rediscovering-the-prophetic/
3. https://rabbibrant.com/2012/02/22/i-support-of-the-presbyterian-church-usa
-divestment-resolution/
4. Jerry L. Van Marter, "GAMC Recommends Divestment from Caterpillar,
Motorola, Hewlett-Packard," press release, Presbyterian News Service, February
17, 2012, http://www.pcusa.org/news/2012/2/17/gamc-recommends-divestment
-caterpillar-motorola-he.
5. Dan Klein, "Presbyterian Church Moves Closer to Divestment from Israel-Related

Companies," Jewish Telegraphic Agency, February 17, 2012, http://archive.jta .org/2012/02/17/news-opinion/israel-middle-east/presbyterian-church-moves -closer-to-divestment-from-israel-related-companies.

6. Simon Wiesenthal Center, "SWC to Presbyterians: Just Say No to Unjust Anti-Israel Divestment," press release, February 20, 2012, http://www.wiesenthal.com /site/apps/nlnet/content2.aspx?c=lsKWLbPJLnF&b=4441467&ct=11631951# .V8r2°1cshg0.

7. Adam Horowitz, "Presbyterian Investment Committee Recommends Divestment from Caterpillar, Hewlett-Packard and Motorola over Complicity in the Occupation," *Mondoweiss*, February 17, 2012, http://mondoweiss.net/2012/02 /presbyterian-church-investment-committee-recommends-divestment-from -caterpillar-hewlett-packard-and-motorola-over-complicity-in-the-occupation.

8. https://rabbibrant.com/2012/10/23/american-christians-dare-to-speak-their -conscience-on-israelpalestine/

9. Jerry L. Van Marter, "Religious Leaders Ask Congress to Condition Israel Military Aid on Human Rights Compliance," press release, Presbyterian News Service, October 5, 2012, https://www.pcusa.org/news/2012/10/5/religious-leaders-ask -congress-condition-israel-mi.

10. Noam E. Marans, "Op-Ed: Christians' Letter Is an Unworthy Tactic," Jewish Telegraphic Agency, October 21, 2012, http://www.jta.org/2012/10/21/news -opinion/opinion/op-ed-christians-letter-is-an-unworthy-tactic.

11. https://rabbibrant.com/2012/05/07/some-final-thoughts-on-the-united-methodist -divestment-vote/

12. Laurie Goodstein, "Methodists Vote Against Ending Investments Tied to Israel," *New York Times*, May 2, 2012, http://www.nytimes.com/2012/05/03/us/methodists -vote-against-ending-investments-tied-to-israel.html?_r=0.

13. https://rabbibrant.com/2012/04/25/united-methodist-divestment-standing-in-solidarity-in-tampa/

14. Anna Baltzer, "BDS Scorecard: Methodists Recommend Sanctions & Boycotts; Reject Divestment," *Mondoweiss*, May 5, 2012, http://mondoweiss.net/2012/05 /bds-scorecard-methodists-recommend-sanctions-reject-divestment.

15. David Fischler, "Methodist Debate on Israel Begins (UPDATE: Divestment Loses)," *Stand Firm*, May 2, 2012, http://www.standfirminfaith.com/index.php /sf/page/28760/comment-sf.

16. Pam Bailey, "Zahi Khouri to Methodist Conference: 'We Don't Need Charity; We Want Freedom to Help Ourselves,'" *Mondoweiss*, April 30, 2012, http:// mondoweiss.net/2012/04/zahi-khouri-to-methodist-conference-we-dont-need -charity-we-want-freedom-to-help-ourselves.

17. Desmond Tutu, "Justice Requires Action to Stop Subjugation of Palestinians," *Tampa Bay Times*, April 30, 2012, http://www.tampabay.com/opinion/columns /justice-requires-action-to-stop-subjugation-of-palestinians/1227722.

18. https://rabbibrant.com/2014/02/05/zionism-unsettled-a-smart-and-gutsy-new -church-study-guide/

19. Israel/Palestine Mission Network (IPMN), *Zionism Unsettled: A Congregational Study Guide* (Louisville, KY: Presbyterian Church [U.S.A.], 2014).

20. Ibid., 5–6.

21. Ibid., 47.

22. https://rabbibrant.com/2014/02/19/reconsidering-zionism-unsettled-an-open-letter-to-reverend-chris-leighton/

23. Christopher M. Leighton, "An Open Letter to the Presbyterian Church," Institute for Islamic, Christian & Jewish Studies, February 6, 2014, http://www.icjs.org/articles/2014/open-letter-presbyterian-church.

24. Philip Weiss, "Defying Hillel Rules, Swarthmore Chapter Invites Anti-Zionists to Come On In," *Mondoweiss*, December 9, 2013, http://mondoweiss.net/2013/12/swarthmore-chapter-zionists.

25. John B. Judis, "Hillel's Crackdown on Open Debate is Bad News for American Jews," *New Republic*, January 6, 2014, https://newrepublic.com/article/116100/hillel-college-campuses-fractures-students-debate-israel.

26. https://rabbibrant.com/2014/02/23/guest-post-rev-chris-leighton-responds-to-my-open-letter/

27. https://rabbibrant.com/2014/02/26/more-heat-than-light-my-response-to-rev-chris-leighton/

28. IPMN, *Zionism Unsettled*, 8.

29. https://rabbibrant.com/2014/06/17/from-the-presbyterian-ga-jews-and-christians-in-support-of-divestment/

30. Margaret Holub, "I'm a Rabbi and I Support Presbyterians' Partial Israel Divestment," *Forward*, June 16, 2014, http://forward.com/opinion/israel/200179/im-a-rabbi-and-i-support-presbyterians-partial-isr.

31. https://rabbibrant.com/2014/06/23/the-presbyterian-divestment-vote-toward-a-new-model-of-community-relations/

32. Laurie Goodstein, "Presbyterians Vote to Divest Holdings to Pressure Israel," *New York Times*, June 20, 2014, http://www.nytimes.com/2014/06/21/us/presbyterians-debating-israeli-occupation-vote-to-divest-holdings.html?_r=2.

33. Jaweed Kaleem, "Presbyterian Church (USA) Makes Controversial Divestment Move Against Israel," *Huffington Post*, June 20, 2014, http://www.huffingtonpost.com/2014/06/20/presbyterian-church-israel_n_5517037.html.

34. Lauren Markoe, "Presbyterians Narrowly Vote to Divest from 3 Companies Involved in Israeli/Palestinian Conflict," Religion News Service, June 20, 2014, http://religionnews.com/2014/06/20/prebyteriansdivestment.

35. Kaleem, "Presbyterian Church Makes Controversial Divestment Move."

36. IPMN, "Voting Guide for 221st GA on Divestment," n.d., http://www.israelpalestinemissionnetwork.org/main/index.php?option=com_content&view=article&id=276.

Chapter 11

1. BBC News, "Gaza Crisis: Toll of Operations in Gaza," September 1, 2014, http://www.bbc.com/news/world-middle-east-28439404.
2. https://rabbibrant.com/2014/08/01/for-tisha-bav-a-lamentation-for-gaza/
3. https://rabbibrant.com/2014/11/10/disruptions-over-gaza-notes-from-a-summer-protest/
4. https://rabbibrant.com/2014/07/20/israel-in-gaza-investigating-the-ethics-of-a-war-of-choice/
5. BBC News, "Gaza Crisis."
6. Stephen Zunes, "Congress Utilizes Myth of 'Human Shields' to Justify War Crimes," *Truthout*, November 9, 2014, http://www.truth-out.org/news/item/27301-congress-utilizes-myth-of-human-shields-to-justify-war-crimes; Amnesty International, "Israel/Gaza Conflict: Questions and Answers," press release, July 25, 2014, https://www.amnesty.org/en/latest/news/2014/07/israelgaza-conflict-questions-and-answers.
7. Jewish United Fund, "Hundreds Stand with Israel at Solidarity Fundraiser for JUF's Israel Emergency Campaign," press release, August 22, 2014, http://www.juf.org/news/israel.aspx?id=429684.
8. Moustafa Bayoumi, "US public support for Israel weakens," Progressive Media Project, August 17, 2014, http://www.centralmaine.com/2014/08/17/us-public-support-for-israel-weakens.
9. Bill Chambers, "Chicago Protesters Disrupt Israel Fundraiser," *Chicago Monitor*, August 22, 2014, http://chicagomonitor.com/2014/08/chicago-protesters-disrupt-israel-fundraiser.
10. Martin Luther King Jr., "Letter from a Birmingham Jail," April 16, 1963, http://abacus.bates.edu/admin/offices/dos/mlk/letter.html.
11. https://rabbibrant.com/2015/07/05/tzedek-chicago-a-new-congregation-puts-justice-on-the-agenda/

About the Author

 **BRANT ROSEN** is a Chicago-based rabbi, blogger, and social activist. He is currently the Midwest Regional Director for the American Friends Service Committee. In 2015, Rosen, who had lengthy earlier experience as a congregational rabbi, co-founded a social justice–focused congregation, Tzedek Chicago.

Just World Books
Timely Books for Changing Times

Just World Books exists to expand the discourse in the United States and worldwide on issues of vital international concern. We are committed to building a more just, equitable, and peaceable world. We uphold the equality of all human persons. We aim for our books to contribute to increasing understanding across national, religious, ethnic, and racial lines; to share more broadly the reflections, analyses, and policy prescriptions of pathbreaking activists for peace; and to help to prevent war.

To learn about our existing and upcoming titles or to buy our books, visit our website:

www.JustWorldBooks.com

Also, follow us on Facebook and Twitter!

Our recent titles include:

White And Black: Political Cartoons from Palestine, by Mohammad Sabaaneh

No Country for Jewish Liberals, by Larry Derfner

Condition Critical: Life and Death in Israel/Palestine, by Alice Rothchild

The Gaza Kitchen: A Palestinian Culinary Journey, by Laila El-Haddad and Maggie Schmitt

Lens on Syria: A Photographic Tour of its Ancient and Modern Culture, by Daniel Demeter

Never Can I Write of Damascus: When Syria Became Our Home, by Theresa Kubasak and Gabe Huck

America's Continuing Misadventures in the Middle East, by Chas W. Freeman, Jr.

Arabia Incognita: Dispatches from Yemen and the Gulf, edited by Sheila Carapico

War Is a Lie, by David Swanson